Economics of the 1%

Economics of the 1%

How Mainstream Economics
Serves the Rich, Obscures Reality
and Distorts Policy

John F. Weeks

ANTHEM PRESS
LONDON · NEW YORK · DELHI

Anthem Press
An imprint of Wimbledon Publishing Company
www.anthempress.com

This edition first published in UK and USA 2014
by ANTHEM PRESS
75–76 Blackfriars Road, London SE1 8HA, UK
or PO Box 9779, London SW19 7ZG, UK
and
244 Madison Ave #116, New York, NY 10016, USA

British Library Cataloguing-in-Publication Data
A catalogue record for this book is available from the British Library.

Library of Congress Cataloging-in-Publication Data
Weeks, John, 1941–
Economics of the 1% : how mainstream economics serves the rich,
obscures reality and distorts policy / John F. Weeks.
pages cm
Includes index.
ISBN 978-0-85728-108-1 (pbk. : alk. paper)
1. United States–Economic policy. 2. United States–Economic
conditions. I. Title.
HC106.84.W44 2013
330.973–dc23
2013047460

ISBN-13: 978 0 85728 108 1 (Pbk)
ISBN-10: 0 85728 108 9 (Pbk)

This title is also available as an ebook.

For Lukas
and his parents Michael and Rachel
in hope he grows up in a better world

CONTENTS

Preface

DR BOB'S THIRD LAW

Not long ago a friend asked me to explain the difference between the public budget deficit and the public debt, and soon after another wanted to know if the Federal Reserve Banks were private, profit-making institutions. I was struck that intelligent and informed people with advanced university degrees would ask such basic questions.

Why, I asked myself, are many people ignorant of simple aspects of our economy? To me, a professional economist for almost fifty years, the answer to that question is simple. It is the motivation for this book. Mainstream economists have been extraordinarily successful in indoctrinating people to believe that the workings of the economy are far too complex for any but experts (i.e., the economists themselves) to understand.

The mainstream of the economics profession achieves this indoctrination by misrepresenting markets or, to be blunt, systematically marketing falsehoods (and I am tempted to use a four letter word beginning with "l"). It was not always so, and I dedicate this book to progressive economists who are not liars, be they Keynesians, Ricardians, Marxists, institutionalists or evolutionists. What we all have in common is that over the last 30 years, when the "econfakers" school of economics (see below) seized the mainstream, it expelled us all as heretics and incompetents.

The incompetence can be found in mainstream economics, burdening the professional with a dead weight of absurd inconsistencies that they present as theory, much like astrologers and alchemists were a barrier to understanding the natural world. There is no policy or economic outcome so reactionary or outrageously antisocial that some mainstream economist will not defend it, and most would lend their tacit support. Among these reactionary absurdities is that gender and race income discrimination is an illusion, unemployment is voluntary and sweatshops are good.

Therefore, I designate the mainstream as *econfakers*, practicing a pseudoscientific *fakeconomics* just as astrologers practice astrology and alchemists alchemy. As I elaborate in subsequent chapters, what makes the mainstream a false paradigm worthy of the term fakeconomics is the assumption that market economies are always and continuously at *full employment*. All theoretical and policy conclusions derive from this fanciful base. It is the unrelenting and unapologetic presumption of full employment, contrary to economic reality, that qualifies mainstream practitioners as "fakers." They propound and zealously defend a fake version of market society.

If, after appropriating the profession, the neoclassical school had driven it into disrepute – rather as if creationists had taken over the field of genetics, astrologers astronomy and alchemists chemistry – their offense would rank as a minor intellectual crime. To the contrary, they have successfully sold their nonsense as an unchallengeable wisdom guiding governments. It is not wisdom. On the contrary, it is nonsense, a virus of the intellect.

Deconstructing what is nonsensical and exposing it as such is the purpose of this book. I am able to do so because of the many intellectually honest and dedicated economists who taught me to be skeptical of the mendacity of what is now the mainstream. Among those humane men and women are Clarence Ayres, H. H. (Lieb) Liebhafsky, Robert (Bob) Montgomery, C. C. (Carey) Thompson, Daniel Suits, Daniel Fusfeld and Wolfgang Stolper, who taught me at the Universities of Texas (Austin) and Michigan (Ann Arbor). Many colleagues encouraged and deepened my skepticism: Emily Taft Morris, Thomas Dernberg, James Weaver and Howard Wachtel at the American University, and Hassan Hakimian, Terry Byres, Ben Fine, Caroline Dinwiddy, Jan Toporowski, Alfredo Saad Filho, Terry McKinley and Costas Lapavitsas at the School of Oriental and African Studies of the University of London. Many other dissidents have influenced me, above all Anwar Shaikh and Alemayehu Geda, Mike Zweig, Simon Mohun and Susan Himmelweit. If the economics profession had a mustard seed of the scientific content it currently claims to have, these men and women would be the mainstream. To all of them and the other dissidents, I dedicate this book. Finally, and most importantly, I thank Elizabeth Dore for her continuous support and intellectual inspiration.

. . .

When I studied economics at the University of Texas in Austin in the early 1960s, students would find in the department an old codger named Robert Montgomery, who retired the year after I took his course in public utility economics. Accused of teaching communism, Doctor Bob was called before an investigating committee of the Texas state legislature in 1948. He was asked if he belonged to any radical organizations. In reply he confessed, "Yes, Senator, I am a proud member of two: the Democratic Party that says people can rule themselves without kings and queens, and the Methodist Church that tells people they don't need a priest to read the Bible."

Likewise, you don't need an economist to understand the basic workings of the economy, a truth I designate "Dr Bob's Third Law," because it was certainly his view. This book is an exegesis on the Third Law of Dr Bob.

Further Reading

Robert J. Robertson, "Montgomery, Robert Hargrove," Handbook of Texas Online. http://www.tshaonline.org/handbook/online/articles/fmodd (accessed 10 October 2013).

Norbert Häring and Niall Douglas, *Economists and the Powerful: Convenient Theories, Distorted Facts, Ample Rewards* (London: Anthem Press, 2012), ch. 1.

Web addresses for progressive economists

International Initiative for Promotion of Political Economy
   http://www.iippe.org
Union of Radical Political Economists
   http://www.urpe.org
Association for Evolutionary Economics
   http://www.afee.net/division.php?page=institutional_economics
World Economics Association
   http://www.worldeconomicsassociation.org/

Introduction

ECONOMIC IGNORANCE

> Any intelligent fool can make things bigger and more complex...
> It takes a touch of genius – and a lot of courage – to move in the
> opposite direction.
>
> (Albert Einstein)

Critics complain that economists arrogantly pretend to understand far
more than they actually do. This criticism is too weak. The mainstream
claims profound knowledge of the economy, understands almost nothing
and obscures almost everything. This assertion may strike the reader as
either shocking or slanderous (or both), rather like accusing engineers of
knowing nothing about mechanical devices.

Nonetheless, it is true and not difficult to demonstrate.

What is difficult is to explain why so many people in so many countries
of the world revere economists as gurus. In part it may come from the
econfaker practice of using in-group terminology whose meaning to
the layperson remains obscurely impenetrable. I treat this misplaced
reverence at some length, because it reflects a stronger version of the
hypothesis attributed to Abraham Lincoln, that most of the people can
be fooled not just some of the time, but most of the time (especially if
the media are in the hands of those who benefit from the mainstream
economic ideology). Perhaps more appropriate to describe the broad
acceptance of the reactionary banalities of economists is "a sucker is
born every minute" (origin highly disputed).

In great part the undeserved credibility of economists results from the
systematic fostering of ignorance over the last 30 years. Understanding
the economy of any society is not simple, but no more difficult than
understanding the political system sufficiently to vote. People regularly
go into voting booths and choose among candidates or reject them all.
The same people would profess a degree of ignorance of economics
that leaves them unable to evaluate competing claims about the state of
the economy.

ECONOMICS OF THE 1%

Discriminating among Economists

If you meet an economist it is almost certain he or she is from the "neoclassical school." Any discussion arising during the encounter is almost certain to be banal, reactionary and tedious, with considerable condescension.

From the late eighteenth to the mid-nineteenth century, people writing on economic issues were usually identified as "political economists" and their field was "political economy." The profession included a great variety of thinkers: Karl Marx the revolutionary through John Stuart Mill the reformer, across to right-wing nationalists. Later in the nineteenth century the mainstream redefined itself as scientific and "value free," renaming the profession "economics." While the pretensions of value-free science characterized the conservative and respectable mainstream, considerable dissent festered outside it.

Then, along came Keynes, the greatest economist of the twentieth century. By his innovations and powerful personality, he remade the profession for almost four decades, 1935–1975. Before, there had been one realm of theory: "microeconomics" (households and companies). From Keynes arose a second: "macroeconomics," the study of society's economic activity as an aggregate, which became the foundation of public policy. It provided the guidelines for governments throughout the world: social democratic, Christian democratic, one-nation conservative (UK), and Republican and Democrat (US).

During those decades generalizations about "economists" would have been few. The mainstream was "Keynesian," and the academy was a broad church, accepting Marxists (only begrudgingly) as well as the pre-Keynesian enclave at the University of Chicago (with some bemusement). The profession would not stay tolerant for long. The last two decades of the century brought a purge of contributions by Keynes and those he inspired. At the dawn of the new century "economics" was again the study of households and companies, with only a superficial veneer of macroeconomics. Those who disagreed suffered banishment to the fringes of the profession, followed by expulsion.

Surrendering the words "economics" and "economist" to the reactionary mainstream insults the largely unheard and unrecognized heterodox progressives who struggle on in a profession that denies their existence. I will not engage in this surrender. The mainstreamers are not economists, they are the alchemists of the social sciences – *econfakers*.

The keystone to the econfakers' fantasy world is a hypothesized state of grace: "perfect competition," in which all buying and selling occurs with full knowledge of the future and with the absence of market power of any type, and full employment of all resources. Their *modus operandi* is mathematics. John Kenneth Galbraith, one of the two great iconoclasts of economics (the other being Thorstein Veblen), recognized the symbiosis of "perfect competition" and mathematics: "In the real world perfect competition was by now leading an increasingly esoteric existence, if indeed, any existence at all, and mathematical theory was, in no slight measure, the highly sophisticated cover under which it managed to survive."

An astoundingly high proportion of the adult population regards the economy and economics as something understood only by experts. It is quite extraordinary that when asked whether monetary policy should be more expansionary, for example, people frequently begin statements with, "Since I am not an economist..." or "Not being an economist..." If asked whether a national health system should be private or public, the same people would not say, "I am not a doctor, so I can't comment." Yet the health system is at least as technically complex as economics.

Somehow the mainstream economics profession, supported by a thoroughly uncritical and credulous media, successfully convinces people, regardless of level of education or political orientation, that economics is a subject so complex and esoteric that the nonexpert is excluded from understanding it. If people do venture opinions on economic issues, it is frequently on the basis of breathtaking banalities and clichés. Common ones are the vacuous "Well, that's the result of supply and demand working"; the old cliché "Too much money chasing too few goods" causes inflation; or, my favorite, "Governments should not live beyond their means."

These are the clichés of the ignorant, repeated shamelessly by the media. Even worse, they are repeated by the "experts" the media bring forth to foster our, and their, continued ignorance. Consider, for example, a typical justification of reducing the government budget deficit by cutting social services when unemployment is high: "The government has to consider the reaction of financial markets." The insight in that banality is equivalent to seeing the terrible photographs of people leaping to their deaths from the World Trade Center towers on 11 September 2001 and commenting, "Well, that's the law of gravity for you."

We find reactionary ignorance even in media purporting to be left-of-center. For example, on 29 November 2012, unsuspecting readers encountered in the *Guardian* (UK) the following "explanation" of the US fiscal deficit: "The US has about $2.3tn of money coming in, and it spends about $3.6tn. So imagine you were making $23,000 a year and spending $36,000. What would happen? You'd be in debt, and you'd have to cut your spending. The US is in the same pickle. Except, instead of a few thousand, it has to cut $1.3tn."

These 57 words were and are unmitigated nonsense, wrong from beginning to end, with the factual errors the least of its sins against clear thinking (the correct numbers for the first sentence are $2.7 and $3.7 trillion). Long before the end of this book the reader will know it makes no sense and why.

In recent decades in most of the developed world, business interests (and with equal frequency governments) have fostered the doctrine of "choice" in almost every aspect of society. People should have the opportunity to choose the schools for their children, so we should pass out vouchers rather than fund public primary and secondary education. Public provision of health restricts the right of people to choose doctors. Social security should be privatized so that people can choose the retirement plan they want. These and other arguments for "choice" come from the presumption that people have the information and specialized analytical knowledge to select among complex alternatives, the *idée fixe* of the economics mainstream.

Consider just the last of these alleged choices: social security and retirement. To make an informed decision among retirement schemes, a person would need to assess the market risk associated with each. This assessment requires knowledge of the past performance of a large number of financial funds. Even with this narrow technical skill and the time to investigate the bewildering range of options, objective, reliable and unbiased information is required. That type of information must be separated from beguiling propaganda. To argue that this problem can be solved by hiring an "expert advisor" is no answer. Which advisor can be trusted?

The media, governments and business interests assure the public that We the People have the knowledge to make these decisions. At the same time, in practice most people are convinced that they are so ignorant of economics that they cannot venture an informed opinion. This is the General Law of Public Ignorance of Mainstream Economics:

> The individual is capable of informed choices in all areas, except for economic policy, which the individual must leave to experts.

The General Law requires the belief in and obedience to specific laws certified by mainstream economics. These include (among many others) the laws of 1) supply and demand; 2) that public sector deficits are inflationary; 3) that taxes are a burden; and 4) that higher wages and better working conditions reduce employment; to name but a few of those more frequently encountered.

The intelligence and curiosity of humans tells us that knowledge is easier to acquire than ignorance is to maintain. The General Law overcomes this obstacle through a combination of professional fraud, intellectual intimidation and service to the interests of the rich and powerful. The professional fraud involves creating an imaginary economy to explain, in place of the one in which humans live. I dissect this in considerable but necessary detail. On the basis of that fraud mainstream economists generate reductionist parables analogous to Aesop's Fables, but with less insight. These parables, such as that taxes are a burden on individuals, are defended on the grounds that they are self-evident, or based on a theory too complex for the layperson to comprehend, and contested only by fools and nutcases.

To put it in a cliché-ridden nutshell: accept the mainstream parables because they are obvious. If they are not obvious to you it is because they are based on theory beyond your expertise. And if you persist in not embracing them your objection is foolish and irrelevant. But, don't they all carry at least a grain of truth? Aren't taxes a burden? Isn't inflation the result of government spending too much money? When wages rise it costs more to employ people, so isn't it obvious that employment will be less? The answers are (in order), *no, no* and *no.*

To understand how and why all but a few people, perhaps begrudgingly, accept these phony parables *and* why they are wrong, is the purpose of this book. So successful has been the free market propaganda that no re-education can hope for success by treating issues piecemeal. The reader has no alternative to beginning at first principles and inspecting the world mainstream economists make for themselves and then sell with great success to the rest of us.

After I show that the building blocks of the free market dogma peddled by mainstream economists are absurd, I can deal with specific propositions produced by those absurdities. I begin with the biggest and most pervasive falsehood of all: market competition is a good thing. The incantation that competition is virtuous provides the basis for misrepresenting markets as inherently benign, and by extension that capitalism, made up of all those competitive markets, is itself inherently benign. Lurking in reserve is the accusation that failure to embrace the virtuousness of the market makes the skeptic a *de facto* supporter of socialist central planning.

With the successful sale of the big lie of benign competition, it becomes possible to take this down to the household level, and preach the absurdly improbable dogma that benign capitalism offers the opportunity of riches to everyone. Like a witch's familiar, along with the false promise of personal riches goes "the consumer." Be you rich or be you poor, you are part of the royal family of capitalism, because The Consumer Is Sovereign.

xviiiECONOMICS OF THE 1%

Once people accept that benign markets can bestow riches upon them and grant a title of sovereignty, the more serious lies that guide the policies of governments follow on closely. Public intervention in markets is bad. Free trade among countries brings cheap commodities and jobs. The source of economic ills is the government, which oppresses you with its arbitrary rules, regulations and taxes. Having taken you this far, the next step, wildly improbable on its own, is an easy sell. Free and unregulated markets result in free and unregulated people. Happy are the people in the land where markets are free.

The truth lies elsewhere. As was well recognized across the political spectrum at the end of World War II, unregulated capitalist competition leads not to a free people, but down the dark road to fascism. Once the bright and flashy promises of free markets are exposed as lies, it becomes possible to construct a capitalism fit for human life. The design involves no reinvention, just common sense, a commitment to a decent society, and adapting and updating what we know. Achieving it requires a profound shift in political power, which I confront in the last chapter.

This book is not an antimarket polemic. I do not carry an agenda for an authoritarian, centrally planned economy that the right wingers see in every reasonable and progressive proposal for social and economic reform. I defend markets as effective social mechanisms, *if and only if* they are regulated through a democratic process for the collective good, not when they are left "free" to concentrate riches in the hands of a few. More on that in the last chapter. First, I expose the lies and myths.

Further Reading

Robert Heilbroner, *The Worldly Philosophers: The Lives, Times, and Ideas of the Great Economic Thinkers* (New York: Penguin Business Library, 1995).

John Kenneth Galbraith, *A History of Economics: The Past of the Present* (New York: Penguin, 1987).

Chapter 1

FAKECONOMICS AND ECONOMICS

This paper, then, is a serious analysis of a ridiculous subject, which is of course the opposite of what is usual in economics.

(Paul Krugman)

Do not be alarmed by simplification, complexity is often a device for claiming sophistication, or for evading simple truths.

(John Kenneth Galbraith)

Idolatry of Competition

From tiny acorns great oaks grow. In a case of dogma imitating nature, from low and banal theory mainstream economists ascend to extreme ideological heights. With superficial and simplistic propositions the economics mainstream constructs a great and complex ideological edifice from which it issues oracle-like judgments over the affairs of humankind (see Box: The Construction of Nonsense). The employment, inflation and antigovernment parables of the current mainstream derive from a shortlist of putatively incontestable propositions which can be found in almost all introductory, and many advanced, textbooks:

1. Desires and preferences are unique to each person;
2. on the basis of these desires and preferences people enter into exchanges of their free will, seeking to satisfy themselves through market exchanges with other people;
3. these market activities, including the exchange of a person's capacity to work, are to obtain the income to buy the goods and services dictated by the person's desires and preferences;
4. many people seeking simultaneously to buy and sell generates competition; and this competition ensures that people buy and sell at prices that are socially beneficial;

5. action by any collective or individual authority, private or public, that restricts the potential for people to buy and sell reduces the social benefits generated by markets;

6. in the private sector monopolies (sellers) and monopsonies (buyers) reduce welfare. Much more pernicious are the welfare-reducing actions of governments, which proclaim good intentions while restricting freedom. These restrictions include all forms of taxation, which reduce people's incomes, alter market prices of goods and services, and lower the incentive to work below its "natural" level (that is, its market level). Many government expenditures have the same effect, such as unemployment compensation reducing the incentive to work, and subsidies to public schools that distort individual choice among potential providers.

I can summarize this shortlist of antisocial generalities briefly. People have a desire for goods and services beyond their current earning capacity, requiring them to make choices. Choice occurs when they allocate their incomes among their wants in the manner that will best fulfill those wants. For all people added together, wants are unlimited and the resources to satisfy them are finite. Economics is the study of the allocation of scarce resources among unlimited wants to maximize individual welfare. Government actions restrict, limit and distort the ability of people to make their choices. Its role should be strictly limited, in order to minimize those restrictions, limits and distortions.

This is the central narrative of mainstream economists, that markets are efficient organizers of economic life. Winston Churchill famously defended political democracy by arguing that "democracy is the worst form of government except all those other forms that have been tried." The mainstream economics profession accepts no such ironic minimalism in its defense of markets.

In the ideological myopia of big money and its economic priests, markets are not only more efficient than alternative methods of allocation and distribution, they are the *only* efficient method. Even more, markets are efficient if and only if they are not regulated in any manner. "Controlled" economies (socialist and communist) are by far the worst, but regulated markets in capitalist countries are almost as destructive of individual welfare.

Economic life organized through free markets is not merely the best, it is the only "good." Irrefutable evidence for this assertion is demonstrated in the fact that markets cannot be eliminated even in the most draconian communist state; they can only be "suppressed." As a result, attempts at the regulation of markets, even more the banning of them, does no more than to drive them underground ("black markets"), distorting the natural tendency of people to "truck, barter and exchange" (Adam Smith). Human activity is market driven: There Is No Alternative, the most fundamental of the many TINA principles so commonly found in the public pronouncements of mainstream economists.

The Construction of Nonsense

The modifier "neoclassical" has a decidedly retrograde origin in economics. In the mid-1930s J. M. Keynes designated his adversaries in the profession the "classicals." This sowed everlasting confusion. When written with a capital C the word refers to those who based their analysis on some version of the labor theory of value – Adam Smith (albeit a confused version), David Ricardo, Karl Marx and John Stuart Mill being the most famous.

By contrast the economists Keynes designated as the "classicals" argued that a society ruled by markets automatically and continuously adjusts to full employment, and efficiently allocates resources and allows individuals to maximize their pleasure through consumption. Keynes considered this Pollyanna-esque analysis at best a description of the special case in which the economy has full employment. This was why he titled his great work *The* **General** *Theory of Employment, Interest and Money* (1936). Almost immediately the priests of free markets launched their counterattack. By the 1950s the "classicals" had seduced most economists into accepting that a combination of the analysis of Keynes and their own reactionary views was both possible and desirable – the "neoclassical synthesis."

This bogus synthesis, the Trojan Horse of the economics profession, would be the vehicle by which the classical nihilists would roll back and bit by bit destroy the theoretical understanding generated by the greatest theorist of modern economics. The current organized neoclassical censorship of alternative ideas is the equivalent of the anti-Copernicans taking advantage of the conviction of Galileo for heresy in 1615 to destroy all evidence of a heliocentric solar system.

If you think that I have descended into scurrilous polemics, read Paul Krugman, winner of one of the Bank of Sweden "Nobel" Prizes:

> We're living in a Dark Age of macroeconomics... What made the Dark Ages dark was the fact that so much knowledge had been lost... And that's what seems to have happened to macroeconomics in much of the economics profession... I'm tempted to go on and say something about being overrun by barbarians in the grip of an obscurantist faith, but I guess I won't. Oh wait, I guess I just did.

Teflon Pseudoscience

The difficulty lies, not in the new ideas, but in escaping from the old ones, which ramify, for those brought up as most of us have been, into every corner of our minds.

(J. M. Keynes)

Many people would disagree with and even be disgusted by the political and policy conclusions of mainstream economics (e.g., all unemployment is voluntary). However, the same people who disagree with the conclusions might reluctantly accept the premises of the argument. These premises should not be accepted. They are wrong – no more than ideological pretenses.

First, market choices by people are not the result of preferences and desires arising at the individual level. An individual has choices in markets as a result of living in a society with a division of labor that has organized its production and distribution in a specific historical manner. The existence of markets is a social phenomenon. Second, whatever the source of people's wants and needs, whether or not they enter into exchanges "willingly" is a matter of definition. For example, no one is forced through physical coercion to forego medical treatment because it is too expensive. Nonetheless it is a choice many people make in most countries, and a choice that would not be presented to a person in a humane society. Third, because preferences arise from a person's social interaction, and many choices are forced upon us, the collective actions of people to improve their society by government intervention cannot be condemned in general as restricting freedom.

Opponents and critical supporters of markets have made these arguments many times. They never "stick." As with cooking utensils made of Teflon, the ideology of the mainstream can be wiped clean of criticism with astounding ease. No appeal to justice or decency has a long-term or fundamental impact on the hegemony of mainstream economic ideology. It should be obvious that this ideology serves the interest of wealth and power. That has been true for 200 years, though the current, absurd version of economics was not always hegemonic. Why now? Before that question can even be asked, I must demonstrate the absurdity of this hegemonic mumbo jumbo.

The ideology preaches that "the market," omniscient and omnipresent, is both tyrannical and benevolent, like one of the ancient gods of the Greeks and Romans. It manifests its tyranny in its relentless control over production, distribution and allocation of the necessities of human life. Its benevolence is sublime, through the boundless pleasure it can deliver in personal consumption of the commodities it distributes. Like all gods it demands disciplined obedience to its fundamental laws. It rewards the obedient with riches and punishes the rebellious with misery in a myriad of forms (e.g., unemployment) that all result from vainglorious attempts to challenge its will.

Like gods, it issues pronouncements – "judgment of markets" – which are accepted in reverent passivity (see below for obvious examples). Be they about executive salaries or the price of heating oil, all the judgments carry the same divine authority: "You can't argue with supply and demand." These are universal laws of human interaction that can no more be altered than water can be prevented from running down hill.

We know that these laws are universal and inexorable because their operation has been theoretically explained and that explanation empirically verified by the science of the market, "economics." At the root of the current triumphant return of the nineteenth-century antisocial arguments for "the market" is the ingrained belief, even among most progressives, of the logical power, technical strength and empirical validity of mainstream economic theory. As much as we may criticize the reactionary views of economists, at the end of the day "you just can't deny market fundamentals."

That is wrong. There are no "market fundamentals" in the sense that the mainstream has coined the phrase. Mainstream, "neoclassical" economics is not logically powerful, technically strong or empirically valid. On the contrary, its logic is contradictory, its techniques sloppy, and the real world economy refutes its generalizations with startling regularity. Concrete examples of the illogic abound, as I shall demonstrate.

In other words, mainstream economics is, as the British would say, rubbish; or, to be less polite, a real load of crap. The rest of this book verifies that hypothesis, beginning with considering how markets operate in reality, followed by an excursion into the Land Where Econfakers Dwell.

How Real Markets Operate

A few characteristics of markets, as obvious as they might appear, need to be made explicit before I can consider the putative scientific content of mainstream "neoclassical" economics. Most purchases and sales do not occur in markets in the literal sense. They occur in department stores, warehouses, online and by telephone, to name the most obvious.

These purchases and sales occur at different times and under different conditions. The motor vehicle sector provides a good example, because it has various stages of production and distribution. When someone refers to the "market for automobiles," the word "market" is used in a descriptively loose sense to refer to all the purchases of automobiles in a specified area during a specific period of time; for example, "the market for new cars in the US in 2011."

This "market" can be divided into its component parts of production and distribution. On the basis of an estimate of sales for the market period, each automobile company hires the workers it requires and arranges for the delivery of the necessary raw materials and intermediate parts. Depending on the specific policies of each company, some or most of the workers will be on contracts longer than the time it takes to produce, deliver and sell the cars. This simplifies hiring while slightly limiting the discretion of management to change wages and working conditions. When production is occurring, the marketing outlets have in their showrooms automobiles produced in the previous period, so production and sale occur concurrently.

Many factors influence total automobile sales, with perhaps the most important being the general level of economic prosperity. If employment is high, households are likely to be in a buoyant mood and disposed to replace their old vehicles; if unemployment is rising, households will be more cautious. How many vehicles each company sells is more complicated to determine, influenced by consumer brand recognition, effectiveness of advertising, and the market power of each seller, among other things.

In this market the prices of automobiles will be set by the companies from recent market experience, judgments as to whether household demand will be strong or weak, and an assessment of the public impression of the advantages of each model compared to its competitors. If most companies are too optimistic, slow sales will result in accumulation of automobiles in showrooms or on the great holding lots by the factories. This accumulation is at no cost to buyers, who might benefit if retailers lower prices to reduce inventories. For the producers and retailers it represents a considerable problem, because the unsold vehicles embody costs that the company owners wish to recover.

If the companies predict sales too pessimistically, many retailers quickly empty their showrooms and make new, urgent orders to the factories. When such a shortage occurs in the automobile market, adjustment comes through several responses. Households can either place themselves on a waiting list, or shift to another model by the same company or a different company. The companies can attempt to reduce production and delivery delays through extra shifts in the factories.

The asymmetry of surpluses and shortages characterizes markets. The surpluses are easy for both buyers and sellers to observe, and carry a substantial explicit cost to sellers. If the commodity is perishable (as with supermarket merchandise) or sensitive to shifting preferences (as in the clothing industry), surpluses can mean a near-total loss of the value of the excess inventory. In contrast, a shortage of a commodity can go unobserved or be merely a matter of opinion. For the company a shortage means missed sales volume, but how much, even whether it is small or large, is speculative. It should be obvious that if offered a choice between certain losses from excessive inventory and notional losses of undeterminable amount from shortages, most companies would choose the latter.

This description of the automobile market, shamelessly realistic compared to the markets of mainstream economics, is extremely simplified. It does not include household access to borrowing, the influence of automobile durability, obsolescence or the role of advertising. Markets for other products would exhibit some of the characteristics described above as well as their own, depending on whether the item is for households or producers, if for households whether it is durable or nondurable, and if nondurable whether it is rapidly perishable.

In spite of this variety, a few generalizations are possible. First, except in unusual times market processes have a tendency to reduce the accumulation of surplus commodities and prevent extreme shortages. The first is achieved by direct observation: when the quantity of a product at the retail level exceeds what the companies consider appropriate, they reduce deliveries and reduce production. Extreme shortages are avoided in great part when buyers shift to similar, alternative commodities, though this is not as clear a signal to companies as the accumulation of unwanted inventories.

Market adjustments to shortages and surpluses are not perfect. A surplus of working men and women – unemployment – is endemic in market economies, occasionally catastrophically high, and the poverty created by unemployment is a shameful offence to civilized values. Nonetheless, market economies are considerably more flexible and effective in organizing production and distribution for both companies and households than the various administrative systems practiced in the Soviet Union, East and Central Europe, and China and Vietnam before the 1990s. On superficial inspection market economies seem more amenable to reform and regulation than administrative systems that have in every case been based on undemocratic regimes. We would certainly be justified in paraphrasing Churchill: "Markets are the worst from of economic organization except all those other forms that have been tried."

While mainstream economists may walk among the rest of us in supermarkets and department stores, that is not the world in which they dwell. They live in another land, where no shortages or surpluses occur, where unemployment is unknown and the past, present and future are the same. Just as every soul in heaven is virtuous, economists dwell in a land in which every market is perfect, and would (and do) say, "Markets are the perfect form of economic organization."

Where Econfakers Dwell

Buying and selling in individual markets appears to eliminate surpluses and shortages because the former are costly to sellers and the latter cannot be directly observed, only inferred from people's behavior. The operation of a market usually results in little or no surplus and with few people desperately pining for more. This makes markets useful but does not mean they are efficient in any sense other than avoiding excessive surpluses and shortages.

Accepting this common-sense view requires a bit of the "backstory" of markets. Markets have existed for thousands of years, and more recently in countries with central planning. Their functions were very limited except in capitalist societies over the last 250 years. To give an example, in Cuba in the early 1990s the government legalized marketing of specified agricultural products from small farms and individual garden plots. These exchanges represented a tiny portion of the food people consumed, most of which was allocated through a rationing system or purchased from government-run shops.

No market for the things required for agricultural products, or "inputs," existed and producers were legally limited to family labor. Further, the produce sold in private markets represented a surplus after government procurement. The small markets for private production did not allocate resources in the agricultural sector. Sellers could not to any substantial extent respond to prices in that market by varying their production, because there was no market in labor, land, credit or other inputs.

This example indicates that markets are a bit like automobiles: if there are no or few roads, then there is no place to drive. The equivalent in market transactions is a formal guarantee of right of ownership. In a society in which economic life is regulated through markets, the sales of commodities provides "signals" to producers. The most important "signal" is the level of sales. For example, if the sales of a book exceed the stock held in a bookstore, more are ordered and vice versa. Prices play a minor signaling role, if any at all.

The increases and decreases in orders prompt changes in the number of people employed by the company printing the book, and, in turn, orders for nonlabor inputs. Prices change, but do so with much less frequency than quantities. In general the "signaling" is from quantities to prices. When a book is "jumping off the shelf," the shopkeeper does not raise the price of those copies that remain; more are ordered. Price only comes into play when the shops give up and offer a book as a "remainder," at a rock-bottom, give-away sale price. I discovered this fact of life one day when I walked by the famous Economists' Bookshop in London and saw an embarrassingly large stack of my first book, marked £1 each, down from £40 (I bought them all).

The reality of "the clearing of markets" is "sell it or smell it," as they say in the supermarket trade. There is very little efficiency in this process, but it has the great advantage that in normal times it is a self-adjustment that requires no organized intervention to tidy up its mess, as would be likely in a centrally planned system. It also has obvious deficiencies. Perhaps foremost among these is the distribution of purchasing power. Many people may want a certain book, but with their low incomes would find it irresponsible to lay out $50 for it in place of medicine for high blood pressure, buying food for the day or paying the car insurance premium. Public libraries are a partial solution to this social inadequacy of the book market.

A further drawback from the buyer's perspective, which everyone has experienced, is the discovery after a purchase that the identical product can be bought more advantageously elsewhere. For many people this represents a minor annoyance, as in "I could kick myself for not shopping around more." For poor households with limited transport facilities, it can be a very serious matter. In 1997, a study for the US Department of Agriculture concluded:

> Low-income households may face higher food prices for three reasons: (1) on average, low-income households may spend less in supermarkets – which typically offer the lowest prices and greatest range of brands, package sizes, and quality choices; (2) low-income households are less likely to live in suburban locations where food prices are typically lower; and (3) supermarkets in low-income neighborhoods may charge higher prices than those in nearby higher income neighborhoods.

Various public policy interventions can reduce this form of price discrimination, from the minimalist, requiring chain stores to post prices in an easily accessible form, to various actions to reduce market power, such as prohibiting wholesalers from setting prices for retailers (called wholesale price maintenance in the US), or the direct regulation of prices.

Still more market inadequacies arise when buyers and sellers, both households and businesses, lack adequate information to engage in a transaction, but have no alternative to doing so, such as purchasing healthcare coverage for the family or employees. The lack of sufficient information may arise because 1) the information is too difficult or expensive to obtain; 2) it is unattainable because the other party in the transaction controls it; 3) the controller of the information may lie; or 4) it is unknowable (e.g., how long you might live).

Collective management of risk, the principle governing both private and public insurance programs, represents one way to deal with these information deficiencies. Examples are the US Medicare program to protect the health of the elderly or deposit insurance to protect savings in financial institutions. The former provides a standardized service whose quality is verified by an independent third party not directly involved in either the delivery or the use of the service or product (a federal government department). In Western Europe people receive almost all healthcare through collective means, organized within a range of public and private institutions. Private sector insurance operates similarly, using actuarial tables – "average risk" – to set premiums.

These well-known, everyday problems with markets – affordability, discrimination and inadequate information – are not fatal flaws. All can be managed in the public interest, and to varying degrees have been. While not fatal, they do imply that markets, as with everything else in this imperfect world are also, well, imperfect. And being imperfect, markets require careful and responsible collective (public) oversight and regulation.

As obvious and reasonable as the previous paragraph may be (i.e., experience makes it obvious that markets are imperfect, so they should be regulated) mainstream economics rejects it out of hand as the superficial babbling of the ignorant. Markets are efficient. They allocate resources to optimal use. They bring consumers what they want, of the quality desired, at prices that correctly signal the social cost of providing those goods and services. Except in extraordinary cases, of which there are very few, regulation of markets reduces human welfare and happiness. So goes the story in the economics mainstream.

How does the mainstream sustain this market liberation propaganda when all experience is to the contrary? More important, why do the vast majority of people in English-speaking developed countries believe it, when their everyday market transactions contradict it? Even turkeys squawk when confronted with their executioners, but not so with consumers, most of whom accept the "iron laws of supply and demand."

The first task of promarket propaganda is to convince people that they lack the competence to assess their own market experiences. Rather like the role of the priest in some religions, those experiences must be interpreted through the intermediation of mainstream economics. We must all accept that our mundane exchange activities – buying food, paying rent or the mortgage, saving for unforeseen events – come about through extremely complex processes that only the experts fully understand. Partial understanding can be granted on a conditional basis to a few, for example bankers and hedge fund speculators, because of their instinctive reverence for unregulated markets. But the masses can never acquire such knowledge, only revere it.

Once people become convinced that experts monopolize knowledge of everyday economic processes, the promarket deed is done. The experts present themselves in unanimous agreement that markets are "good." As proof of unanimity, the mainstream economists identify dissenters as fools and nutcases. A process of elimination establishes the proof of the "goodness" of markets. Eliminate every possible source of problems that markets might generate and, contradictory to direct experience, perfection becomes the only possible conclusion. I stress that what the mainstream calls competition is not some subtle, counterintuitive process such as quantum mechanics, analytically accessible only after years of training. On the contrary, competition involves a complicated but easily understood process that requires no esoteric terminology or specialized knowledge to explain. True to their calling, econfakers obscure the simple with a façade of unnecessary complexity.

The process of elimination proceeds as follows. First, treat distributions of wealth and income as independent of the operation of markets themselves. Distribution represents "initial conditions" about which each person may hold a subjective opinion, but that opinion has no role in judging markets. I hardly need point out that this treatment of distribution is absurd. The structure of household and business demand determines the composition of production, and the distribution of income and wealth determine the structure of demand. Were there no billionaires, there would be no private seagoing yachts or jet planes.

It is not surprising that when an economist sings the praises of markets, he or she rarely prefaces with, "By the way, I am assuming that the distribution of income has no impact on markets."

This "assumption" proves very convenient. It dismisses all market problems and outrages that result from unequal access to economic power. People enter market transactions with what they have, and questioning of distribution degenerates the analysis into antiscientific subjectivity. This is the deadly sin of "normative" assessments in a "positive" science, a distinction made the keystone of mainstream economics by Paul Samuelson (see Box: "Nobel" Prizes for Nonsense). When to this we add the "assumption" that all exchanges are voluntary, the space for criticizing markets because of inequalities shrinks to zero.

Having ruled out qualms arising from the inequalities generated by markets, we turn to the problems of access to information. The free marketeers can dismiss this with ease. Assume that every market participant enjoys access to true and full information about every aspect of every potential exchange now and in the future ("perfect knowledge and foresight"). If treating distribution to be independent of markets was absurd, this one is a howler. Misrepresentation of products, misleading advertising, insider trading, even the cost of acquiring information – forget them all and forge ahead in free market bliss. The mainstream might justify this analytical trick under more apparently respectable names, such as "rational expectations," the "efficient market hypothesis," and "cost benefit of acquiring more information." These are alternative hoots from the same howl.

The nagging problem of widespread market discrimination due to the power of large buyers or sellers remains. Some background is necessary before confronting this issue. A person may have true and full information (I know relatively few that do), but still be cheated because he or she cannot access better market conditions, though they exist. This problem results because exchanges for any product happen at different times and places. All measures of sales by necessity refer to some specific time period, as in "food sales in August."

Even in the absence of discrimination and fraud, the same item can be sold at different prices within a short period of time in the same place. An obvious example is when supermarkets discount to "move" merchandise quickly. The commonly observed variations in prices show that markets may be flexible, but they are not "efficient." Buying and selling the same product at different times and places creates the basis for capricious exercise of market power. What appears as market flexibility, prices allegedly "adjusting" to changing conditions, may actually represent exercise of market control by powerful enterprises. For this reason, mainstream economics insists that competition will insure that one and only one price is offered for the same product – the so-called Law of One Price.

To summarize, the mainstream says that the prices thrown up by markets indicate the true underlying cost of producing and distributing a commodity. If powerful companies and individuals can manipulate markets, this cannot be true. The "markets tell us the true cost" story lacks credibility even in the absence of obvious market manipulation. If a package of lettuce sells at $2 when the supermarket opens, then at $1 an hour before closing time (again, the "sell it or smell it" rule of pricing), which represents the true cost? If we take an average, are all sales equally representative, or are the later (or earlier) ones the more accurate "signals"? Mainstream economists cut this Gordian Knot – markets send *too many signals too often* to buyers and sellers – by an additional assumption: that exchanges occur simultaneously in one big market place, which by definition allows only one price for each transaction.

You might think that this journey into the absurd has reached its limit by now: 1) wealth and income distribution is ignored; 2) buyers and sellers know everything that need be known; and 3) all exchanges occur simultaneously. However, there remains a serious procedural problem. Who sets the price in these transactions? Because both the buyer and the seller seek to maximize gain from the transactions, neither can be trusted by the other to set the price. Haggling back and forth cannot be allowed because it creates the possibility that the exchange will be influenced by market power, with the result that the agreed price will deviate from the "true" cost of production and distribution.

In 1961 Joseph Heller, himself a former crew member of a B-25 bomber during World War II, published a best-selling book, *Catch-22*. The title referred to an apocryphal rule in a US Air Force manual stating that anyone claiming dispensation from combat because of mental instability was by definition sane enough to realize that he suffered from instability, therefore fit to fight. The question of how a price is set in competitive market transactions represents the Catch-22 of mainstream market theory.

It is, indeed, a quandary. Buyers and sellers mutually agree to exchanges, but either making a concrete offer calls the purity of markets into doubt. For example, consistent price setting by the seller, as for almost all actual exchanges, in shops, stores, online or by telephone, may signal the presence of market power, suggesting need for public oversight. This oversight could be mild, through a consumer protection agency, or aggressive, by laws that limit the market shares of companies and preventing collusion among buyers and sellers.

Escaping the logic for public regulation requires that the mainstream economists exclude from their models of markets even the possibility of market power. Buyers and sellers cannot be permitted to discuss prices among themselves. We require something dramatic and innovative to square this circle of competitive price setting. The salvation comes in the form of the auctioneer. Amid all the buyers and sellers, who wait eagerly to make their exchanges, stands the auctioneer, who shouts the price for all exchanges. When the auctioneer barks out a price, it immediately becomes the price, accepted passively and dutifully by all buyers and sellers.

As in Heller's novel when Yossarian marvels, "That's some catch, that Catch-22," the auctioneer is truly awe inspiring. The prices supplied must have a very specific outcome. They must result in no surpluses, no shortages, and leave every buyer and seller happy. This is the imaginary land constructed by economists, in which markets function perfectly and public oversight is not only unnecessary, it is "bad," because any regulatory intervention prevents the outcome that leaves everyone content. The reader should sniff the odor of circularity – by assumption the econfakers construct a concept of markets in which those markets function to social perfection, then argue that public regulation pollutes this perfection.

The fanciful argument achieves contentment for all buyers and sellers by passing through the looking glass into a land of the imagination of economists. This economic version of Cloud Cuckoo Land has no production, only buying and selling which occurs simultaneously in one big market. In the Aristophanes play *The Birds* (414 BC), from whence the term comes, two characters, Pisthetairos and Euelpides, construct a perfect city suspended in the sky, with the name Cloud Cuckoo Land. It would be difficult if not impossible to find a more precisely appropriate term for the market analysis offered so fervently by the economics mainstream.

In that great neoclassical economics megamarket, people come with a variety of commodities that they do not want, to exchange for ones they do want. The market operates according to the following inflexible rules:

1. It is supervised by an all-powerful auctioneer;
2. the auctioneer announces to the buyers what is for sale, to the sellers what the buyers seek to purchase, and to both the prices at which exchange can occur; and
3. all exchanges are at the same moment, and none occurs without the explicit approval of the auctioneer.

In this marketplace buyers and sellers have no influence on prices, because the neoclassical economics theorist does not permit them to.

The discriminating reader might well ask why I present this ridiculous farce, a market of simultaneous exchanges that never produces surpluses or shortages, and no haggling over prices occurs. This absurdity is farcical because the absence of surpluses, shortages and haggling is purely *deus ex machina*. It results from no interaction of traders. The superficially efficient outcome results from the imaginary auctioneer overseeing equally imaginary exchanges. To put it bluntly, this market has no surpluses, shortages or haggling because I have not allowed them. Similar to the methodology of the Bellman in Lewis Carroll's "The Hunting of the Snark," these markets have no surpluses or shortages because "what I tell you three times is true."

I present this credibility-challenged fantasy market because, as hard as it may be for the layperson to believe, it serves as the theoretical foundation of mainstream economics. Formally known as Walrasian general equilibrium theory, elaborating its absurdities could win the apostle a Bank of Sweden "Nobel" Prize (see Box: "Nobel" Prizes for Nonsense), the gold medal of economic theory. In case the reader thinks I made all this up, go to a typical website devoted to explaining economic theory and read: "Some of the problems with Walras general economic equilibrium theory included the fact that the perfect competition assumption was, of course, invalid. Also, how would new prices get established in the first place? Walras assumed that an auctioneer or 'crier' would announce prices."

Mainstream economists have no theory to show that unregulated markets produce socially beneficial, efficient results. Even more, as strange as it may seem to the layperson, mainstream economics has no explanation of prices themselves.

This excursion into farce masquerading as theory does not demonstrate how a market economy is guided by the "invisible hand," which Adam Smith used to justify simultaneously the avarice of the 1% and the virtues of markets:

> The rich...are led by an invisible hand to make nearly the same distribution of the necessaries of life, which would have been made, had the earth been divided into equal portions among all its inhabitants, and thus without intending it, without knowing it, advance the interest of the society.

Far from being guided by forces impersonal and out of sight, the Walrasian theory of markets that informs mainstream economics has a very visible and heavy hand, a mythical auctioneer whose intervention prevents markets from descending into disarray. There is no invisible hand, in practice or in theory.

Referring to the free market advocates that preceded him, J. M. Keynes famously commented, "Even the most practical man of affairs is usually in the thrall of the ideas of some long-dead economist." I regret

---

"Nobel" Prizes for Nonsense

In 1968 the Central Bank of Sweden, Sveriges Riksbank, instituted the Sveriges Riksbank Prize in Economic Sciences in Memory of Alfred Nobel. The long-winded title gives the impression that the award is a Nobel Prize alongside those for Peace, Physics, Chemistry, Medicine and Literature. It is not, though by practice (imitation and aspiration?) it is announced at the same time.

In 1999 Barbara Bergmann, a prominent US economist, explained the "contributions" of recent winners as follows:

> The prize frequently occasions embarrassment, since we have to explain to the public what the achievement of the newest laureate is. That achievement is usually...a totally made-up, simplified representation of some process we all know takes place. People snickered when they heard that James Buchanan's prize was for telling us that politicians and bureaucrats act in their own interests, Robert Lucas's was for telling us that people do the best they can in doping out what to do, and Franco Modigliani's was for telling us that people save and spend their savings at different times in their lives.

Referring specifically to Robert Fogel, who in 1993 won for demonstrating the economic "rationality" of slavery, and to Gary Becker for the insight that the subordinate role of women in the labor force is optimizing behavior (1992), Bergmann wrote: "Fogel's and Becker's awards were not just in bad taste. Those prizes honored work that distilled complicated and sometimes painful phenomena into simplistic representations of cheeringly optimal processes."

The "contributions" of Buchanan, Lucas, et al. seem seminal compared to later ones. In 1997 Myron Scholes and Robert C. Merton garnered the Sveriges Riksbank Prize for their breakthroughs in the theory of capital markets ("break" being singularly appropriate). Using their contributions to science they helped create in 1994 a scheme for high-stakes speculation, Long-Term Capital Management (LTCM). In one of those outcomes a critic couldn't make up, the scheme of the laureates went spectacularly bust in 1998, losing $4.6 billion. To my knowledge, no one at Sveriges Riksbank expressed embarrassment, much less an apology.

There have been outstanding recipients, Jan Tinbergen (1969), Gunnar Myrdal (1974) and Amartya Sen (1998). However, if via a time machine you were to gather all the winners in the same room, the vast majority would strike you as crashing bores and decidedly reactionary.

to say that most of the economists defending the virtues of markets are very much alive and have proved to be as brilliant at free market propaganda as they are at their banal and trivial theorizing. The rest of this book attempts to dispel the confusion and disinformation that their theory has marketed through smoke, mirrors and illusions, easily outdoing the Wizard of Oz.

Fakeconomics and Economics: Name and Shame

> While they prate of economic laws, men and women are starving. We must lay hold of the fact that economic laws are not made by nature. They are made by human beings.
>
> (Franklin D. Roosevelt)

For the rest of the book I shall not use the term "mainstream economics," in part because of its inherent ambiguity. I shall apply the more accurate term "fakeconomics" (pronounced "fake-economics"). The opposition between alchemy and chemistry, and astrology and astronomy suggested this term to me as singularly appropriate. In order that this word not be interpreted as a mere term of abuse and insult (which it certainly is), I will carefully define it.

Fakeconomics is the study of exchange relationships that have no counterpart in the real world and are endowed with metaphysical powers. These exchanges are voluntary, timeless and carried out by a large number of omniscient creatures of equal prowess. These creatures know all possible outcomes and the likelihood of every exchange, so they are never surprised (they are omniscient, after all). In fakeconomics no difference exists among the past, present and future, and full employment always prevails.

The people who analyze the economy and how it operates in practice are dismissed by the econfakers as vulgar empiricists, ignorant and blasphemous. The econfakers frequently attribute this vulgarity and ignorance to insufficient use of mathematics and lack of technical skills in general. With or without mathematics, a useful way that the nonspecialist can appreciate the role of fakeconomics in society is as a religious sect with an extremely doctrinaire priesthood that zealously guards its doctrines, the most important of which is the magic of markets.

With fakeconomics properly defined, I should not refer to the "fakeconomics school of economics," any more than I would the alchemy school of chemistry or the astrology faction within astronomy.

Further Reading

Price discrimination

Phillip R. Kaufman, James M. MacDonald, Steve M. Lutz and David M. Smallwood, *Do the Poor Pay More for Food? Item Selection and Price Differences Affect Low-Income Household Food Costs* (Washington: USDA, 1997). Online: http://www.ers.usda.gov/Publications/AER759/ (accessed 13 November 2013).

Nonsense-free economics

Robert Heilbroner and James K. Galbraith, *The Economic Problem* (New York: Prentice Hall, 1990).

Steve Keen, *Debunking Economics: The Naked Emperor of the Social Sciences* (Sydney: Zed Books, 2001, revised 2011).

Norbert Häring and Niall Douglas, *Economists and the Powerful: Convenient Theories, Distorted Facts, Ample Rewards* (London: Anthem Press, 2012).

A bit technical

John Weeks, *The Irreconcilable Inconsistencies of Neoclassical Macroeconomics: A False Paradigm* (New York: Routledge, 2012).

The nonsense itself (approach with great care)

Gregory Mankiw, *Principles of Economics*, 5th edition (Stamford, CT: South-Western Cengage Learning, 2011).

Yoram Bauman, "Mankiw's 10 Principles of Economics, Translated for the Uninitiated" (lecture at the AAAS Humor Session, 16 February 2007). Online: http://www.youtube.com/watch?v=VVp8UGjECt4 (accessed 10 October 2013).

Chapter 2

MARKET WORSHIP

What Is Competition?

People of the same trade seldom meet together, even for merriment
and diversion, but the conversation ends in a conspiracy against
the public, or in some contrivance to raise prices.

(Adam Smith)

Competition has been shown to be useful up to a certain point and
no further, but cooperation, which is the thing we must strive for
today, begins where competition leaves off.

(Franklin D. Roosevelt)

I suspect that most people understand "competition" to mean a process
in which more than one person wants an outcome that cannot be gained
by everyone seeking it. This interpretation of competition follows
that found in the Merriam-Webster dictionary, which offers "rivalry"
as the first definition and "contest among rivals" as the second. The
Cambridge dictionary has a more aggressive definition: "a situation in
which someone is trying to win something or be more successful than
someone else," and *a* competition is "an organized event in which
people try to win a prize by being the best, fastest, etc." The explicit
implication of these definitions as well as the common-sense view is that
in competition someone wins and most lose.

Econfakers reject this definition and all it implies. Where they dwell
competition is quite different. First and foremost, it is an outcome,
not a process. Second, and equally fundamental, it is not a rivalry in
which a few win and most lose. It is continuous harmony of economic
coexistence, a romantic dance to market forces. It is a game of musical
chairs with enough chairs for all.

In its own perverse way, this competition-as-its-opposite has a mad logic. If competition is a good thing bringing cheaper commodities to households and efficiency to businesses, it cannot be a contest of rivals. Were market competition among companies similar to a tennis match or the World Cup of football, the rivalry would inevitably produce one winner or collusion among a few survivors.

For example, the user of a cell phone might have many "providers" to choose among. Competition among these companies could at first drive down prices to the benefit of cell phone users. From the perspective of the companies the purpose of the competition is to eliminate rivals and increase market share. The low prices serve as the vehicle by which the contestants fight the competitive struggle. What looks like a good deal to the user (a low price) serves as a selection mechanism to eliminate higher-cost companies. This would be all to the good if that process of elimination resulted in permanently lower prices, but the world of competition does not work that way. If the selection process eliminates all but a few companies, the surviving few gain the power to control prices to the detriment of users.

For mainstream economists the continuous ebb and flow of competition finds no place in their analytical world. In that world, competition exists as a state of grace, neither waxing nor waning, always harmonious, stable and unchanging. I do not wish to be accused by incredulous readers of attributing absurdities to the profession. Therefore, I quote from a mainstream source, which proves considerably more absurd than I or any critic could make up:

> The theoretical free-market situation [occurs when] the following conditions are met: (1) buyers and sellers are too numerous and too small to have any degree of individual control over prices, (2) all buyers and sellers seek to maximize their profit (income), (3) buyers and sellers can freely enter or leave the market, (4) all buyers and sellers have access to information regarding availability, prices and quality of goods being traded, and (5) all goods of a particular nature are homogeneous, hence substitutable for one another. Also called perfect market or pure competition.

If the reader thinks that I have selected with intent to ridicule, I offer another, in even more teeth-grinding detail:

> Competitive markets operate on the basis of a number of assumptions. When these assumptions are dropped – we move

into the world of imperfect competition. These assumptions are discussed below:

1. Many suppliers, each with *an insignificant share of the market* – this means that each firm is too small relative to the overall market to affect price via a change in its own supply – each individual firm is assumed to be a price taker.
2. *An identical output produced by each firm* – in other words, the market supplies homogeneous or standardized products that are perfect substitutes for each other. Consumers perceive the products to be identical.
3. *Consumers have perfect information* about the prices all sellers in the market charge – so if some firms decide to charge a price higher than the ruling market price, there will be a large substitution effect away from this firm.
4. All firms (industry participants and new entrants) are assumed to have *equal access to resources* (technology, other factor inputs) and improvements in production technologies achieved by one firm can spill over to all the other suppliers in the market.
5. There are assumed to be *no barriers to entry and exit of firms* in the long run – which means that the market is open to competition from new suppliers – this affects the long run profits made by each firm in the industry. The long run equilibrium for a perfectly competitive market occurs when the marginal firm makes "normal" profit only in the long term, where "normal" means the absolute minimum that keeps a business in operation.
6. No externalities in production and consumption so that there is no divergence between private and social costs and benefits.

No Microsoft, ExxonMobil or Walmart in the econfakers' Cloud Cuckoo Land, which, it seems, we find contiguous to the principalities of Oz and Never Never Land (and perhaps on the continents of Atlantis or Mu). It is blindingly obvious that encountering a market in which just one of these conditions holds would involve quite a search, and coming up with them all would be as likely as encountering a hen with dentures.

But, wait, the mainstream has an answer to my fecklessly superficial appeal to reality:

Many economists have questioned the validity of studying perfect competition. However, the theory does yield important predictions about what might happen to price and output in the long run if competitive conditions hold good.

There are still markets that can be considered to be highly competitive and in which competition has strengthened in recent years. Good examples of competitive markets include:

- Home and car insurance
- Internet service providers
- Road haulage

The writers at *tutor2u* must not buy their insurance and internet services in the market that I do. The competitiveness of specific markets I dissect below, and here I make a more general point. It is a lame argument that 1) concedes its lack of validity, then claims to usefulness nonetheless; and 2) defends itself with examples.

The authors note that some economists "question" the validity of perfect competition, which is rather like reminding us that some zoologists doubt the existence of unicorns. "However, the theory does yield important predictions." Look back at the assumptions. There is no theory, nothing that can yield anything analytical. We are offered a laundry list of nonexistent characteristics, all of which are required to produce a nonexistent concept. That is not a theory. We are presented with this list and told that from its nonexistent components we can produce "predictions" about reality. The "theory" produces one clear prediction: if you believe it you will believe anything.

Concrete examples can provide strong support for an argument, but they cannot be the *basis* of an argument. Arguing from example results in challenges through counterexamples and bickering over whether the supporting examples do, in fact, support. For an argument to be generally valid, this generally must be credible prior to citing examples.

The assertion that perfect competition helps understand real markets cannot be verified. We need go no further than its first assumption to reject it. Not by accident is the assumption of "many suppliers, each with an insignificant share of the market" always listed first. To be precise, the condition is "many suppliers *and many buyers.*" If this characteristic is not manifested in real markets, the applicability of the perfect competition concept is zilch.

At this point Adam Smith aids our understanding. His empirical and practical analysis of competition refers to a society before large-scale production based on joint-stock companies emerged as important.

His was a eulogy of competition among the small, "atomized" buyers and sellers. This treatment of competition became decreasingly credible as capitalism developed and companies grew, requiring intricately esoteric and absurd specifications to maintain the competitive fiction.

Many myths exist about unicorns. To my knowledge no zoologist suggests that the anatomy of a unicorn guides an understanding of horses or any other real animal. Perfect competition is a myth at best. At worst it misguides us into believing that markets inherently tend toward perfection, with occasional impurities. Accepting this market myth is equivalent to believing that creatures from other planets exist and visit the Earth (apparently over half of adult Americans do, which is not encouraging).

Jean-Jacques Rousseau, eighteenth-century philosopher of the Enlightenment, began *The Social Contract* with the famously dramatic sentence "Man was born free, and he is everywhere in chains." Fakeconomics shifts the shackles from humankind to markets: "Markets are born perfect, but they are everywhere in the chains of government regulation."

Why Markets Go Bad

> Once it is realized that business monopoly in America paralyzes the system of free enterprise on which it is grafted, and is as fatal to those who manipulate it as to the people who suffer beneath its impositions, action by the government to eliminate these artificial restraints will be welcomed by industry throughout the nation.
>
> (Franklin D. Roosevelt)

No great insight is required to understand how and why markets produce antisocial results. The ingenuity lies in explaining why they rarely or never do, or even if they do, why they should not be regulated. Fakeconomics embraces this challenge with zeal. To combat the resultant nonsense, I turn away from the fakeconomics of markets, to the *economics* of markets.

What we call "markets" are not places or events, they are processes. These processes involve the interaction of people separately or in concert, in the context of rules defining appropriate behavior. As everyone knows, many market transactions occur with the purpose of personal or corporate gain. This is not true of the vast majority of purchases that people make. Few people enter a supermarket with the intent to maximize their pleasure from consumption, though most compare prices of different brands of the same product while also influenced by perceptions of quality. The typical shopper fills the supermarket basket with items from a list, goes to the checkout line and pays.

While most transactions are not and need not be carried out for commercial gain and profit, when they are they create the temptation to cheat. A small minority of market participants, mostly rich individuals and companies, hit "the market" with the intention of personal gain. When buying and selling they come under considerable pressure to break the rules, to the detriment of others involved in the transactions. Succumbing to this pressure results more from circumstance than malevolence of character. In practice, market transactions can bring out the worst in people.

To take a rather benign example, a salesperson in a clothing store who receives a commission on each sale may find it difficult to resist the temptation to claim more for the product than it can deliver, as in "This raincoat is 100% waterproof." Considerably less benign is the car salesperson who feloniously resets the odometer on a vehicle to disguise the real mileage.

A moment of nonfakeconomic thought shows these minor and major frauds result from the pressure of individual gain aggravated by rivalry. Competition in the specific sense of many buyers and sellers has an ambiguous and unpredictable effect on the motivation for gain and profit. Consider an example of a bank seeking deposits. If there are few banks, they may collude among themselves to keep deposit interest rates low and restrictions on withdrawals strict. If there are many banks, depositors may initially enjoy higher interest rates and more flexible conditions. These apparent benefits to depositors are likely to result from some of the banks engaging in risky speculation with the deposited funds, as dissenters from the mainstream have repeatedly argued and demonstrated.

The competition that generates the higher interest rates also results in very narrow profit margins. The combination of risky speculation and a narrow margin of commercial safety is a recipe for disaster. Among these disasters is the savings and loan crisis in the US of the late 1980s, which caused the bankruptcy of over 20% of these institutions. In relative terms much more catastrophic was the banking collapse in Iceland that destroyed the country's economy, as well as wiping out billions of dollars in savings of households, companies and local governments in the UK. In April 2012 the Icelandic financial disaster prompted the criminal conviction of the country's prime minister, Geir Haarde, for his part in the fiasco.

In one of those profound insights that only an econfaker could produce, shortly before the Icelandic banking collapse of 2008, Richard

Portes, erstwhile head of the UK Royal Economic Society (and former colleague of mine at Birkbeck College), registered for posterity a cheery assessment in his report for the Icelandic Chamber of Commerce, for which he was paid £58,000: "[Iceland has] an exceptionally healthy institutional framework. The banks have been highly entrepreneurial without taking unsupportable risks. Good supervision and regulation have contributed to that."

The debacle of the "exceptionally healthy" Iceland proved a harbinger of bigger things to come when the great financial collapse hit the North American and Western European banking systems in 2008–2009. The roll call of econfakers who failed to anticipate this unnatural disaster would challenge the length of a telephone book of a smallish town.

These disasters suggest that the consequences of behavior by people and companies under the pressure of competition can be as bad as or worse than the abuses caused by excessive market power. The rational response to this obvious lesson (that market power is the Devil's own work and free competition the Devil himself) is to regulate markets in the public interest. We regulate the pharmaceutical industry to prevent bogus concoctions being sold as diet pills, the sale of used cars to stop scammers from peddling dangerous clunkers, and to avoid the many varieties of insurance fraud that challenge the imagination (see Box: Markets on the Make).

When men and women go to war as soldiers, they kill and maim other men, women and frequently children. Harming other members of humankind does not come naturally to people. We engage in such pathologically antisocial action because of the circumstances in which we find ourselves and the training we receive to behave in those circumstances. Similarly, people do not by their natures engage in commercial fraud and deception. On the contrary, all but a tiny portion of population in any country would vigorously condemn such behavior. Analogously to war, people defraud other people, perhaps even their friends, neighbors and relatives, because commercial gain in markets generates strong incentives to do so.

Market fraud occurs for the same reason that athletes attempt to cheat by taking performance-enhancing drugs. Through the "rules of the game" authorities attempt to restrict such behavior. Similarly, market regulations eliminate, to the extent possible, cheating, fraud and deception in transactions among households and businesses. Public regulation of markets involves nothing more than legally setting the "rules of the game" to protect people against fraud and to make markets "user friendly." Taking opposition to the regulation of markets to the point of principle because it "restricts freedom of choice" represents, in effect, a blanket endorsement of commercial crime.

Some legal rules may be dysfunctional, unenforceable or out of date. For example, the legal requirement in the US that some documents be endorsed by a public notary is unnecessary. The UK and other countries eliminated this practice years ago. By contrast, no sane person would oppose motor vehicle inspections because they limit the freedom to drive. That is their purpose, to keep unsafe cars and drivers off the road. Public regulation of markets by a community, city or country through its elected representatives should and do specify the "rules of the game."

Opposing public regulation on the argument that markets operate efficiently ignores their social nature. It is the equivalent to arguing that doctors and medicines are unnecessary because the body is a perfect regulator of itself. Opposing regulation in principle endorses in practice the freedom to cheat and defraud – freedoms that no stable market society allows.

The general principle is simple and straightforward. The rules regulating commerce and finance should be chosen on pragmatic considerations. The obvious considerations include whether public interventions are necessary, and if necessary how they are best designed to maximize their effectiveness and minimize undesirable side-effects. This principle is so obvious and reasonable that by comparison the deregulationist arguments of the right-wing libertarians and Tea Party true believers seem barking mad, to use a British cliché. Why would anyone even think up, much less take seriously, demands for the elimination of the US central bank (the Federal Reserve System), moves to repeal the rights of people to join together voluntarily to bargain over wages and conditions, and an end to laws protecting the quality of the air?

These rabid insults to common sense and decency, what might be called the peddling of political madness, I deconstruct in subsequent chapters. As the more immediate task I consider some very real and concrete market processes, with all their warts and imperfections: those for finding work, for money, credit and finance, and for foreign trade. The first is in this chapter and the other two I dissect later.

Before these market excursions, I point out the obvious: that descent into deregulationist insanity becomes possible only if you believe in the perfection of markets – the doctrine of fakeconomics. The alchemists of olden times allegedly believed in the existence of a substance, the

Markets on the Make

Pharmaceutical fraud

Should anyone suggest that the health industry is excessively regulated, go to the Internet and search "pharmaceutical fraud." Examples vary from the criminally grotesque to the larcenously mundane. An infamous case of the former was thalidomide, a sedative drug with horrific affects on fetal development.

Qualifying for the mundane is Lipoban, an alleged diet pill introduced in the 1990s, which was no more than a placebo. It proved an extremely profitable placebo, used by over 130,000 people and bringing the scammer $10 million. In a defense that ranks among the best in chutzpah, the dietary con man who peddled Lipoban pleaded for leniency on grounds that he had dedicated his life to crusading for dietary supplements.

Used car scams

Research suggests that one out of every three used car sales involves fraud of some type. These include the well-known scams of concealing that a vehicle has been in an accident, selling stolen cars, and peddling an automobile that carries the liability for the debt of a previous owner. You might say that the market for used cars is not one in which the buyer is likely to have perfect knowledge.

Insurance larceny

The insurance business offers the potential for fraud by both sides of the transaction. The policy holder can go for bogus claims, though not usually for big money. The policy seller has more options, from the nominally legal use of proverbial "small print," to refusing to pay legitimate claims. Many Hollywood films feature insurance scams: Erin Brockovich (2000, health insurance, Julia Roberts), *The Verdict* (1982, malpractice, Paul Newman), and *Double Indemnity* (1944, life insurance, Fred MacMurray, Barbara Stanwyck and Edward G. Robinson).

Further reading

"Diet Pill Fraud Nets 20-Year Below-Guideline Federal Sentence (and Ads for Diet Pills)," Sentencing Law and Policy (blog), 27 February 2013. http://sentencing.typepad.com/sentencing_law_and_policy/2010/02/diet-pill-fraud-nets-20year-belowguideline-federal-sentence-and-ads-for-diet-pills.html (accessed 13 October 2013).

Chris Nickson, "Used Car Scams," Safe from Scams, 12 December 2012. http://www.safefromscams.co.uk/usedcarscam.html (accessed 13 October 2013).

Insurance Fraud Investigators Group. http://www.ifig.org/

philosopher's stone, that turned base metal into gold. The econfakers offer a substance in exchange that magically turns the base motivations of greed and deception into commercial virtue, their fantasy of "perfect competition." The philosopher's stone and the econfakers' competition are equally imaginary, equally useless guides to policy.

The "Labor Market"

When people shop they use the word "market" to mean a specific place, as in "the local farmers' market" and "the supermarket." The word is also used in a vague manner: "I haven't found the house I want, and I am definitely still in the market." Econfakers use the word with a very specific metaphysical meaning, a transubstantiation through exchange that occurs instantaneously among perfectly informed and equally powerless participants.

If we think back to the discussion of the automobile market, we see that the fakeconomics view of markets bears some, but very little, similarity to the buying and selling that people and companies actually do. The few things that idealized and real markets have in common include price, money, buyers and sellers. However, where the econfakers have in mind a specific, magic outcome, the rest of us employ the word "market" in a metaphorical or commercial sense. By a stretch of the imagination and flexibility of language, we speak of markets for apples, automobiles, computers, and bonds, while knowing that all of these are ongoing processes, not events. Using "market" in this way, for commodities and services, involves oversimplification, but is not actively misleading if we do not interpret it literally.

The term "labor market" is quite different. Despite its common use, it *is* actively misleading and inherently invalid. It is a false metaphor embodying an erroneous generalization. The term should not be used because what is "marketed" is the capacity to work (the fakeconomics term is "labor services"). It is not bought and sold in a manner remotely resembling other commodities. The term "automobile market" is a fiction of some limited use for understanding the economics, production and distribution of motor vehicles. The "labor market" is beyond fiction, a gross misrepresentation that portrays a social activity as something it is not. It is a term that misrepresents what actually happens, presenting the search and acquisition of work as what the agents and principals of politically reactionary capital wish it to be, and do all in their power to bring about.

To achieve analytical progress we have to banish "labor market" from our vocabulary. "Jobs market" offers a considerable improvement, with the great advantage of explicitly identifying the exchange as one between employers and employees. The sloppy term "labor market" is frequently used to include the self-employed, which is a clear case of mixing apples and oranges. In the jobs market people sell their capacity to work, unlike in a slave system where people themselves are sold, or self-employment that involves selling directly what you produce. The modifier "jobs" clarifies the social character of this exchange, between the employee and the employer.

Jobs markets only occur in capitalist societies. They are the defining characteristic of such societies (see Box: Donald Duck on Capitalism). Because a person is inseparable from his or her capacity to work, it is fundamentally different from all other commodities. This the *sine qua non* of the so-called labor market. You can't separate yourself from the work you do. You must be there to do it, and doing it requires that you be there. The implication is profound and impacts on all aspects of the exchange between employer and employee.

Donald Duck on Capitalism

Donald Duck collects his wages from the pay window of McDuck General Enterprises at the end of work on Friday. He drives to the McDuck Self-Service to fill the tank of his car, and he just makes it to the McDuck Rental Bureau before closing time and pays his rent. From there he drives to his local branch of McDuck Supermarkets to do his food shopping.

He arrives home where his nephews (Huey, Dewey and Louie) greet him and ask how his day went.

DONALD: I spent my entire paycheck before I got home – I'm broke!
NEPHEWS: Uncle Scrooge will still be in his office, go ask him for an advance on next week's salary.

Off Donald goes to ask his uncle, Scrooge McDuck (sole owner of McDuck Enterprises), for an advance. In the posh office of his uncle, there occurs the following exchange:

SCROOGE: Well, what is it this time, Donald?
DONALD: Could you advance me half of next week's salary, I am completely broke.
SCROOGE: What you do with your money is a complete mystery to me, Donald. You never find me broke at the end of the week.

MORAL: Donald sells in order to buy (i.e., his working time for the necessities of life). Scrooge buys in order to sell (i.e., Donald's working time that produces the gasoline, food, etc. that he sells). Donald is a worker and Scrooge is a capitalist.

For all other commodities, the interest of the seller ends with the sale, except for those commodities involving guarantees of some sort. This is because for all but the capacity to work, what is sold can be physically separated from the seller. The farmer, supermarket owner and checkout staff have little interest in what happens to a sack of potatoes after it is sold. A skilled cabinet maker may hope that the purchaser will not abuse a chair he or she has carefully made, but is unlikely to lose any sleep over the possibility. The overwhelming concern of the seller of all but the capacity to work commodity is price and revenue. Concern about its quality, durability and suitability the seller leaves to the buyer.

Because a person accompanies him- or herself to work, the conditions of work, pace and duration are important, along with price (wage or salary). The inseparability of work and worker implies a further uniqueness in buying and selling the capacity to work. Unlike all other inputs into production, the use that the employer can obtain from work is variable. In contrast, a computer runs on electricity, and for a specific type of computer, the electricity it uses to operate for a specific length of time is technically determined.

The effort that an employer extracts from an employee is not technically determined. An inherently conflictual social process determines how long an employee works and at what intensity. The process is inherently conflictual because the employer's costs decrease when people work longer and harder for the same pay. In contrast, the employee's income per hour worked declines and so too may his or her state of health. The actual duration and pace of work reflect in great part the relative bargaining power of the employer and employee. It is for this reason that Franklin D. Roosevelt commented, "If I were a worker in a factory, the first thing I would do would be to join a union," because a trade union is the vehicle by which employees strike a mutually beneficial compromise with employers on remuneration, duration and pace of work.

The impossibility to separate work from worker means that, unlike for the *producer* of a commodity, it can never be in the interest of a person to sell cheaper. If an apple farmer cannot sell all apples harvested, a reduction in the price will in general add more to revenue than to cost, so profit increases. This statistical property – "elastic demand" in the jargon – characterizes most commodities. Because the seller of the apples is interested in profit, a lower price can bring a benefit.

The same can never be true for the sale of the capacity to work. A wage or salary cut with the same working hours and conditions leaves the employee worse off. A pay cut and longer hours is a double blow. The employee's time is worth less with more of it to deliver. As strange as it may seem, I once had an academic colleague who claimed that for the economy as a whole, lower wages would generate more employment and everyone would be happier. The formerly unemployed would be delighted to have work and the formerly employed would be pleased to have higher incomes (he was an econfaker, of course, and not notably collegial). The higher incomes would result because, like apples, the demand for the capacity to work is alleged to be "price elastic." This argument (one cannot compliment it with the word "analysis") is so absurd that it leaves any economist (in contrast to the econfaker) wondering "what kind of an enterprise I've devoted my life to" that would generate such *prima facie* rubbish.

Yes, absurd. Shall I count the ways? The first absurdity is the implicit suggestion that the demand for the capacity to work is determined similarly to the demand for consumer commodities. Cut the price of apples, cars, computers, beer, and the seller's revenue is likely to go up. Cut the price of working and the employee's income goes up. Right? *Wrong*, totally wrong, not even a little bit right. Preferences, needs and income determine consumer demand, which is a demand for final use (eat it, read it, drive it, etc.). In complete contrast to this, a private employer buys the capacity to work in order to produce, distribute or sell something. To use one of the less obscure economic terms, the demand by employers for workers (or any input) is a *derived* demand.

A consumer buys a good or service motivated by personal or household need or pleasure. The employer buys a good or service because he or she thinks it will result in the production or distribution of something that can be sold. This derived demand has two aspects that play no role in consumer demand. First (quite literally), the technology of production determines the demand for employees and other inputs, with very little flexibility. Technical considerations even determine employment in retail commerce with little flexibility, as any one who has ever stood in line at a supermarket can testify.

There is a favorite fakeconomics fairytale that more than any other solidifies its kinship with alchemy. The story goes that when the unit cost of employing people changes, companies ("firms" as econfakers love to call them) can change their technologies of producing or distributing a good or service. This might be dubbed the "shape-changing" or *lycanthropic* theory of production. This fairytale underpins all fakeconomics wage theory. It should be dismissed with the contempt it so richly deserves.

Households can at short notice change their consumption patterns in reaction to changes in prices. The price of gasoline goes up, take the bus. The specifics of the buildings and machines employers use to produce the good or service that they sell determine the extent to which they can hire more people. If a company's management anticipates sales sufficient to use its buildings and equipment to the maximum feasible level, there is little discretion over the number of people to employ. This takes us to the second big difference between company and household demand. Since the demand for employees derives from the demand for what they produce, companies set their production level and number of employees primarily by what they anticipate their sales will be.

The econfakers would jump forward to tell us that the same is true for households, which consume not on the basis of their income now, but their anticipated income. An econfaker received the "Nobel" Prize for carrying this nonsensical idea to its limit and demonstrating to his satisfaction that people consume on the basis of their *lifetime* incomes. This prize-winning insight brings to mind Oscar Wilde's suggestion that madness lies in carrying an argument to its logical conclusion. Grimm did a considerably better job of fairytales than the econfakers.

Leaving this and the shape-changing argument to the priests and acolytes of fakeconomics, I can summarize: what companies do in markets is quite different from what households do. Households receive paychecks and spend them. Having spent them, they return to the factory, office or home computer to earn the next paycheck. The composition of their spending is sensitive to prices.

Companies spend on inputs including employees, produce goods and services, and sell them. To no substantial degree in the short term do the prices of inputs affect their use except in rare cases of extreme changes. The revenue from sales becomes what companies spend on inputs for the next production period. As a great economist of the twentieth century, Michał Kalecki, famously wrote, workers spend what they get and capitalists get what they spend (again, see Box: Donald Duck on Capitalism). Insightful statements of that variety do not garner prizes from the Bank of Sweden.

There is a still further difference between the market for the capacity to work and all others. Only a fraction of all working people enter the jobs market at any moment. In 2011 the US and the UK suffered from close to 10% of the labor force being unemployed, and Spain had the highest rate among the large Western European countries at well over 20%. These numbers mean that even in the worst economic circumstances since the Great Depression of the 1930s, 90% of the labor force was employed in the US and UK, and over 70% in Spain. This is not presented as a "cheer up, folks" argument, but to emphasize that in the worst of times the vast majority of people are not "in the market," and in the best of times very few are.

This is true of no other commodity. If a seller cuts the price of apples or even automobiles, that can force other sellers to do so, because the annual crop of apples and the new automobiles are sold over more or less the same time period (or the sellers hope so). The equivalent for employment – a wage cut leads to more jobs – is less than unlikely, it is impossible. It is impossible because

1. on the demand side, over short time periods (certainly up to a year) maximum potential employment in the private sector is technically determined by the machinery and other equipment in place;
2. on the supply side, a person with a job has no incentive to accept a lower wage, because it results in a lower income or a lower return per hour worked; and
3. in the jobs market the vast majority of the commodity (the capacity to work) is not on sale (most people have jobs).

The twenty-first century has demonstrated the consequence of the successful campaign by reactionaries with econfakers in the ideological vanguard to treat the capacity to work as if it were any other commodity. This contributes to stagnant and falling real wages, intensification of work and occupational injuries (see Box: Wages and Poverty in the Land of Opportunity). We have returned to a bygone age of occupational tyranny, succinctly described by Franklin D. Roosevelt: "The hours men and women worked, the wages they received, the conditions of their labor – these had passed beyond the control of the people, and were imposed by this new industrial dictatorship."

Wages and Poverty in the Land of Opportunity

If you live in the US and the American dream is passing you by, you are not alone. Median household income (sometimes called income of the "typical" household) is the level that equally divides the employed by their incomes (the 50:50 divide, as in "Half the class made above 70 on the exam and half made lower"). The average is total income divided by the population (as in "The average grade was 73" – aka the "mean").

From 1981 to 2000 the average rose by 51%, while the median increased only 19%. From 2000 until 2008 (the end of the growth boom), the average continued to increase by a further 15%, but the median fell by 3%. How can the average rise and most people be worse off? Because the incomes of people above the 50:50 divide rose and the incomes of those below it fell. Why? The decline of unions and rise of finance capital would be good places to start for an explanation.

With the real value of wages and salaries falling for the majority after 2000, it is hardly surprising that during the "prosperity" of the "new economy" in the 2000s the proportion of US families in poverty rose, then went through the roof in 2008–2011 (see below).

What's going on in the USA? Average household income is up, income of the typical household is down and poverty is rising!

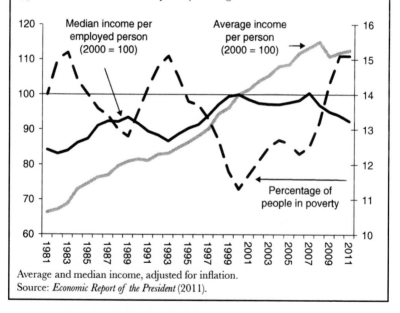

Average and median income, adjusted for inflation.
Source: *Economic Report of the President* (2011).

Workers Cause Their Unemployment?

Granted that the term "labor market" is not entirely appropriate, is it not still the case that higher wages, either by collective action (unions) or legislation (legal minimum wages) cause unemployment? As any fool can see: higher pay means lower profit, which discourages companies from employing more workers. Alternatively, companies may raise their prices in response to higher wages. Just as water runs downhill, higher wages directly lower employment, or do so indirectly through higher prices for the consumer who buys less. Both add up to workers themselves being the cause of their unemployment.

Actually, no. While water runs downhill, only in the ideological world of the econfakers do wage increases always result in lower employment and/or higher prices. Empirical evidence of the wage–employment "trade-off" has been unsuccessfully sought by generations of number-crunching econfakers using "fake-econometrics," in contrast to the real thing: econometrics (the application of statistical techniques to economics). When the accumulation of evidence began to undermine the trade-off hypothesis, the right-wing econfakers (forgive the redundancy) went ballistic.

In a comment to the *Wall Street Journal* about the work of David Card and Alan Krueger that showed a possible *positive* relationship between minimum wages and employment, faux Nobel Prizer James M. Buchanan asserted,

> No self-respecting economist would claim that increases in the minimum wage increase employment. Such a claim, if seriously advanced, becomes equivalent to a denial that there is even minimal scientific content in economics, and that, in consequence, economists can do nothing but write as advocates for ideological interests. Fortunately, only a handful of economists are willing to throw over the teaching of two centuries; we have not yet become a bevy of camp-following whores.

In nonideological pursuit of scientific inquiry, Professor Buchanan's value-free contribution to economics was to demonstrate to the satisfaction of econfakers that politicians are inherently self-seeking and act contrary to the general interest. To demonstrate further his scientific objectivity he became a Distinguished Fellow of the Cato Institute, whose mission statement reads,

> ...to increase the understanding of public policies based on the principles of limited government, free markets, individual liberty, and peace. The Institute will use the most effective means to originate, advocate, promote, and disseminate applicable policy proposals that create free, open, and civil societies in the United States and throughout the world.

In seeking "effective means" the institute is aided by funds from the billionaire Charles G. Koch, whose "overall concept is to minimize the role of government and to maximize the role of private economy." One of those camp-following whores that Buchanan might have had in mind, Paul Krugman (also a faux Nobeler), responded to the self-defined nonideological Buchanan:

> [Card and Krueger] found no evidence that minimum wage increases in the range that the United States has experienced led to job losses. Their work has been attacked because it seems to contradict Econ 101 and because it was ideologically disturbing to many. Yet it has stood up very well to repeated challenges, and new cases confirming its results keep coming in.

By what logic do econfakers conclude that wage increases reduce employment and why is it contradicted by reality? The logic, if one might call it such, is from the same full-employment fantasy world as "supply and demand," dissected in Chapter 4. As in that discussion I have to begin with clear specification of the fakeconomics trade-off hypothesis. It does not assert that a wage increase in a specific company will reduce employment. The precise hypothesis is: "From an initial position of full employment for an economy that produces only one commodity under conditions of perfect competition, an increase in the real wage will reduce employment."

A rational person might ask: why on earth state a simple proposition (wage up, employment down) in such an absurdly complex manner? They do so because the proposition is not simple. It is valid only under extremely restricted conditions. The hypothesis begins with the economy as a whole, not individual companies or industries. This reason for this will soon be clear. The full-employment caveat is necessary in order to exclude the effect of the most important determinant of the level of employment and unemployment: the total expenditure, public and private, in the economy as a whole (aggregate demand).

As should be obvious, if the analysis begins in conditions of unemployment, an increase in real wages could contribute to an *increase* in employment by increasing consumer demand. The econfakers exclude this possibility by starting from full employment (maximum output), so any increase in demand could only cause inflation.

But starting at full employment means that the analysis cannot apply at the level of individual companies except as part of the economy as a whole. This implies that the trade-off hypothesis has no relevance to real-world decisions made in companies about employment levels.

Moving on to the next absurdity, allowing the economy only one output is an unavoidable technical requirement. With only one product, either there is no input or the input is the output itself (which is quite strange when you think about it). The following example reveals why the econfakers enter into such contorted illogic. In an economy with an output that has an input different from itself (e.g., wheat and fertilizer), the result of a wage increase in both industries cannot be predicted. A possible logical (and practical) sequence might be as follows: the higher wage prompts farmers to use more fertilizer to raise yields and make labor more productive. Employment in the production of fertilizer increases, with little change in labor used on farms, so total employment expands. In a real economy with thousands of products, the result of increases and decreases in wages can only be known after the event.

This is no abstract, arcane issue. The unpredictable outcome of a general wage increase can be easily demonstrated using what are called "input–output" tables. These tables are available via the Internet for most countries of the world. They show the flows of inputs throughout the productive system, which eventually result in what are called "final products" – those bought by households and governments, and businesses for investment.

Finally, the trade-off hypothesis requires a competitive economy in which no collusion exists among employers or employees. This condition ensures that the demand for labor varies independent of the supply (more on this in Chapter 4), which rules out a feedback from higher wages to higher employment.

What seemed so simple and obvious – lower wages, cheaper labor, more employment – proves impossible to establish as a general rule. For an individual company reducing wages may result in more employment. That is not the issue. At the level of the company, lower wages may allow for lower prices, and the lower-wage company takes business away from its rivals. The "higher wages cause unemployment" accusation is quite different. It alleges a fakeconomics *faux* law that a general increase in wages for the economy as a whole will reduce employment (and vice versa). This allegation cannot be established in theory, nor is it supported by empirical evidence. It is an ideological construction intended to justify lower wages and higher profits, and to blame unemployment on workers themselves.

In practice the econfakers and those they have indoctrinated trumpet this argument as a law of nature, and use it against all attempts to improve the conditions and hours of work. For example, laws that regulate working hours and require additional pay for overtime allegedly reduce employment because they increase labor costs. The same ideological illogic applies to workplace protection, health and safety legislation, and protection of vulnerable workers. They all raise the cost employing people. Therefore, they must contribute to unemployment. All attempts to improve the conditions of labor, either through the collective action of workers or legislation, are self-defeating. These arguments are wrong, technically, empirically and morally. In civilized societies all people are paid decently and work in healthy conditions to the extent that the level of economic development allows. This is a simple and straightforward hypothesis that requires no fanciful assumptions to establish.

The econfakers look back to Adam Smith as their intellectual ancestor and their inspiration for the free market. However, the great contributor to the Scottish Enlightenment had no truck with "labor markets":

> What are the common wages of labour depends everywhere upon the contract usually made between [workers and employers]… It is not, however, difficult to foresee which of the two parties must, upon all ordinary occasions, have the advantage in the dispute, and force the other into a compliance with their terms. The masters, being fewer in number, can combine much more easily, and the law, besides, authorizes, or at least does not prohibit their combinations, while it prohibits those of the workmen… In all such disputes the masters can hold out much longer.

Anyone familiar with the union-busting campaigns of the closing decades of the twentieth century in the US and Europe would recognize the similarities with the closing decades of the eighteenth century.

Further Reading

How markets work

Ha-Joon Chang, *23 Things They Don't Tell You about Capitalism* (London: Penguin, 2010).

James K. Galbraith, *Created Unequal: The Crisis in American Pay* (Chicago: University of Chicago Press, 2000).

Philip L. Rones, Randy E. Ilg and Jennifer M. Gardner, "Trends in Working Hours since the Mid-1970s," *Bulletin of Labor Statistics*, April 1997. Online: http://www.bls.gov/opub/mlr/1997/04/art1full.pdf (accessed 13 October 2013).

Susan E. Fleck, "International Comparison of Hours Worked," *Bulletin of Labor Statistics*, May 2009. Online: http://www.bls.gov/opub/mlr/2009/05/art1full.pdf (accessed 13 October 2013).

Chapter 3

FINANCE AND CRIMINALITY

And Jesus went into the temple of God, and cast out all of them
who sold and bought in the temple, and overthrew the tables of the
moneychangers.

(Matthew 21:12–13)

Why a Financial Sector?

When I grew up in East and Central Texas, people disparaged another
person's judgment with the comment "If you believe that, I'd like the
chance to sell you a used car." In that spirit, I might ask if there remains
anyone in the known world other than an econfaker who believes in the
efficiency of financial markets. If so, he or she should not enter a used
car lot unaccompanied.

In the 1930s the Great Depression brought banking collapse to
North America and Europe. In 1929 on the eve of collapse, over 26,000
banks operated in the US. When the newly elected president Franklin
D. Roosevelt suspended banking operations on 5 March 1933, the total
was less than 15,000, with 5,000 bankruptcies (quite literally) in 1932
alone. The suspension brought a temporary end to a nationwide run
on banks by depositors. On 9 March the US Congress rapidly passed
the Emergency Banking Relief Act in a first move toward substantial
restrictions on private financial institutions.

Three months after the emergency law, Congress passed the Banking
Act, commonly known as the Glass–Steagall Act of 1933 (not to be
confused with the relatively trivial Glass–Steagall Act of 1932). It is the
mildest of exaggerations to say that we owe the Glass–Steagall Act the
distinction of preventing another US banking collapse for 50 years.

For most Americans, the importance of the act lay in the creation of
the Federal Deposit Insurance Corporation, which protected households
against loss of deposits when a bank collapsed. But the protection of

Financial Fiascos in Our Times

Senator Glass and Representative Steagall, 1933.
Where are you when we need you?

In the early 1980s several major developing countries, especially in Latin America, staggered to the brink of default on loans taken from the major US banks, defaults that would have bankrupted the US financial sector. The origins of this, the sovereign debt crisis, came well before the dismantling of the Glass–Steagall Act. The debt crisis of the 1980s demonstrated the clear need for strict regulation. The unsustainable lending by commercial banks to governments resulted because this activity was *not* regulated by Glass–Steagall.

Free from the prying eyes of the regulators, the big banks – Wells Fargo, Citicorp (as it is known now), Bank of America and others – could make loans to foreign governments as recklessly as they wished and did so. Had the US government not saved them from folly through several interventions, they would have gone the way of dodos (though less mourned). The debt crisis had two clear lessons: 1) if the government does not regulate it, the banks will make a mess of it; and 2) the clearing and cleaning of the mess must be done by the public sector. Neither lesson would be remembered in the years to come:

1987   Black Monday, the largest one-day decline in US stock market history, due in great part to the Securities and Exchange Commission's nonregulation of new stock-trading practices (e.g., computer-based trading).

1989–91 The savings and loan crisis, costing what would prove to be a rather modest $90 billion.

2001–02 The "dot.com" speculation bubble bursts, wiping as much as $5 trillion off the value of the funny-money "e-stocks," driven by reduced public regulation of financial institutions.

2008 → The mother of all financial crises swept the globe and we are still counting the cost, which unlike previous crises includes mass unemployment, inspiring a documentary narrated by Matt Damon, *Inside Job* (2011).

depositors was not what prevented another systematic banking crisis for half a century. That great achievement came from the act's strict and direct regulation of bank behavior. Perhaps most important, the act prohibited banks from engaging in a range of speculative activities, including playing the stock market. Making banking a safe and relatively dull function represented its greatest achievement. Today, with US representatives and senators from the Old South almost all reactionaries, it comes as a surprise to many that Senator Carter Glass hailed from Virginia and Representative Henry Steagall from Alabama.

The first important step towards reversing Glass–Steagall came with the Depository Institutions Deregulation and Monetary Control Act of 1980, which, far from controlling anything, ended regulation of interest rates on deposits by the Federal Reserve System. This encouragement set the US financial system off and running to its first crisis in over fifty years, the savings and loan debacle.

In a textbook demonstration of the Law of Unintended Consequences, the end of the Federal Reserve System's regulation of interest rates resulted directly in the collapse of almost 750 of the 3,234 savings and loan associations in the US. This collapse cost the public budget about $90 billion, or $150 billion at 2012 prices (getting on toward 2% of national income). Modest this would seem compared to the financial devastation of the late 2000s.

As a general rule, financial crises never lack a silver lining for the financiers themselves. The savings and loan disaster had the beneficial effect of reducing competition, which set the large US banks on a path to market dominance, albeit beyond their hopes as long as the Glass–Steagall Act was in full operation.

Even if we restrict ourselves to cases in the US, the list of financial fiascos remains impressive (see Box: Financial Fiascos in Our Times). What makes financial markets so unstable? If we clear away the propaganda fog from the financiers themselves, propaganda enthusiastically endorsed by the econfakers, the answer is quite simple. It has two parts, the nature of finance and the nature of speculation. We need to begin, as they say, at the beginning. Why is there finance, and why are there banks?

The media and the econfakers would have us believe that the gambling speculators that chase after a fast buck are "investors." This implies the absurd, that buying a Greek bond to sell it within the hour is a "investment." Not withstanding this loose usage, sensible people understand the word "investment" to mean the creation of new productive capacity, which is a major source of the sustainable growth potential of an economy. In a market economy a very specific difficulty faces a company that wants to invest in expanding its current production facilities or creating new ones.

For the economy as a whole, new investment cannot exceed business profits over any prolonged period, and typically falls considerably below this. The profit constraint is obvious if we think of the economy as one big company. After it pays its bills to suppliers (itself in this case) and its employees, what remains is profit. If the company distributes part of the profit to shareholders, potential new investment will be considerably less than profit. After World War II in both the US and Western Europe governments employed tax measures to discourage payments to shareholders and increase the incentive for companies to invest. In the 1980s this began to change. In the US dividends paid to stockholders accounted for 39% of corporate income in the 1960s, and almost 65% in the 2000s.

Real economies consist of many companies, some that expand, others that contract, a few that flatline, and some newly created. New enterprises need to borrow, as do existing ones. If an existing company wants to invest beyond its current profits it must either squirrel away its profits from previous investments, or raise funds from outside the company. Companies do this either by borrowing or creating ownership shares which they sell to the public (mostly to the rich). Households take a mortgage to buy a house because they cannot issue shares. Both the borrowing and selling of newly created stock brings about the redistribution of the economy's total profit from declining and flatlining companies to expanding ones. This redistribution requires borrowing and lending, essential for the dynamics of a market economy.

Borrowing to invest creates the need for institutions that specialize in this function. This first developed on a substantial scale in Western Europe and the US in the mid-nineteenth century. Institutions superficially similar to investment banks existed previously, lending for trade rather than funding productive facilities. Credit-financed investment frees a company from the limits of its profits, and facilitates the rise of the strong and the decline of the weak.

Credit produces its own problem: institutions (banks) whose profitability requires lending on uncertain outcomes. Bank lending is inherently uncertain. Banks have limited control over the business decisions of the borrower, and almost no control over the environment in which the borrower operates. Extreme circumstances, such as the financial crisis of 2008, may make repayment impossible no matter how wisely or foolishly the borrower may behave.

Uncertainty is inherent in the financing function in a market economy, and frequently misunderstood or misrepresented. Robust growth dramatically reduces market uncertainty. At the operational level uncertainty remains about the distribution of the aggregate growth among companies seeking to maintain or increase market shares. But when "all boats rise," as the cliché says, winners outnumber losers in the commercial struggle. When a recession strikes, the uncertainty goes viral with a vengeance and the losers swamp the winners. More than anything else, the state of the economy determines risk and uncertainty. What appears as bold entrepreneurship – grabbing an opportunity and becoming rich from it – is the luck of the draw in most cases. It is one thing to "float" the shares of a new company in a boom, and quite another to do so during a recession (e.g., Facebook in the summer of 2012).

Many people, not least financiers themselves, consider lending by banks a noble activity essential to the health, wealth and happiness of economies. A concrete example dismisses this self-praise. Consider the case of a company that develops a new product, such as an easily portable touch-screen computer. Partly with its profits from other products and partly with a bank loan, the company brings together the skills, plant and equipment to turn the design into a product ready for the buyer.

Through its own retail stores, via the Internet or in the retail outlets of other companies, the company markets the new product. The product that the buyer receives by mail or collects from a store represents the work of many people, those who *designed* it, those who *directly produced* it, those who *supervised* the design and production, those who *transported* it, and the online or in-store people who *sold* it.

What did the bank do? The bank *did not* design, produce, transport or sell anything. The bank certainly did not create any of the resources by which the product arrived in the lap of the buyer. The role of the bank was important but modest. It helped bring together the new plant, equipment and employees by providing credit. The bank provided credit through a bureaucratic process. It first created a checking account for the company, and then assigned a specific amount that the company could withdraw. The company used these withdrawals to pay suppliers, employees and other costs associated with the prospective investment. The bank did not lend the company "its own" money. It created credit on the basis of country-specific legal rules governing the relationship between its assets (such as government bonds) and its liabilities (its outstanding loans).

In practice banks lend far more than what they receive from depositors. In all market societies, governments restrict banks to lend a legally specified multiple of their deposits. In the US the ratio in the 2010s was 10:1 for all but the smallest lending institutions. Banks extend borrowers credit that they, the banks, create literally out of thin air. This is the case no matter what the deposit ratio might be, because the "reserves" cannot themselves be lent – if you must hold it as a "reserve," it cannot be lent. The credit created on the basis of government regulations allows the borrower to spend more than his or her current income flow. While this is a very useful function, it is a quite minor one that could be carried out through many types of institutions that need not and have not always been driven by the profit motive.

Taking profit on money created out of nothing would not seem an activity worthy of great status. Quite consciously I do not write of "earning" profit. If the word "earning" has a useful meaning, it refers to a productive activity, which finance, necessary as it might be, is not. The garbage collector that works in the hot sun or bitter cold all day earns his or her pay. The same verb should not apply to the financier who shifts entries in an electronic database, or the word loses all meaning.

Speculation comes about by banks and other financial institutions creating their own uncertainties independent of the productive investment process. The lure of profits induces financiers to create this uncertainty or risk, by which they accrue gains of a very specific and peculiar type: *speculative profit*. The difference between speculative financial profit and the profit generated out of sales among businesses and between businesses and households is simple and straightforward.

A company produces a commodity or service and sells it. From the sales it pays its workers, suppliers and other claimants, and what remains is profit. The difference in prices at the wholesale and retail level results from services that must be compensated, such as transport, storage or marketing. There are several theories to explain profit and all of them agree that its source is production. Therefore, it exists before the product is sold, and profit is realized or appears in the sale. Disagreement arises over which elements of production generate the profit and over the process by which distribution of profit occurs throughout the economy. These disagreements need not divert us from an inspection of speculative profit.

While a company must produce something to generate profit, speculators can lose or gain through buying and selling without producing anything. They achieve this profit grab by betting on changes in prices. Most people at some time or other speculate on prices. For example, in most parts of the US in 2008 the canny house buyer would wait, anticipating a decline in property prices. However, this would probably bring no profit, because most buyers purchase the house to live in it. Grabbing profit through exchanges requires that you buy for the purpose of selling. The clumsy and old-fashioned way to do this involved actually buying the thing whose sale would bring the speculative gain. At an auction the primitive speculator buys a sack of potatoes, carries it off, brings it back to the auction some time later in hopes of selling it at a higher price.

To avoid the bother of transporting, storing and transporting again, the speculator takes an "option" on potatoes, a piece of paper (very twentieth century) or an electronic document (twenty-first century) guaranteeing the right to purchase a specified amount of potatoes at a specified price on a future specified date. I purchase a contract that requires a potato farmer to sell me one ton of potatoes in Des Moines, Iowa, on 31 January for $275. The farmer is "hedging" against potato prices falling below that price, while I am betting that prices will go above $275. On 31 January, if the price of potatoes in Des Moines has risen to $350 (the "spot price"), I am in the chips (though not potato chips, because I plan to sell the spuds on). People who actually want potatoes for some useful purpose would be willing to pay me up to $350 for my contact. Without approaching a spud within intent to stew, fry or boil, I make a profit on potatoes. If, on the contrary, the end of January price has dropped to $125, I find myself stuck with a lot of very expensive potatoes or a contract worth less than half what I paid for it.

This speculation using "derivatives" (something linked to something else) occurs without personal contact with the object of the speculation. The imagination of econfakers and financial charlatans provides us with various justifications of speculation, all of which allege that such market exchanges protect against risk and uncertainty. They peddle the improbable argument that by purchasing "options" to buy and sell at various prices a person or company can "hedge" (protect) against unpleasant market surprises. If anyone accepted such improbable optimism before mid-2008 (and many did), I hope that they learned their lesson.

When the price of potatoes in Des Moines goes to $350, from where does my profit come? The answer is quite clear: I gain what the farmer would have received had there been no derivative contract. It is a straight redistribution of profit between the producer and the speculator. Less clear is the source of my loss when the spot price falls to $125. I suffer a loss ($150 maximum), but having produced nothing, I cannot be the *source* of the loss.

Income from some useful activity in society must cover my loss. The gain-and-loss process is not symmetrical. The speculator's gain comes from a specific useful activity (the production of potatoes in my example). The loss is borne by useful activity in general, with the rest of you carrying the can.

If it seems fanciful that speculators can grab profits from the useful activities of society, and that those useful activities must cover their losses, reflect on the great financial fiasco of 2008. In March 2008 employment in the US was 146 million men and women. When time came to celebrate the Christmas holidays in 2009, total employment was 138 million, a fall of over 8 million men and women (5.6% lower). As everyone knows, that particular Christmas present resulted from the collapse of the financial sector. This, the sector that boasted of bringing us the new economy that hedged against uncertainty and generated prosperity without end, had collapsed under the moribund and unproductive weight of its Ponzi schemes of speculative mania. The result was a massive transfer of income and wealth from useful and productive Americans to useless and feckless finance. (Read more on these losses in the next section.)

Financial speculation involves no productive activity on the part of the speculator. It is economically and socially unproductive in another, more basic sense. Almost all of the risk and uncertainty that feeds profit to speculators need not exist. It is not inherent in a market economy. Purposeful public regulation of markets comes close to eliminating all the important opportunities for unproductive and destabilizing speculation.

Perhaps the largest of these opportunities arises in currency markets. Each day trillions of dollars, pounds, euros, etc. chase each other in a frantic race for the impossible – creating profit out of nothing. The Bank for International Settlements, a global institution serving national central banks (located in Basel, Switzerland, about eighty kilometers west of the Gnomes of Zurich), estimated that the average daily turnover in currency markets in 2010 was about $4 trillion. At a generous estimate perhaps 10% of this turnover involved exchanges related to a useful activity, such as a company switching currencies to pay suppliers. From the start of speculative trading at a minute past midnight on a Monday (these markets dysfunction 24 hours a day), the trading turnover would have matched *total annual commercial sales* in the US or the EU sometime before breakfast on the Thursday of the same week.

A great myth about currency speculation presents it as a competitive market free from manipulation, conspiracy and collusion, something close to the "perfect competition" of fakeconomics. From this mythologizing comes the fiction that currency changes result from impersonal market forces. This view qualifies as pure propaganda. While there are many currency traders, a few large global banks carry out the vast majority of transactions. Both in the US and in Europe the limited competition and collusion in currency markets has prompted calls for regulation.

In the mid-2000s, the banking expert Hugh Thomas did the numbers on banking concentration and reached the following conclusion:

> [The largest] 100 banks include over 67 percent of the world's banking assets. Within the top 100 banks, there is also substantial concentration, with the top 20 banks accounting for 50 percent of profit and 45 percent of the aggregate assets and capital. Bank concentration is likely to increase in the future as national boundaries to the flow of capital decrease and nationally fragmented institutions, markets and instruments succumb to globalization.

Global finance is not an exciting field in which bold young traders seek the thrill of survival-of-the-fittest competition. Assets and power are highly concentrated, and these powerful institutions use their assets in unproductive speculation in markets cynically managed through fraudulent collusion. In 2012 the grossness of this cynicism became obvious by the revelation that the masters of finance, with Barclays Bank in the lead, had for years conspired to manipulate global interest rates. One expert called it the largest commercial fraud ever: "This dwarfs by orders of magnitude any financial scam in the history of markets." It is a price-fix deal that indirectly affected (and affects) everyone who borrowed from credit institutions – for mortgages, automobiles, you name it.

Adam Smith famously wrote, "People of the same trade seldom meet together, even for merriment and diversion, but the conversation ends in a conspiracy against the public, or in some contrivance to raise prices." For no trade is that truer than finance.

Cost of the Financial Crisis

> But the banks are made of marble, with a guard at every door,
> And the vaults are stuffed with silver that we have toiled for.
>
> (Les Rice, "The Banks Are Made of Marble")

Hurricane Irene will most likely prove to be one of the 10 costliest catastrophes in the nation's history, with damage estimated at US$ 7–10 billion.

(New York Times, 31 August 2011)

How much did the financial crisis of 2007–2008 cost Americans (not to mention the rest of the world)? I can confidently assert that no hurricane, earthquake or other act of nature has ever or will ever approach the potential of financial markets to generate human disasters, not even the deadly Indian Ocean tsunami in December 2004. To match the devastation, suffering and dead-weight loss of the Great Depression of the 1930s and the recent financial crisis, we move into the league of wars, famines and pogroms.

Lest you think that I exaggerate, I let the statistics speak. From the beginning of 2000 through the middle of 2008, US total output ("gross national product" or GNP) grew at an annual rate of 2.3%. Three years later in 2011 total output stagnated still below the peak of mid-2008. Had the US economy "enjoyed" no growth over those three years, and output held at the level of mid-2008, the cumulative income gain would have been almost $800 billion compared to the finance-driven debacle, or about $2,000 for every person in the US – all 311 million.

Every person losing $2,000 to the follies of finance is appalling. Worse, it is a gross underestimate, because during no three-year period since the end of World War II had the US economy stagnated at zero growth, even less had it declined. That $800 billion may far exceed the estimated cost of any earthquake or hurricane in the history of humankind, but it is a considerable underestimate of what out-of-control finance can do and has done, before our eyes in real time.

What if US output had continued to grow at 2.3%, as it did in the 2000s before the catastrophe? Despite all the prattle about a "new economy," this rate was not unusually high, well below the average of 1946–1999, which was 3.6%. What if finance had not torpedoed the rather modest rate of growth of 2.3%? The answer is shown in the chart below. It measures GDP (gross domestic product) at the price level of 2013, eliminating increases resulting from inflation.

Had the "natural" working of financial markets not reeked havoc and the economy continued to grow at 2.3%, GDP for 2013 would be almost $16 trillion, rather than the actual level of $14.9 trillion. The accumulated loss for 2008–2013, dead weight because it can never be recovered, is $6.5 trillion (the striped region in the chart). If magically recovered from the ether (i.e., the bankers), at the end of 2013 the dead-weight loss would have provided a bonus of over $20,000 for every man, woman and child in the US.

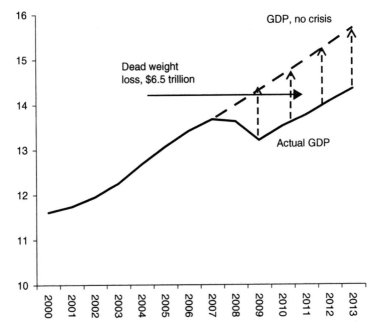

Actual US GDP during 2000–2013 and what it would have been without the financial crisis and with the same growth rate as 2000–2007 (trillions of dollars adjusted to prices of 2011)
Source: *Economic Report of the President* (2013), table B-4.

What about employment? The chart offers a simple way to estimate the effect on jobs of high finance. The trend rate of GDP growth from 2000 until the financial catastrophe was 2.3%, and this was associated with an unemployment rate of 5%. It is highly likely that if the trend had continued, the same unemployment level would have also continued. It is simple arithmetic to subtract the trend-implied unemployment from actual unemployment, and obtain the dead-weight employment loss.

During 2009–2011 when the collapse was at its worst, total unemployment averaged 15 million men and women per year, and the rate never fell below 9% of the labor force. Almost exactly half of this unemployment, an annual average of 6.7 million, was above the trend.

This half of the unemployment resulted directly from the financial crisis. Imagine, if possible, a natural disaster that could so devastate the society that it throws almost 7 million people out of work for four years, a loss of almost 25 million working years. It would be the mother of all hurricanes. Its name is Market Forces.

There are big differences between hurricanes and financial market catastrophes. First, the financial market catastrophes are much more devastating. Second, we can prepare for hurricanes but we cannot prevent them. In contrast, market catastrophes can be prevented. They need never occur except as minor annoyances. Over six decades, 1950 through 2008, annual unemployment rose above 9% in only two years, 1982 and 1983. At the end of 2011, the count went from two to six. The ways to prevent such market catastrophes are known – tight regulation of financial markets and "countercyclical fiscal policy" (see Chapters 7 and 9).

Unemployment is the scandal of market economies. Unemployment wastes human skills and means vast quantities of goods and services are never produced. Idle, rusting factories are an eyesore. Idle people in despair due to a social system's failure to provide livelihoods qualifies as a crime. The high unemployment in many developed countries in the twenty-first century demonstrated a failure of institutions and democratic mechanisms to ensure all people who wish to work can work. In his once-famous "Four Freedoms" speech to the US Congress in January 1941, Franklin D. Roosevelt explained this with eloquence:

> The basic things expected by our people of their political and economic systems are simple. They are: jobs for those who can work; equality of opportunity for youth and for others; security for those who need it; the ending of special privilege for the few; the preservation of civil liberties for all; the enjoyment of the fruits of scientific progress in a wider and constantly rising standard of living.

If they wish to serve their constituents, "jobs for those who can work" would be a minimalist start for the politicians of the twenty-first century throughout the developed world. I explain concretely how to meet this commitment in the final chapter.

To end on the follies of finance, why are financial markets inherently unstable and suitable candidates for strict regulation? Because financial activities are in themselves potentially useful but unproductive, and if left to themselves financiers abandon the useful to run rampant with the unproductive.

The philosopher George Santayana wrote, "Those who cannot remember the past are condemned to repeat it." For bankers and speculators this should be rephrased: "Those who profit from the past are delighted to repeat it." In 2007, profits of all US corporations were less than 13% of national income, falling to 10% in the depth of the recession two years later. By the end of 2012 the corporate barons were doing quite handsomely again, with profits above 14% of national income.

Those businesses foolish enough to try to make money by producing and transporting things saw an increase of a paltry 12% from 2007 to 2012, while the lords of finance weighted in with an increase in their hard(ly)-earned speculative rewards of over 30%.

It worked once. After coming out of a disastrous collapse and public bailout smelling like roses, the bankers say: why not try it again if nobody stops us?

Financial Markets: Folks like You and Me

> The thief or swindler who has gained great wealth by his delinquency has a better chance than the small thief of escaping the rigorous penalty of the law.
>
> (Thorstein Veblen)

> Well, as through the world I've rambled, I've seen lots of funny men
> Some rob you with a six-gun, some with a fountain pen
> As through this world you ramble, as through this world you roam
> You'll never see an outlaw drive a family from its home
> (Woody Guthrie, "Pretty Boy Floyd the Outlaw," c.1935)

With so much power bestowed on financial markets by the econfakers and the media, it comes as no surprise that their worshippers should personify them. This personification serves as an essential part of the defense of a market economy free from democratic oversight. We find it applied across all types of markets, quite memorably by US presidential candidate Mitt Romney, who assured us that "corporations are people." The most fervent application of this anthropomorphic principle appears in the financial sector, where "financial markets" are presented as independent, collective (anti)social actors.

Treating financial markets as a person instead of real people as market participants helps to perpetuate the mythology of competition. Personification is nothing more than a restatement of the absurdity that people individually have no market power. It is integral to the justification of a socially dysfunctional financial system, national and global. Very much in the spirit of the global financial crisis of 2007–2008, personification functioned as a key element in the misrepresentation of the disastrous speculation in eurobond markets during 2009–2011.

In a so-called analysis article, Timothy Heritage, a Reuters journalist, wrote that "The European Union is struggling to convince financial markets it has got what it takes to save the currency." Presenting a speculative run on bonds and currencies as a test of wills between government and markets ideologically defines the plight of the euro as human fecklessness versus elemental forces, with the inevitable winner obvious (recall that "you can't buck market forces").

An article by a certain Toby Heaps, who describes himself as president of Corporate Knights, the Company for Clean Capitalism, is characterized by a heart-rending personification of markets: "Nothing makes presidents or CEOs quake in their boots quite like the wrath of bond markets. That's because bond markets have the power to cut off oxygen. When bond markets are unhappy, they hit where it hurts in the form of higher interest payments on debt."

"Unhappy" bond markets would seem but a step away from addressing to the Securities Exchange Commission (the US financial regulator) Shylock's famous challenge: "If you prick us, do we not bleed? If you tickle us, do we not laugh? If you poison us, do we not die? And if you wrong us, shall we not revenge?" The last would indeed seem relevant.

Markets do not bleed, laugh or die, and their personification diverts attention away from the real world of speculators. It transubstantiates financial fraud into a force of nature. It facilitates the mythology that the dysfunctional financial system arises not from the work of men and women (mostly the former) within institutions with antisocial rules and norms. On the contrary, personification of markets would have us believe that speculation comes from the inexorable operation of the laws of nature that no government can change. This naturalization of speculative behavior manifests itself in assertions that "bond markets want" the US/UK/Greek deficit reduced, or that outrageously high executive salaries result from the impersonal operation of a mythical international market for "talent."

If fiscal deficits result in increases in the cost of public borrowing, this reflects the actions of specific financial speculators whose behavior can be controlled through regulatory measures. Astronomical executive salaries have a more transparent cause and cure. They result from the power of top company officials combined with the institutionalized weakness of stockholders. Something as seemingly simple as changing laws on corporate governance would reduce those salaries (find the specifics in the book by William Lazonick listed at the end of this chapter).

"Financial markets" do not in themselves cause a problem in any country. The weak and inappropriate rules and constraints on markets cause the problems. This weakness allows speculators, fraudsters and all-purpose crooks to behave recklessly with the confidence that they will not be held accountable (caught, tried and locked up). To take but one appalling example, in response to all the corporate crimes perpetuated by financial speculators in the US leading up to the global crisis of 2008, the US government prosecuted not one fraudster from a large bank. Even run-of-the-mill financial fraud seemed to enjoy a postcrisis holiday from justice, with total federal prosecutions in 2011 at a 20-year low.

Rules are so weak because those that perpetrate the fraud have themselves been writing the "reform" legislation, not only in finance, but in other sectors. The philosopher David Hume in the eighteenth century marveled at "the ease with which the many are governed by the few." Similarly, I marvel at the ease by which a system of financial fraud created by a few goes largely unchallenged by the many. In the next chapter I go after the Big Lie of fakeconomics and free market ideologues, in hope of provoking such a challenge.

Further Reading

John Kenneth Galbraith, *The Great Crash 1929: The Classic Account of Financial Disaster* (New York: Penguin 1954).

James K. Galbraith, *The Predator State: How Conservatives Abandoned the Free Market and Why Liberals Should Too* (New York: Free Press, 2008).

Ha-Joon Chang, *23 Things They Don't Tell You about Capitalism* (London: Penguin, 2010).

William Lazonick, *Business Organization and the Myth of Market Economy* (Cambridge: Cambridge University Press, 1991).

For the technical stuff simply presented

Jan Toporowski, *Why the World Economy Needs a Financial Crash and Other Critical Essays on Finance and Financial Economics* (London: Anthem Press, 2010).

Chapter 4

SELLING MARKET MYTHS

Designing Deception

The first man who, having fenced in a piece of land, said "This is mine," and found people naïve enough to believe him, that man was the true founder of civil society. From how many crimes, wars, and murders, from how many horrors and misfortunes might not anyone have saved mankind, by pulling up the stakes, or filling up the ditch, and crying to his fellows: Beware of listening to this impostor; you are undone if you once forget that the fruits of the earth belong to us all, and the earth itself to nobody.

(Jean-Jacques Rousseau)

People will believe a big lie sooner than a little one; and if you repeat it frequently enough people will sooner or later believe it.

(Office of Strategic Services, describing
Hitler's psychological profile)

All over the globe people experience frustration when buying and selling. Not infrequently the frustration involves more than a hint of fraud, as in "I was gypped!" Criminal fraud in buying and selling is quite common. More common are the day-to-day disappointments that result from believing what you read in advertising propaganda.

Despite these repeated disappointments while shopping, an amazingly large number of people oppose government restrictions on markets, for the apparent reason that these regulations would limit the benefits markets allegedly deliver. This combination presents a perplexing contradiction. Everyday experience informs people that markets are fraught with disappointment and fraud. Many if not most of these people believe that markets should be regulated only in exceptional circumstances. People know concretely that markets can cause harm, but believe them benign in the abstract. Why?

It is not uncommon for people to believe things contradicted by experience and common sense. For example, everywhere sports fans enter a new season with hope their hapless team will win a championship. A large proportion of Americans think creatures from outer space visit the Earth. Unlike the faith in markets these illusions have relatively little impact on everyday behavior and household welfare.

Perhaps we can explain the faith in flawed markets as the flip side of a profound distrust in the effectiveness of public policy (aka "government" as in "Big Government" or the "nanny state"). There can be no doubt that this distrust represents a fundamental belief of the majority of people in the UK and US. The *Guardian* (UK) reported in 2012 that an entity with the rather suspect name of the "Edelman Trust Barometer" found that 38% of those polled in Britain "trusted" government institutions. A higher proportion was reported for the US (43%), which suggests that we should not take such polls too seriously.

Whatever the accuracy of that polling, the distrust of the private sector seems equally intense in both countries. A Gallup poll of June 2011 reported that only 19% of those questioned in the US trusted "Big Business." Even if it were the case that people trust big business, this unlikely discovery would do no more than substitute one enigma (faith in markets) with another (faith in big business). Reading the tea leaves of polls does not seem a promising approach to explaining the enigma of opposition to the regulation of markets.

A more promising route to reconcile the apparent contradiction might start by asking why people reject a noncontradictory skeptical position. People directly experience the follies and frauds of markets. They could conclude that flawed markets provide adequate solutions to many problems only if appropriately regulated. This can be summed up as: Markets are OK, but "curb your enthusiasm," as Larry David might say.

What argument would dissuade people from this pragmatic view to an endorsement of markets as essentially benign? For some this endorsement has a religious component. A fifth of the respondents in the same US Gallup poll I cited above believed that "God [is] actively engaged in daily workings of the world with an economic conservative view that opposes government regulation and champions the free market as a matter of faith." As I shall show, the hypothesis of divine intervention by a right-wing God provides an explanation of market operations considerably more believable than Adam Smith's famous "invisible hand." That oft-invoked hand proves not only invisible but, like most invisible creatures, nonexistent.

The obstacle to convincing people of the virtues of markets is reality – everyday experiences with buying and selling. Among themselves the econfakers finesse this confrontation with reality through the creation of a fantasy world. In this fantasy world everyone is employed, markets are flawless, and "traders" have perfect and complete information. But what satisfies a practicing priesthood may not convince a layperson that reality is false and fantasy is real.

For those determined to negotiate the opaque and arcane small print of buying and selling, a more creditable story of market operations is required. The econfakers do so with their version of the Myth of the Good King. In colonial Spanish America, the oppressed majority consoled itself in the face of an arbitrary and venal bureaucracy with the rationalization that local functionaries caused their oppression. Encouraged by priests, they had faith that if the king knew, he would stop the abuses. I recall being told exactly this by friends when I visited Cuba in the late 1990s and early 2000s. Faced with repeated bureaucratic frustrations, my friends would often say, "Now, if Fidel knew…"

The fakeconomics equivalent of the Myth of the Good King is the Inherent Virtue of Competition. The Inherent Virtue doctrine deals with complaints by market victims at two levels. As the first line of defense the doctrine maintains that competition ensures fair and efficient markets at the global operation of the system, but this need not imply that every specific market and every individual's market experience will be fair and efficient. If you are overcharged or sold faulty goods, you have suffered from an unfortunate but rare exception to the Inherent Virtue doctrine (the Occasional Exception).

If you suffer from market maladies with alarming regularity and the Occasional Exception argument leaves you unimpressed, the Inherent Virtue doctrine falls back on the principle of public ignorance (see Introduction). This Experts-Know-Best defense stresses the complexity of markets. Nonexperts cannot expect to understand and correctly interpret the manifestation of virtuous market operations. What may appear to the layperson as unfair represents a misunderstanding due to ignorance. For example, to the noneconomist it may appear that child labor is a shameful abomination robbing the vulnerable of the joy of their youth and the benefits of education. If someone thinks about it from a *fakeconomics* point of view, he or she realizes that the labor of children brings the family income, representing a rational decision by parents to maximize household welfare. A prohibition on child labor would take away income from the household and drive it deeper into poverty.

By contrast, the *economics* of child labor is obvious. Children are hired because their weak or nonexistent bargaining power drives wages down. The elimination of child labor leaves the jobs to be filled by adults, and incomes rise throughout society including for the parents of the erstwhile child laborer.

You might grumble (or worse) after exiting a central city supermarket, having paid considerably more for almost every item than you would have paid at a suburban branch of the same corporation. The econfaker tells you that higher rents, transport costs, etc., associated with central cities, force the local branch of the corporation to charge different prices for the same item. Otherwise, the urban branch would not be viable (the TINA principle, see Chapter 1). Pay more than the suburbanites with a spring in your step, knowing that the market provides for you.

By contrast, the *economics* of this flagrant price discrimination is obvious. The food marketing corporation takes advantage of the relative immobility of households to extract the price in each submarket that will maximize its profits across all markets.

The ideology of fakeconomics sustains the Big Lie (that Markets Are Good) by 1) trivializing people's day-to-day encounters in markets with tautological rationalizations, and 2) inculcating in people the belief that understanding how markets work is far too difficult for any but the expert. Should these arguments fail, the business interests and the academic ideologues that serve them play their trump card: would you prefer communism? If you are so critical of your local supermarket, laundry, gas station, would you prefer that the government take them over, restricting your freedom to choose, as well as bringing unimaginable inefficiencies? Take your local markets with all their warts and imperfections, or suffer the horrors of socialism/communism, where freedom disappears and humanity descends to misery.

This crass line of defense of markets and capitalism combines several invalid arguments. The warning against dire communism uses the technique of the false dichotomy – that only two possibilities exist, with no middle ground. One of the possibilities is unconscionable, so there is no alternative to the other. This type of argument manifests itself frequently: either you are for me or you're against me; one puff of grass and you're a drug addict; a little inflation leads to hyperinflation.

A variation on the "no middle" scam is the "disaster through unspecified causality" argument. This debating technique manifests itself in statements such as "You cannot go against market fundamentals," "In the end, markets decide," or "Policies must not unsettle financial markets." The pseudostrength of these statements comes from not specifying any causal mechanism and no method by which to assess the degree of danger involved. Is going against markets black and white – make one little market-unfriendly step and all hell breaks loose – or is it more likely that some actions have major consequences and others so minor that the impact can be ignored? If it is the second, the "markets must be free" defense is quite weak.

With these bone-headed arguments considered, I can now summarize the Big Market Lie. Capitalism is a system of efficient markets. It may not appear so to you because you only see a small part of the entire system *and* you lack the expertise to assess what you do observe.

I Do Not Make It Up: False Trading

Most religious systems include the myth that the world we observe is false and some imaginary state of existence is true; e.g., heaven is "true" and the world into which we are born is a perverse distortion of it. In common with many religions, this conviction lies at the core of fakeconomics, which offers "general equilibrium full employment with perfect competition" as the true state of being. What occurs in practice is judged as false.

> The market prices at any given date are…seen as "*false* prices." It is the market process, driven by the competition of profit-seeking entrepreneurs, that modifies those false prices and tends to ensure that they are replaced by prices more closely and "truthfully" reflecting the underlying preferences of the consumers.
>
> (I. M. Kizner)

> The simplest case is the one where we assume that…the supply and demand curves are unaffected by the actions of individuals in the market. That is to say, the effects of trading at "false prices" must be…ignored.
>
> (P. Lewin)

I can summarize this gibberish in simple language. We can construct in our minds an economic system in which markets function perfectly, generating prices of goods that accurately account for the social as well as the private cost of producing them. These prices are the result of the independent decisions of a very large number of people about what to consume and how much to work. This is the system of *true prices*. The everyday world is not perfect. As a result, it generates a system of *false prices*.

Those convinced of that line of argument should take up fakeconomics as their profession or enroll in a religious sect (which is much the same career path).

For those cases in which serious market imperfections might possibly exist, any attempt at government intervention leads down the dark road to communism, from which there is no return.

The Big Market Lie represents an unholy symbiosis of the pseudointellectual abstractions of the fakeconomics profession – the respectable partner – and the extremist rants of the political Right – the nutcase partner (or do I have them reversed?). This marriage of banal theory and venal politics spawns subsidiary lies that I now dissect. A middle ground exists, alternatives exist, and many of the alternatives are far, far better than where we find ourselves now.

Resources Are Scarce

> Economics is the science which studies human behaviour as a relationship between given ends and scarce means which have alternative uses.
>
> (Lord Lionel Robbins)

The ideology of fakeconomics derives from a major illogical inference, a syllogism: the resources of each country and the world are insufficient to meet human needs, and, therefore, decisions on how to allocate those limited resources for human satisfaction dominates human existence. Economics is the science that studies the allocation of limited resources to achieve unlimited human needs.

Can any sane person disagree that resources are limited? The effect of human activity on the global climate should alone make that obvious. Scarcity is equally obvious when you reflect on the challenge of meeting the basic needs of the increasing population in face of natural resource limits (e.g., "peak oil"). This scarcity is compounded by the aging of the population that leaves fewer workers to support more retirees. Because scarcity is real, economics must study how to set the guidelines for allocating our limited resources to best achieve the needs of all humanity.

This definition of the economic problem confronting humanity is the *raison d'être* of mainstream economics. It is the intellectual virus that drove its mutation into fakeconomics. The analytical importance to fakeconomics that scarcity rules human existence cannot be exaggerated. It is the necessary foundation of the market parables summarized in the phrase "supply and demand." The principle of scarcity underpins commonplace statements of the type "Executive salaries are determined by supply and demand" or "Supply and demand dictate the prices at supermarkets."

Supply and demand statements are incantations that convey messages at several levels of consciousness, some of which we do not completely realize. Most profoundly (profanely?) they attribute a naturalism to markets, that the commercial relationships we observe, and the prices associated with those relationships, do not result from the arbitrary actions of men and women. Supply and demand stories preach that natural laws of economics control us and dictate specific outcomes. Because they arise from forces beyond individual discretion, tampering with these specific outcomes leads to an accumulation of economic maladies too disastrous to contemplate. The comparison to religious dogma should be obvious.

Incantations of "supply and demand" also ward off market critics much like Doctor van Helsing used the cross to repel Dracula in Bram Stoker's famous novel. These incantations expose critics as ignorant dreamers of a communitarian Never Never Land or the nefarious purveyors of authoritarian collectivism. The naïve and the nefarious have ignorance in common, perhaps willful ignorance, of basic human nature that manifests itself in the mundane setting of the supermarket.

The prices we pay result from unlimited human wants and finite resources to satisfy them. Further, buying and selling are inherent in human nature like the instinct to mate. An authority for this economic naturalism is Adam Smith himself, the malappropriated icon of the econfakers, who wrote, "The propensity to truck, barter and exchange one thing for another is common to all men." The human propensity to exchange implies that markets arise from human nature itself. From this naturalism to the conclusion that regulating markets ("interfering") contradicts human nature is a short step.

The natural tendency of individuals to exchange produces the Law of Supply and Demand, though only the expert (econfaker) can fully understand the operation of the scissors of wants and resources. I provide a child's guide to help the untutored grasp the great natural forces of supply and demand, which we might call the Fable of the Virtuous Market.

The human problem: People want many things. As consumers they demonstrate what they want through markets. As producers they observe these wants and purchase the resources to obtain the goods and services in order to produce the things other people want.

These resources are limited in supply. This means that people and nature together cannot produce all the things people want.

If the story ended at this point, it would be a quite sad and unsatisfactory: unlimited wants, scarce resources, and most people left unsatisfied and unhappy. However, market magic provides for a happy ending.

The market solution: Being both consumers and producers, people find themselves in a virtuous circle. As producers we sell our scarce resources (laboring time and "entrepreneurship"). This sale provides us with incomes that allow us to realize our wants through consumption. Guided by market prices, each of us decides how much he or she wishes to work. That decision determines the overall supply of productive resources. It also establishes each person's income. As a consumer each person allocates his and her income to obtain the combination of purchases that bring the greatest personal satisfaction.

The dual function of people as producers and consumers allows for a state of grace that all humankind can achieve:

The Magical Optimum: Through the simultaneous choices of work and consumption, each person achieves the maximum potential for happiness, allocating the scarce resource (working time) to fulfill unlimited wants to the maximum possible.

To put the matter simply, we cannot have everything we want, but by balancing work and leisure, and allocating our expenditures rationally, we can achieve the best outcome consistent with the scarcity inherent in nature and infinity of human desires. Few people understand this subtle and sublime optimization process even when they act it out in real time. Little does the individual realize that each trip to the supermarket, excursion to a department store and stop to fill the tank of the car is but a small part of a grand scheme to resolve the tension between the scarcity of resources and the infinity of wants. Though individuals may grumble at the prices they pay to achieve their state of grace, those prices are the outcome of millions of people seeking bliss through market relationships.

The Fable of the Virtuous Market is false. Every part of it is wrong. Resources are not scarce, except for what Marx named "the produce of the earth," a real scarcity that the econfakers almost always deny. Wants are not unlimited. There is no Law of Supply and Demand. It is all nonsense – figments of the imagination of econfakers.

The Supply and Demand Scam

The phrase "supply and demand" is used in daily discourse to convey the idea that economic events are beyond the influence of individuals, determined by "market forces." For example, in March 2007 in the *Farmer's Guardian* (UK), an article invoked the Law of Supply and Demand to "explain" grain prices in the UK, with details left to the reader's imagination:

> The reasons behind the price surge [in grains] are well documented, world shortages and perceived increased demand from the supposedly burgeoning biofuel industry are putting a true floor in the wheat commodity market as more buyers come to the market. Fortunately the laws of supply and demand that I learned in my formative years still hold true.

We find similar insight (that a price rises when more people want more of something) in discussions of petroleum prices. Here it appears that it is price that affects demand, rather than demand affecting price:

> Supply and demand remain among the most influential components of oil-market behavior. Unlike in most other markets, though, drastic changes in oil prices do not necessarily kindle changes in demand. "Prices can fall a long way without stimulating demand," says Tim Evans, an energy analyst at Citigroup.
> Supply issues, on the other hand, can have considerable impact on oil prices. Geopolitical events that threaten oil supplies, such as troubles between Venezuela and the United States or Turkey and Kurdish Iraq, can spook investors and lead to price volatility.

In the same rather incoherent vein, we could read in the *Economist*: "Two factors determine the price of a barrel of oil: the fundamental laws of supply and demand, and naked fear." These statements have implications both proscriptive and ideological, that markets produce "fundamental" outcomes that are beyond the power of individuals, groups or governments to change, and that they have done so as long as people have traded things. Attempts to interfere with "the fundamental laws of supply and demand" are misguided and doomed to failure.

To evaluate this market fundamentalism, I restate the essence of these quotations without using the words "supply" and "demand":

> When businesses and people want to buy more of something at the current price, that price is likely to rise. If a business cannot sell all of its inventory, it can lower its price and might sell more. How much more depends on the characteristic of each commodity.

As predictions of actual behavior these assertions may or may not be true. For example, in 2011 the exhaustion of retail inventories of iPad 2 devices in the UK did not result in an increase in price. This was because the producer, Apple, used its market power to hold retail prices constant. Was this a violation of the "fundamental laws of supply and demand," or proof of its operation? Or both?

Whether true or false, the quotations above bear no relationship to what economists or econfakers mean by "supply and demand." "Naked fear" may or may not impact on the price of oil as the *Economist* speculates. Without knowing fear of what, it is impossible to assess this banality. But no competent economist (and few econfakers) would suggest that "the fundamental laws of supply and demand" determine the price of a barrel of oil, as I shall explain.

The "supply" of a commodity or service and the "demand" for it are theoretical constructions. These theoretical constructions exist only in the imaginary world of perfect competition, a noncredible concept that I dissected previously. Sufficient here is to explain that buying and selling, prices rising and falling, and gluts and shortages of commodities are not the operation of any economic law, and certainly not something that could legitimately be called the Law of Supply and Demand, or the "law" of anything.

Commodities are produced and delivered to wholesale and retail distributors. People, companies and governments demonstrate how much they want of these commodities by purchasing them from the distributors. In this simple, everyday sense commodities have a supply and there is a demand for them. The words mean nothing more than "someone sells" and "someone buys." The real world activities of buying and selling are not the Law of Supply and Demand made infamous by econfakers, and are eagerly misrepresented by free market ideologues in popular outlets such as the *Economist*.

Real world production, distribution and exchange are subject to manipulation through market power by both buyers and sellers. To take the obvious example, producers of petroleum do not passively accept prices. They manipulate prices directly through collusive agreements or indirectly by adjusting what they offer for sale. Supply and demand do not determine oil prices. Quite the contrary, monopoly-administered oil prices determine how much will be bought, and the petroleum producers match their "supply" to that demand.

As any freshman learns in introductory economics (more accurately, introductory fakeconomics), the "supply" in the Law of Supply and Demand does *not* mean an amount. The word refers to a list of quantities of a commodity that a producer would *offer* for sale at different prices. These are not actual sales or deliveries to the retailer. The quantities on the list or schedule are planned or anticipated amounts that might be supplied were various anticipated prices to appear in the market. They are quantities for hypothetical prices when the actual selling price is *unknown* to the vendor.

For example, a tailor might plan to produce and deliver five custom-made shirts over a week at a price of $50 each, eight if the price rises to $60, and so on. It might appear obvious that a producer will offer more when prices rise. This simple relationship proves extremely difficult for the econfakers to establish as a general rule, as I shall explain.

These offers and the anticipated prices cannot be observed. They are imaginary, sometimes called "notional" supply in the fakeconomics jargon. When producers match the imaginary quantities with imaginary prices, this matching has an extremely important property. The producer must believe that each planned quantity will be entirely sold at the anticipated price (i.e., the price in the quantity–price match). Formally stated, the "supply" of "supply and demand" consists of the quantities of beer, computers, etc. that each company offers at each conceivable price, firm in the belief that sales are potentially unlimited. But if potential sales have no limit, from where come the quantities to match the prices? Why not "supply" until the tailor shop operates 24 hours a day with as many assistants that the master tailor can pack in? "Aye, there's the rub," as Hamlet might say were he an economist – a very serious rub, pursued below.

The layperson can justifiably ask what relationship does this imaginary matching of quantities and prices have with actual production and distribution of commodities and services? The answer is "none." Any CEO or sales manager acting on the belief that whatever offered will be sold would soon be seeking alternative employment, having driven his or her company bankrupt. As unlikely as a belief in no sales limit might be, let me pursue this illogic of fakeconomics to the end of the story, because it yields the true tale of supply and demand.

If each unit of an item a company produced were the same, for example a DVD of *Titanic*, we would expect each unit to have the same cost of production as output increases. Let us try combining this reasonable generalization about unit costs with the improbable idea that companies decide their supply offers firm in the belief that they have no sales limit.

The combination of constant unit cost and unlimited sales implies that the profit-seeking DVD company would run its machinery 24 hours a day, 365 days a year, producing all it possibly could. We should observe producers, from the tailor to the multinational, operating continuously at maximum capacity. But we do not observe this – quite the contrary. Idle capacity shows itself frequently, even continuously. Either the logic is incomplete or it is wrong.

As for almost every fakeconomics generalization, what began as an apparently simple idea (that markets generate prices determined by the supply and demand for what people buy and sell) proves exceedingly difficult to establish in logic, much less in practice. The solution to the supply and demand puzzle requires additional pieces unanticipated when we began, some with very strange shapes. With unlimited demand and constant unit costs, there would be only two levels of production (supply). If the selling price is below unit cost, the company makes losses and drops the product from its sales list (zero supply). If the price rises above unit cost, the company produces at full capacity output.

Any other production level, between zero and maximum, would mean that the quantity produced and offered came from an estimate of the company's anticipated sales. While this inference seems reasonable and realistic, it has a devastating impact on the "fundamental law of supply and demand." When anticipated sales not anticipated prices determine production, the anticipated quantity demanded dictates the actual quantity supplied – *supply and demand are the same thing.*

This tautology makes the putative Law of Supply and Demand no law at all, just a banal redundancy. If company owners believe they have no sales constraint, then they will keep building larger and larger production facilities until one, or very few, of them controls the entire market. At that point, the buyers find themselves the passive recipients of prices posted by powerful monopolies or "oligopolies" (one seller or a few sellers, respectively).

If supply and demand determine prices, then supply and demand must be independent of each other. The scissors of supply and demand must have two blades, not one. Buyers (consumers) determine demand and sellers determine supply. If constant unit costs characterize a company's production, anticipated (predicted) sales determine supply. Supply and demand coincide. Independence of supply from demand (predicted sales) requires that the company believes that the demand for its product is limitless. If demand is limitless and unit costs constant, supply is independent of demand, but we have only two possible outcomes: zero and maximum.

To repeat the dilemma yet again, the famous Law of Supply and Demand paints itself into a tautological corner. If at the going price sales are potentially unlimited, then production will always be at full capacity. As a result, supply is one unique amount, unaffected by price unless it falls below unit cost. If price is above unit cost, price increases have no impact on the amount produced (supply), they affect only unit profit. If sales are not unlimited, the amount supplied is not known until after sales are made. Supply and demand are the same thing.

An escape route exists from this descent into market concentration, if we get rid of constant unit costs. We must be careful in doing so, because a misstep out of constant costs can have fatal consequences. Consider the opposite cases: rising unit costs and falling unit costs. If a company's unit costs continuously rise as output increases, then it does not have long to operate. Under pressure of price competition, the company managers would discover that to lower unit costs they must reduce the level of production, driving output and sales down, down, until closure. The opposite case is, if anything, even worse for the putative Law of Supply and Demand. Continuously declining unit cost leads to monopoly. Each company will increase its scale of operations until one company can satisfy the entire market. Railroads in the US during the nineteenth and first half of the twentieth centuries provided clear examples of falling unit costs, as the huge fixed investment spread over larger and larger scales of operation. As a result, the railroads in every country in the world are either a public monopoly or publicly regulated private monopolies.

What can salvage the Law of Supply and Demand from tautology? Constant unit costs cannot generate a meaningful supply curve, nor can falling or rising unit costs. The process of analytical elimination leads to a solution, albeit rather absurd. We require a plausible explanation of why unit costs might first fall, then level off, and subsequently rise, resulting in "U-shaped" unit cost. If this unlikely sequence could be justified and generalized, it provides hope for the concept of "supply." A "U-shaped" company would have a minimum unit cost resting somewhere between the falling and rising portion.

A supply and demand story might go as follows. On the belief that they can sell as much as they can produce, companies set their production at the cost level that maximizes profit for each price. As the market price increases, this compensates for rising unit costs and induces the company to offer a larger quantity for sale. Over time, competition among producers forces companies to their lowest unit cost point. If the level of output for each company at the minimum unit cost contributes a small fraction to total consumer sales, then the industry can support many companies.

The mechanism to avoid monopoly on the one hand and zero production on the other has been found, in the simple letter "U" applied to unit costs. An unfortunate difficulty remains. U-shaped unit cost structures do not exist in the real world. The "solution" is a shamelessly *ex machina* step. In the absence of a known mechanism for such a cost structure, econfakers make one up and repeat it endlessly as if it were credible. The inventive creation is the fakeconomics Law of Diminishing Returns. This new law states that if we combine more of a "variable input" (i.e., workers) with a "fixed input" (plant and machinery, "capital"), output increases, but at a diminishing rate. Out of thin air this "law" generates the U-shaped production story so desperately needed.

Before going further, I must stress that this putative law, snatched like a rabbit from a hat, bears no kinship with David Ricardo's early nineteenth-century concept of diminishing returns, though econfakers invoke him for credibility. In his famous work, *Principles of Political Economy and Taxation* (1817), Ricardo argued that the fertility of land in every country varies. Capitalist farmers will first plant on the most fertile land, which generates the highest profit, then move to the less fertile where profit will be lower, which is the principle of "decreasing returns at the extensive margin," to use the jargon.

Economic and social historians have demonstrated beyond doubt that Ricardo was wrong, due to social and cultural constraints on the allocation of land. But at least the idea has some superficial credibility, which U-shaped unit cost does not (sometimes given the dignity of the phrase "diminishing returns at the *intensive* margin"). Anyone knowledgeable of the work of Ricardo must feel sympathy for a great thinker largely remembered through gross misrepresentations of two of his ideas: diminishing returns and "comparative advantage" (the next chapter confronts the latter).

To return to the absurdity at hand, this approach ("We need U-shaped unit costs, let's call it the Law of Diminishing Returns") should not impress a rational person. How to make it believable? Wikipedia gives a try:

> A common sort of example is adding more workers to a job, such as assembling a car on a factory floor. At some point, adding more workers causes problems such as getting in each other's way, or workers frequently find themselves waiting for access to a part. In all of these processes, producing one more unit of output per unit of time will eventually cost increasingly more, due to inputs being used less and less effectively.
>
> The law of diminishing returns is one of the most famous laws in all of economics. It plays a central role in production theory.

The last two sentences are true. The rest is garbage. I infer that the Wikipedia author visited some quite unusual car factories. It may well be that as more and more workers squeeze into an automobile plant, they begin to step on each other's toes and generally disrupt operations. I doubt that any factory manager has experimented to find out. Companies staff their factories on the basis of technically determined equipment-to-worker rates, on farms, in offices and at other places of work.

The famous Law of Diminishing Returns suffers from misnaming, because "diminishing returns" do not yield the necessary U-shape for costs. This magical shape requires that "returns" first *increase* (the declining or first part of the "U"), then begin to decrease or "diminish" (the rising or second part of the "U"). Mere "diminishing returns" leave the company with a fatal case of continuously increasing costs, discussed above. The Law of Increasing-then-Diminishing Returns is imaginary, a Rube Goldberg attachment to a Heath Robinson "Law of Supply."

The Law of Supply and Demand that allegedly determines market prices has no existence except in the feverish imaginations of econfakers. The "supply" part cannot be logically specified or empirically verified. If companies believed they have no sales constraint, they would always be at full capacity. If they estimate their sales constraint, then the amount offered and sold are the same. The solution to this quandary is the Diminishing Returns scam. The (in)famous supply and demand find relevance only in a very special and absurd case, when a company's production unit costs show a U-shape as output grows. A little nonideological common sense reveals as nonsense all that complicated stuff about supply and demand, unnecessary obfuscation of how companies make decisions and markets operate.

Something akin to economic "laws" exist, but they are deeply embedded in the institutions of society, which I treat in the last chapter. The costs and prices of commodities and services are not arbitrary. They have objective constraints. The amount of goods and services people and corporations buy and sell are not arbitrary. But simplistically viewing production and distribution as solely economic and determined by natural forces beyond the control of people and their collective actions comes from the metaphysics of fakeconomics, not sound thinking. I am hardly the first economist to point that out: "If the wealth distribution which the automatic working of the system brings about is accepted [uncritically], behavior that interferes with the adjustment of relative prices is dysfunctional...and can be condemned on ethical grounds. Academic economists have been the high priests of this ethic."

To most people, and certainly all econfakers, the name Karl Marx provokes dark images of socialism and communism. Be that as it ideologically may, Marx provides important insight about the fakery in the adulation of "supply and demand." Using the term "vulgar economy" for what I call fakeconomics, Marx wrote that it "confines itself to systemizing in a pedantic way, and proclaiming for everlasting truths, the trite ideas held by a self-complacent bourgeoisie with regard to their own world, to them the best of all worlds."

Replace "bourgeoisie" with "1%" and we see how little has changed in fakeconomics over 150 years.

Resources Abundant, Wants Limited

For idle factories and idle workers profit no man.

(Franklin D. Roosevelt)

As illogical and contradictory as supply and demand may be, a more serious problem faces fakeconomics. The generalization that resources are scarce underpins its entire analytical structure. The problem is that resources are not scarce in a market economy. To the contrary, they are abundant. As for wants being unlimited, that comes from the pipe dreams of marketing departments.

The people of a country and their working capacity constitute the most important resource in every society. This is a rare case in which fakeconomics displays some link to reality, because its use of the words "scarce resources" always refers to what it calls the "labor input." Within this framework labor can produce all the other resources or substitutes for them. Scarcity of human labor implies an overall scarcity of goods and services, because every product requires labor.

To assess whether labor is scarce, I look first at statistics from the US, which cover in a consistent manner a longer time period than in any other country. During the Great Depression of the 1930s, civilian unemployment in the US reached a peak of 25% of the labor force in 1933 – one out of every four working people. It persisted in double digits, 10%, until 1941, the eve of the US entry into World War II (Congress declared war in early December). During 1943–1945 the rate edged below 2%, and would never again fall so low. For 62 years, 1950–2011, the annual unemployment rate dropped below 4% in only eight years, and not once after 1969. If that record seems inconsistent with full employment, consider unemployment for African Americans. During the 52 years of 1960–2011, the African American rate never fell lower than 6%, and not once lower than 7% after 1970.

In 2007, on the eve of the great financial collapse, after almost fifteen years of steady economic expansion, 4.5% of all males 16 or older and the same percent of females were unemployed. Many econfakers would argue that 4.5% unemployment is actually full employment, with those 4.5 people out of every 100 "between jobs," lacking the skills to match what employers seek, or waiting for a better offer. So, perhaps we should use 5% as "full employment," in which case 18 years since 1950 would qualify, or 5.5%, which divides the six decades equally with 31 years above and 31 below?

Could US society suffer from an extraordinarily large number of shirkers, living high on unemployment benefits, so that 6% unemployment brings everyone willing to work into work? If this were true, why is it that from 1950 through 1979, 6% or more of the labor force "chose" unemployment in 15% of the years (about one year out of every seven), and during 1980–2011 this occurred in almost 36% of the years (more frequently than one in three). Could we be observing a long-term rise in laziness? Should the term "unemployment rate" be

Idle Factories and Idle Workers

50 years of idle men and women in the US and the UK, 1963–2013

These are the so-called harmonized or standardized rates reported by the Organisation for Economic Co-operation and Development (www.oecd.org). The rates for 2013 are for January–June.

Spot the trend: 50 years of factory idleness in the US, 1960–2012 (percentage)

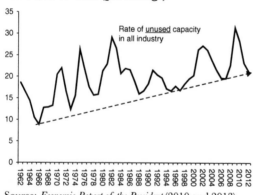

Source: *Economic Report of the President* (2010 and 2013).

Unemployment rate, USA and UK

From 1963 through 2011, the US civilian unemployment was above 5% in 36 of the 50 dull years with an average of 6.1%. In only 10 of 50 years did it fall below 4%.

In the UK the average was almost the same (6.2%), with lower rates than the US before 1980 and higher rates subsequently. During the 33 years after the election that made Margaret Thatcher prime minister, unemployment fell below 5% only twice (2004 and 2005, under "New Labour" prime minister Tony Blair).

Industrial utilization, USA

People find themselves unemployed because companies lay them off (not rocket science). From 1962 through 2012 the factories and other producing units in the industrial sectors of the US economy operated on average with 20% or more of their capacity idle in 27 years. Looking at it the other way, in only 7 years did private industry have 15% or less of its buildings and equipment idle, and 10% or less in one (1966).

The trend towards increasing idleness is obvious and helps explain the declining US investment rate.

replaced with "shirkers' index"? The laziness epidemic seems to infect management as well. Since 1960 the level of utilization of productive capacity has shown a downward trend. Capacity utilization declined during each successive boom and bust, with both the maximum and the minimum lower with each business cycle. (See Box: Idle Factories and Idle Workers.)

The laziness malady must also affect the UK, though with wider swings from maximum to minimum (perhaps due to different definitions of unemployment or laziness in the two countries). During 41 years, unemployment fell below 4% in only 4, all consecutive (1971–74). After 1974 unemployment averaged almost 7.5% of the labor force.

For all reasonable observers (which excludes econfakers) a more obvious answer than laziness presents itself. Some major change occurred after the 1970s to render society less capable of providing employment for those who seek it. That change occurred as a result of the implementation of fakeconomic policies by governments all over the world – policy imitating bad theory. With an average unemployment rate since 1990 of 6% in the US and 7% in the UK, only econfakers and their business patrons look over the land and see scarce resources (and probably not the patrons, who, after all, live in the real world).

When something is in surplus, it is not scarce. The remote possibility that labor could suffer from a shortage at some time in the future does not make scarcity economics plausible. If you cannot use all of something, it should be obvious that there is no danger of running out of it. In most countries in most years we find no scarcity of labor and no lack of the machinery to employ that labor. Only rarely does the problem of how to allocate scarce resources confront a market economy, usually during wars. How to mobilize and use productively the available resources plagues market economies. As long as one cares to look, statistics demonstrate that markets do not solve the problem.

Econfakers respond to the obvious absence of labor scarcity by attempts to show that any level of unemployment, no matter how high, is actually zero. Whatever the statistics might show to the contrary, market economies always enjoy full employment in the eyes of the mainstream. The always-full-employment arguments fall into three categories: the tautological, the statistical and the absurd. All three derive from the dubious division of unemployment between voluntary and involuntary. Beginning with this false dichotomy, the econfakers proceed to demonstrate their own satisfaction that all of the unemployment we observe is "voluntary."

The "voluntarily unemployed" themselves fall into three categories. First and least reprehensible are those between jobs ("structural unemployment"). Second, we find the lazy, politely described as rejecting work because they assign a high price to their leisure time. Third come those who do not work because of the lavish benefits bestowed on them by the nanny state in unemployment payments, disability benefits and welfare handouts in general.

In February 2011 the prominent British television presenter John Humphrys provided BBC viewers with examples of the second and third forms of voluntarism, in a program titled *The Future State of Welfare*. The enticing trailer for the program informed the prospective watcher, "[John Humphrys] returns to the area where he was born – Splott in Cardiff – to show how attitudes to work and welfare have changed in his lifetime. When he was growing up, a man who didn't work was regarded as a pariah; today, one in four of the working-age population in Splott is on some form of benefit."

The BBC broadcast the program when Mr Humphrys was 67 years old. A bit of arithmetic implies that he was "growing up" in the 1950s. Mr Humphrys neglected to mention during his hour-long program that when he was growing up (during the postwar boom), about 3% of the labor force in Wales was unemployed. He might have compared this to close to 10% in 2011 (also reported on the BBC, though not in the same program). During the worst recession in 80 years, one of the leading broadcasters on a publicly owned television station attributed unemployment to personal motivation. In Mr Humphrys the econfakers have a potential follower.

In fairness I should add that two years later the BBC management took Humphrys to task for the program: "The BBC Trust said that a programme called the *Future of Welfare* [*sic*], written and presented by John Humphrys, breached its rules on impartiality and accuracy. It found that the programme had failed to back up with statistics claims that there was a 'healthy supply of jobs.'"

The presenter's patronizing slander of the unemployed calls to mind an article in the *Guardian* in late 1931, citing a speech by then prime minister Ramsay McDonald. In the depths of the world depression, the prime minister explained to the nation that the growing number of people out of work resulted from the onset of the holiday season:

It is not, however, likely that the [unemployment] figure will continue at quite this level, as the rise is to a large extent owing

to the temporary closing down of works for extended holiday
stoppages...

A large increase in the "temporarily stopped" always occurs in
the last week of the year, and a temporary rise of a quarter of a
million is not unusual.

The ideology of scarcity demands the "voluntary" or "temporary"
unemployment absurdities of the econfakers, because the political
stakes are so high. If people (including television presenters) come to
recognize the reality of unemployment, then what passes for economic
wisdom would be recognized as ideology.

Resources may not be scarce, but surely the other half of the
fakeconomics definition is true, that people's desire to consume is
unlimited. Marketing shysters all over the world strive to turn this
assertion into fact. It should be viewed very skeptically. If I stop a large
number of people on the street and ask if they want to improve the
quality of their lives, the vast majority would answer "yes." To equate
or reduce this hope for improvement to an unlimited desire for things
that can be bought and sold turns a triviality into a slander on human
nature.

A shockingly large proportion of the populations of the most
developed countries in the world lives in poverty. Whether or not their
"wants are unlimited" is foolish and reactionary conjecture. Poverty
means that people lack the income or means to the income that would
purchase the minimum required for a decent life. The desire to change
that should surprise no one, nor would any intelligent person interpret
that desire for change as demonstrating some universal truth about
consumption behavior.

At the top of the income and wealth scale, households have the
opposite problem. While austerity reigns for the poor, overindulgence
guides the rich. How do you spend $1.3 million (the average for those in
the top 1% in the US) or £1 million (about that of the UK) *in a year*? The
rest of us are left to imagine the *angst* of those at the top as they come to
31 December and discover, yet again, income unspent.

Nonsense of Consumer "Choice"

The *market*, in its majestic equality, forbids the rich as well as the
poor to sleep under bridges, to beg in the streets, and to steal bread.

(Anatole France)

The great thing about free markets is that they offer choice. People are free to choose what to buy, and through this choice to fulfill their lives. Work hard, earn a decent income, spend it according to your personal choice. The gross vulgarity of this banality (that many things to buy brings freedom) is exceeded only by its pretensions to profundity.

This attempted transubstantiation of the banal into the sublime took the famous form in a less gender-aware age: "Free markets, free men." On 17 October 1974, before an extremely receptive audience of businessmen (and all men they were), Milton Friedman, he of the faux Nobel Prize and an icon of fakeconomics, laid it all out in not-so-sublime detail:

> You can say with great certainty that free markets make free men and that controlled markets destroy free men... My proposition is far more obvious for the more material components of freedom – the freedom to decide how to spend your money, what to do with your time, where to work, what job to take, where to live. Those material aspects of freedom are all associated with free markets, and they are no less important to most people than freedom of thought, of speech, of political persuasion... The absence of free markets destroys free men, and presence of free markets makes free men.

Compare this vision (that freedom equals choice in markets) with that in Franklin D. Roosevelt's Second Bill of Rights: "We have come to a clear realization of the fact that true individual freedom cannot exist without economic security and independence. 'Necessitous men are not free men.' People who are hungry and out of a job are the stuff of which dictatorships are made."

Friedman's "freedoms" – to decide "what to do with your time," "where to work," "what job to take" and "where to live" – require that a person have a job or be out of work with many jobs to choose among. No doubt all of the well-heeled businessmen hanging on his every word were employed and enjoying quite handsome rewards for that employment. But what of the 5.6% of the US labor force that was unemployed in October 1974, and the 12% below the miserly official poverty line?

In 2012 almost fifty million US households struggled below the poverty line, with seventeen million of them suffering from hunger ("food insecure" is the polite term). With one in ten working people unemployed and one in six households in poverty, the "choices" of what to do with your time, where to work, what job to take, where to live, and how to spend your money are not complicated. You spend your time looking for work if you are unemployed. If employed you hang onto the job you have for dear life. You live where you can afford the rent or mortgage. And you spend your money on shelter, food and transport to the job you cannot afford to lose, and hope you have some funds left for the relative luxuries of healthcare and schooling. In the UK the deprivation was worse, with one in five households below the official poverty line, and an overall unemployment rate in 2011 of 9.2%, rising to 25% for "young adults" (aged 16–24). With a similar unemployment and a higher poverty rate, the economically marginalized in the UK had at least one tremendous advantage over their colleagues in the US: a national healthcare system "free at the source."

When on his various UK visits, Professor Friedman would make his contempt for the National Health Service (NHS) crystal clear, for it was the antithesis of market choice (Margaret Thatcher adored him). To verify the principled opposition of the faux laureate to almost every humane measure implemented in the public sector, visit the surreal Becker Friedman Institute of Research in Economics. This organization was known as the Milton Friedman Institute until outrage among the faculty and students at the University of Chicago forced its reorganization, including the addition of an equally reactionary econfaker, Gary Becker, in the center's moniker.

The faux Nobel winner identified not rights, but the privileges of a wealthy minority. Without doubt every "free man" (and woman) should enjoy these privileges. Markets, much less "free" markets, do not provide them for everyone, far from it. On the contrary, in Europe and the US a large minority lives in poverty, and a substantial minority perches so close to poverty that a commonplace misfortune such as the illness of an income earner plunges it into destitution. A further substantial minority has an adequate, if modest, income flow, but lives in constant anxiety of unemployment.

In a decent and humane society all citizens would enjoy the privilege to choose. Through cooperation, not individual acquisition, they can guarantee themselves fundamental social rights. In the words of Franklin Roosevelt,

> We have accepted…a second Bill of Rights under which a new basis of security and prosperity can be established for all – regardless of station, race, or creed. Among these are:
> The right to a useful and remunerative job in the industries or shops or farms or mines of the nation;

The right to earn enough to provide adequate food and clothing and recreation;

The right of every farmer to raise and sell his products at a return which will give him and his family a decent living;

The right of every businessman, large and small, to trade in an atmosphere of freedom from unfair competition and domination by monopolies at home or abroad;

The right of every family to a decent home;

The right to adequate medical care and the opportunity to achieve and enjoy good health;

The right to adequate protection from the economic fears of old age, sickness, accident, and unemployment;

The right to a good education.

All of these rights spell security… We must be prepared to move forward, in the implementation of these rights, to new goals of human happiness and well-being. America's own rightful place in the world depends in large part upon how fully these and similar rights have been carried into practice for all our citizens.

We find much the same sentiment in the 1945 election manifesto of the UK's Labour Party, that would help make Clement Attlee prime minister in a landslide:

The Labour Party stands for freedom – for freedom of worship, freedom of speech, freedom of the Press. The Labour Party will see to it that we keep and enlarge these freedoms, and that we enjoy again the personal civil liberties we have, of our own free will, sacrificed to win the war. The freedom of the Trade Unions… must also be restored. But there are certain so-called freedoms that Labour will not tolerate: freedom to exploit other people; freedom to pay poor wages and to push up prices for selfish profit; freedom to deprive the people of the means of living full, happy, healthy lives… The price of so-called economic freedom for the few is too high if it is bought at the cost of idleness and misery for millions.

The "freedom to choose," whether in the crass ideology of Friedman or the banality of the supermarket ("Tesco/Safeway offers more choice"), requires the chooser to have the income to make choices. Markets are the barrier, not the vehicle, to the freedom to choose, because they do not generate decent employment and incomes for all.

Further Reading

Steve Keen, *Debunking Economics: The Naked Emperor of the Social Sciences* (Sydney: Zed Books, 2001, revised 2011).

Norbert Häring and Niall Douglas, *Economists and the Powerful: Convenient Theories, Distorted Facts, Ample Rewards* (London: Anthem Press, 2012), ch. 4.

Chapter 5

RICHES, "SOVEREIGNTY" AND "FREE TRADE"

Even You Can Be Rich

> I tell you the truth, it is hard for a rich man to enter the kingdom
> of heaven. Again I tell you, it is easier for a camel to go through the
> eye of a needle than for a rich man to enter the kingdom of God.
>
> (Matthew 19:23–4
> It is obvious that Matthew
> never took a course in fakeconomics)

> Two elderly women are at a Catskill mountain resort, and one of
> 'em says, "Boy, the food at this place is really terrible." The other
> one says, "Yeah, I know; and such small portions."
>
> (Woody Allen)

For all its failings, supporters of an unregulated markets system believe it has one great saving grace. This virtue trumps all its sins. In an unregulated market economy anyone can become rich if he or she has the necessary drive, commitment and optimism. Government interference through taxes and regulations on market behavior rob people of the opportunity to be graced with that reward for diligence, prudence and enterprise.

Of course, *everyone* cannot be rich. The fakeconomics myth is not that simplistic and naïve. The shining path offered, what might be called the Sendero Luminoso of the econfakers, recognizes that only a few can, but anyone, even you, could be among the few. This fable teaches that accession by the few is not a lottery, but the direct result of individual effort. In a sentence: If you want it, go for it, and you'll get it unless the government stops you through its socialist meddling.

For this fable to be taken seriously, as in corresponding to reality, it must specify the process by which through individual effort the nonrich, even the poor, become rich. I begin the explanation by clarifying the state of grace under pursuit. The market dream does not promise mere improvement; that is the minimum-expectations dream. Father and mother work as factory hands, son and daughter become school teachers, and the third generation "rises" to be doctors, lawyers and professors. That is nothing but the old liberal/socialist "mixed economy" path of moving up by sucking up to the government through university grants and similar handouts. The grace bestowed by the market means *getting rich*. The task is to identify the "free market" route to *riches* for the enterprising few.

Starting rich and making yourself richer, the Bill Gates path to wealth and fame, is definitively not the market (aka American) dream. In its purest form, the hero in the market dream story starts poor and ends rich. The rags-to-riches route requires that the rag person begins small and up-sizes roughly at the rate of Jack's beanstalk. The twenty-first century evidence for success is not encouraging. During the booming 2000s before the great financial collapse, "voluntary closures" of companies plus bankruptcies averaged over 90% of new small business start-ups. During the last three years of the 2000s, with the economy in decline and stagnation, that rose to 125%. This figure means that substantially more small businesses disappeared than started (i.e., over 100%).

Anyone Can Be Rich in the USA (If You Are Already in the 1%)

Growth in after tax constant price household income by quintiles, 1979–2007

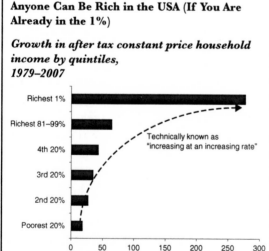

Source: Congressional Budget Office (US).

Over the 28 years of 1979–2007, the average (mean) American household enjoyed an increase in real income of slightly over 60%. Less happy was the meager 37% increase for the median household (the one in the middle of the distribution). Very happy indeed was the richest 1%, which could take unabashed delight in an increase of 278% (3.5% per year).

Very limited in their delight would be the poorest 20% with an 18% increase (a hardly noticeable 0.6% a year).

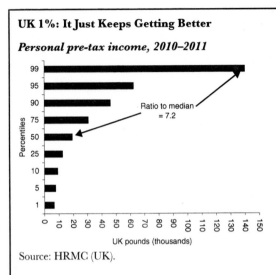

UK 1%: It Just Keeps Getting Better

Personal pre-tax income, 2010–2011

Ratio to median = 7.2

Percentiles: 99, 95, 90, 75, 50, 25, 10, 5, 1

UK pounds (thousands)

Source: HRMC (UK).

While inequality is not exclusively a characteristic of English-speaking countries, the USA and the UK do their part to make it so. From relatively low inequality during 1954–1980, Britain under the neoliberal regimes of Margaret Thatcher (Conservative) and Tony Blair ("New" Labour) managed to make society safe for the ultrarich. In 1993 the entry level of the 1% Club was a meager 5.5 times median income, and in barely fifteen years this rose to 8.1, a considerably more respectable level of elite avarice.

Maybe, just maybe, those bankruptcies and closures refer to old businesses, while the new ones hang in there and after a few years challenge Microsoft, Amazon and Google. While not as bleak as the inscription at the entrance to Dante's Hell ("Abandon hope, all ye who enter here"), the statistics tell a cruel story. Dun and Bradstreet ("the world's leading source of business information" the website tells us) reports, "Businesses with fewer than 20 employees have only a 37% chance of surviving four years and only a 9% chance of surviving 10 years." Only a minute fraction of the minority of survivors made their bold entrepreneurs filthy rich.

Still, 9%, almost one in ten, were winners (or, at least, hanging on). In most countries successful self-enrichers tend to be university graduates. Some attend but dropout, such as the Facebook savant Mark Zuckerberg, erstwhile Harvard student. His success indicates that it is better to drop out of Harvard than to graduate from Slippery Rock Community College. For those that hope to follow in the byte-strewn path of the successful dot.com-ers, it is worth recalling that all of these winners came from families in the upper 20% of the US income distribution (most from the upper 10 or 5).

It seems that the chances of anyone making big money starting a new enterprise in the US is considerably less than one in ten. What are the chances of markets bestowing this happy outcome on someone near the bottom of the social order, with limited education, no elite contacts and zero start-up capital? Well, don't bet the ranch on it (though the poor are more likely to be landless cowboys).

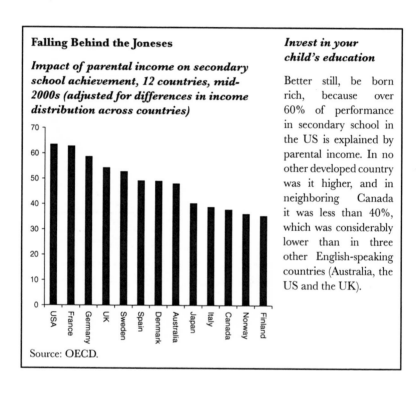

Falling Behind the Joneses

Impact of parental income on secondary school achievement, 12 countries, mid-2000s (adjusted for differences in income distribution across countries)

Source: OECD.

Invest in your child's education

Better still, be born rich, because over 60% of performance in secondary school in the US is explained by parental income. In no other developed country was it higher, and in neighboring Canada it was less than 40%, which was considerably lower than in three other English-speaking countries (Australia, the US and the UK).

After this brief excursion into the Cloud Cuckoo Land of rags-to-riches through do-it-yourself (DIY capitalism, perhaps), it is instructive to "get real," as the cliché recommends. Income mobility in the US is abysmally low. Over 60% of student achievement in US secondary schools is associated with parental income, a statistic that does not include differences in the quality of schools. Strange as it may seem, the better off do not send their children to bad schools.

A study by researchers at the hardly socialist Federal Reserve Bank of Boston compared a large sample of households in 1988 and 1998 with the purpose of investigating income mobility. During these ten years national income increased at over 3% per year, almost exactly the post

World War II average. It qualifies as a "normal" decade of economic growth. Of households in the poorest fifth of the population, over half remained at the bottom ten years later, and a quarter moved into the next fifth (the quintile second from the bottom). This represented progress but not riches. Three out of one hundred households made it from the bottom fifth to the top fifth. "Curb your enthusiasm," because in 1998 at 2010 prices a family reached the richest quintile with a rather modest $67,000 (see Box: Income Mobility in the US).

A second study, by the Department of the Treasury, published in 2007, indicated that after 1998 the distribution of income grew more unequal and mobility declined compared to 1988–1998. In addition to less mobility across quintiles of the distribution, the treasury dissected the richest 20%, with results that could induce insomnia among those whose somnambulant activities feature the American dream. For every 1000 adults in the lowest quintile in 1996, 17 made it into the top 10% of income recipients; 9 reached the richest 5%; and one Lone Ranger climbed into the infamous 1% (reaching the last had an annual cover price of almost $325,000).

For someone smack in the middle in 1996 (median income), the numbers were considerably better, 32 out of 1000 into the top 10%, 12 into the high 5%, and a whopping 3 joining the elite 1%. If you like those odds, 3 out of 1000 for the typical family, step up and vote for those market-loving politicians who will keep taxes low for the billionaire you will become, and do not cast a ballot for some liberal do-gooder who would raise taxes on the rich at the cost of our freedom to choose.

Meanwhile across the pond, a detailed mobility study sponsored by several major UK private foundations covered eight European countries plus the US and Canada. Released in 2011, it came to the not-so-shocking conclusion that income and wealth inequality has a negative impact on social mobility:

> The findings [of the research] suggest that concerns that higher inequality might reduce equality of opportunity and intergenerational mobility appear to be well founded. Countries with large gaps between the rich and poor such as the US and UK look set to remain the least mobile in the future. Income inequality and educational inequality can feed off each other in a cycle of ever decreasing mobility, as those with higher earnings are able to invest ever greater resources into education of their offspring to maintain their advantage in society.

Income Mobility in the US

1988 to 1998

Income quintile	Bottom	Lower middle	Middle	Upper middle	Top
Bottom	53	23	13	8	5
Lower middle	25	38	23	10	5
Middle	13	20	28	28	13
Upper middle	8	15	23	30	25
Top	3	5	15	25	53
Sum	100%	100%	100%	100%	100%

Source: Federal Reserve Bank of Boston.

1996 to 2005

Income quintile	Bottom	Lower middle	Middle	Upper middle	Top
Bottom	55	24	11	7	4
Lower middle	25	37	22	11	5
Middle	11	23	34	23	9
Upper middle	6	11	24	38	21
Top	3	5	9	21	61
Sum	100%	100%	100%	100%	100%

Sources: Federal Reserve Bank of Boston / US Department of the Treasury.
Guide: Reading down is 1988 or 1996. Across is 1998 or 2005. For example, in 1998, 53% of families in the bottom fifth of the population in 1988 were still there, 25% moved up one fifth, 13% rose into the middle, 8% into the penultimate, and 3% gained the top.

Most of the poor stay poor and most of the rich...

From 1988 to 1998 the poorest 20% of families had something in common with the richest 20%. Between 1988 and 1998 they were equally likely to stay in their income group. After ten years, over half the poorest were right where they started (53%) and almost 80% stayed in the lowest two categories. Just 3 in 100 families "made it to the top."

Since 1998...

Less mobility than for 1988–1998, with 55% of the poorest stuck in the lowest quintile and at the top up to a robust 61% from the previous 53%. The rate at which the middle and upper middle quintiles climbed the ladder declined. In the earlier period 38% of those in the middle rose higher, compared to 33% during 1996–2005.

In case you are suspicious of the motivation of do-gooder foundations, a review of existing evidence funded by the UK Department of Business Innovation and Skills came to the same conclusion: "We know that countries with higher income inequality tend to have lower social mobility."

In summary, "Yes, Virginia, there is [an American market dream] Santa Claus," but unlike the Ancient Mariner who "stoppeth one of three," the red, white and blue market bell ringer hails down only one in a thousand and about the same in the UK. Woody Allen's joke at the beginning of this chapter sums up the experience of the vast majority of people in the UK and the US with the market system: it tastes terrible and they don't get enough of it to live decently.

Consumer Is Sovereign

Everybody knows and only fools and knaves doubt that the stuff we find in supermarkets, shops, online retailers and any other sales outlet are only there because we demand them. "[Consumer sovereignty means] that consumers ultimately determine what goods and services are produced and how the economy's limited resources are used based on the purchases they make. Consumers thus reign over the economy as sovereign rulers."

Those Big Macs rest on their trays and the Rolls Royces gleam in grand showrooms because consumers buy them. Is this obvious? The first step to verify the sovereignty hypothesis is to ask: What is a "consumer"? And what is sovereignty when commercial propaganda approached $1000 a head in the US in the 2000s?

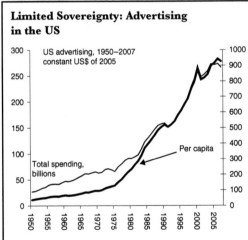

Limited Sovereignty: Advertising in the US

In the US in 1950 companies spent less than $40 per person on advertising to inform "sovereign consumers" of all of the wonderful spending opportunities for them to seize upon (inflation adjusted to prices of 2005). It appears that by 2007 companies had considerably more information to convey to their sovereigns, requiring over $900, increasing by a multiple of 24.

This information, most of it lying on a spectrum from inaccurate to fraudulent, increased the average price of goods and services by over 3%.

Perhaps most impressive, advertising expenditure in 2007 was $280 billion, compared to total private sector research and development outlays of $267 billion. This suggests it is more expensive to convince people to buy a product than to develop it.

Sources: Business Roundtable and the United States Council Foundation / Douglas Galbi.

Since society began, mobilizing the resources to obtain the necessities of life has been the central task of humanity. Most people would not describe hunting and gathering groups to consist of a bunch of consumers. The word has been relevant for approximately the last 250 years at most. During that time the typical household found to an increasing extent that it could no longer produce its necessities, but acquired them through monetary exchange. People became purchasers of these necessities because they and their neighbors could no longer produce them in the household.

Today households cannot produce what they need because almost everyone in the high-income countries and an increasing majority in the other countries work for someone else. A few employ the many to produce goods and services for market exchange. Even more, the categories of goods and services that people in high-income countries purchase have increased inexorably. Child care, previously provided within the household, represents a relative new addition to the commodity list.

The historical back story of household expenditures reveals the relatively new specification of people as "consumers." More recent still is the application of the term "consumer" to activities which were previously identified by their specific attributes or functions. Previously, a person who flew in an airplane considered him- or herself a "passenger," a newspaper buyer was a "reader," and a visitor to a medical specialist a "patient" (the origin of which should be obvious to any person who has spent an extended period in a doctor's aptly named waiting room). Now, they are all "consumers." In the same vein, and especially in Britain, terminology has transubstantiated recipients of public services into consumers.

In an innovative initiative in June 2009, the public health organization in Britain, the NHS, held a conference in London: "Achieving Excellence in NHS Customer Care." The conference corresponded to a survey that revealed that "100% of NHS leaders concede that the NHS is not sufficiently *customer focused* at present" (emphasis added), with the "leaders" in question being NHS chief executives. This survey was reported in an NHS "white paper," given the commercially engaging title "Customer Service in the NHS." One could read:

We all need to learn from the best to deliver a first class, customer-focused NHS fit for the 21st century.

So who do we mean by the best?

The best companies. The best individuals, externally and internally. The best pleased customers. And, crucially, the best learning professionals, in order to facilitate learning and ensure change is implemented and maintained.

The organization and realization of the document and the conference represented the good work of a personnel management company with the quintessentially neoliberal name "you:unlimited" (I have not made it up), who recognized that the concept of "customer service" might strike the uninitiated as possessing an excessively commercial resonance:

> There is a *cultural resistance* to such a change within a lot of [NHS units]. Typically, criticisms of the approach to "seeing patients as customers" centre around the use of business philosophies in the publicly funded NHS. "Giving an impression that the NHS is a business or market-led could encourage the charging of patients for treatments," as Karen Jennings of Unison [the NHS employee union] suggested.

But no need for the culturally backward in the NHS to worry, because "Acknowledging such concerns and addressing them along the way is key to ensuring staff, new and established, successfully embrace this new way of thinking." Certainly about time, one would think, because no such Luddite opposition to sound business values would be found in the US healthcare business (and a profitable business it is). An important step to change the cultural resistance would be to move doctors and nurses away from the antiquarian prejudice that they exist to improve health rather than hospital balance sheets.

The Labour government under the neoliberal Tony Blair (and his grumpy understudy Gordon Brown) did its best to foster the "new way of thinking." Over the 13 misspent years of New Labour, overall employment in the NHS rose at a bit less than 3% annually. NHS chief executives and their administrative underlings increased by double the average, over 6% per year. In 2000 one NHS managerial bureaucrat had over forty health workers to order around, and this fell to barely thirty in 2010. One presumes that they keep themselves busy boning up on "business philosophies," an oxymoron to join the distinguished company of "open secret," "just war" and "for-profit universities."

To be fair, we remain in the early days of the consumerization of British healthcare. In one example, you:unlimited refers to the "mission statement" of a US health consultancy group:

> Baird Group, Inc. is a results-oriented consulting group specializing in customer service improvement and mystery shopping for healthcare organizations... Since 1991, it has provided healthcare clients [aka corporations] with target solutions for customer-service challenges.

The "target solutions" refer to recruiting faux "customers," which is where "mystery shopping" comes in:

> Mystery shopping, or secret shopping, is a tool used by companies in a wide range of industries to measure the quality of their products and services. Secret shoppers pose as normal customers to gather information about shopper experiences. In the healthcare industry secret shoppers pose as patients or patient friends and family members to assess the quality of patient experiences.

It would appear that an essential element of maintaining good health is a cadre of medical-consultant James Bonds in drag and mufti checking out the competition. And, what's wrong with it? Shouldn't those who provide healthcare focus their work on the needs of recipients and judge success by the satisfaction (or lack thereof) of those recipients?

To keep the answer simple: *no*. The purpose of providing healthcare is not to leave people feeling satisfied, not even to make them happy. The purpose is to cure people of what ails them, or, failing that, to make their lives as bearable as medical science and practice can achieve. In general, trying to achieve "customer satisfaction" does not contribute to good health. On the contrary, "consumer service" schemes aimed at inducing satisfaction can undermine provision of good healthcare. This happens by piling bureaucratic "monitoring" tasks onto staff who would otherwise be directly involved in healthcare. Anyone who has used US private healthcare (not that there is much else in the country) must at some point speculate: how much better would health in the US be if the time spent on processing charges, payments and claims were spent on curing illness?

If any general truths about social behavior exist, surely one is that people do not go to clinics, hospitals and other medical facilities with a customer mentality. We do not consider paramedics, nurses and doctors to be sales staff in a medical supermarket. Very few people suffering from an ailment are likely to telephone around or browse the Internet to find the cheapest "provider." You might be willing to use the cheapest dishwashing soap, but you want the best (or, at least, appropriate) health treatment, be it the cheapest or not. If people were "consumers" of healthcare, we might as well run all "providers" as profit-making companies and put them on the stock exchange (see Box: Bond Rating the NHS).

Except in rare cases, people have no basis for judging good health advice from bad, even less a good doctor from a bad one. That rare creature,

---

Bond Rating the NHS, or: Is Curing People Profitable?

In one of those things that no leftist critic would make up, the right-wing British government announced in January 2012 that it would change existing legislation on how the operations of the NHS would be assessed.

No doubt inspired by the downgrading of the French government the previous month, the Tory-dominated coalition had the same in mind for the NHS:

> Under the proposals, any provider, either a hospital trust or private company, that failed to achieve an "investment grade" rating – BBB− by Standard & Poor's, Baa3 by Moody's and BBB− by Fitch – would risk losing its license to operate in the NHS... A similar system works in the electricity market, giving the regulator warning of financial difficulties building up in the system.

Immediately some questioned the competence of a bunch of financial sector lackeys to judge the quality of healthcare: "It beggars belief anyone would countenance bringing in the self-appointed, and spectacularly failed, referees of the financial system." Though the probable effect of this policy would be for the rating agencies to force "financially unsound" hospitals to close, thus reducing access to healthcare, it would have the great advantage of allowing a person undergoing heart surgery, for example, to know whether the hospital doing the operation would be a sound investment should he or she live.

---

a nonreactionary winner of the "Nobel" Prize in economics, Kenneth Arrow, demonstrated that buyer ignorance implies that markets are an inappropriate vehicle for allocating medical treatment. He wrote, "It is the general social consensus...that the *laissez faire* solution for medicine is intolerable," which if true in 1963 (when Arrow wrote it) was not so under New Labour or anywhere in the US in the twenty-first century.

There is a more fundamental point: people consume, but they are not consumers unless indoctrinated to be so. The intellectual and cultural revolutions of the second half of the eighteenth century in Europe, the Enlightenment, established the principle that democracy derives from the consent of the governed. This consent is achieved through participation in the political process, one form of which is elections. With this participation people assert themselves as citizens of the democracy. To state the relationship simply, democratic government comes from "citizenship," the active participation of people in their governance.

Why do I go into this apparent digression into simplistic political philosophy? I do so because especially in the US, the interests of business, big capital, have successfully redefined the nature of political and social existence. In place of "citizens," people are defined as "consumers" and "taxpayers." While these categories may seem blandly descriptive, they are profoundly ideological. The interaction of people with the institutions of their governance sustains democracy. As citizens, people participate in the formulation of laws and regulations that protect them against the Hobbesian "state of nature." In the state of nature, no legitimate authority exists to prevent antisocial behavior (such as in Somalia and Liberia when they had no government, and in Mexico racked by drug crime). Participation creates rights and also obligations, the most obvious to obey the laws that participatory citizenship endorses.

Social divisions based on class, ethnicity and forms of organized superstition (religion being the most obvious) continually threaten this triad of participation–rights–obligations. Democratic societies have sought to contain these threats through legislative constraints on the power of capital, antidiscrimination laws and enforcement of secularism in politics. From the end of World War II into the late 1970s, the social democratic period in the West, political debate and conflict in democratic countries focused on these core issues: the extent to which economic power would be regulated, protecting minorities consistent with majority rule, and rationality versus faith. In general, reactionary forces sought to erode laws limiting the power of capital, opposed egalitarian measures (especially when they implied costs for business), and encouraged superstition rather than rationality in political debate.

In the 1980s and foremost in the US, the forces of reaction initiated a shift in ideological strategy. In addition to attacks on specific measures, such as progressive taxation, the Right sought to undermine the basis of democratic society, the concept and practice of citizenship. Two terms play central parts in this antidemocratic propaganda war: "consumer" and "taxpayer." The first comes directly from fakeconomics, which focuses almost exclusively on buying and selling. As shown in Chapter 1, fakeconomics propagates the fiction that first and foremost people seek to maximize their individual enjoyment. If fakeconomics uses the word "society," it refers to the numerical sum of individuals, not a collective interaction. Consumption of commodities provides the vehicle by which individuals achieve satisfaction. Therefore, each person's primary existence or function is as a consumer, a buyer of commodities. Only secondarily do people exist as family members. Their participation in any social activity other than buying commodities is of little analytical, practical or political importance.

Treating people as consumers and convincing them that this constitutes their existential role brings profound political implications. It generalizes the rhetoric of commodities to every aspect of social intercourse. Rail and airline passengers become "consumers" of the fictitious commodity "transport." One suffers through university classes as a consumer of the degree, not for the knowledge (though the more dedicated may "consume" the knowledge as well). I make a visit to a doctor for the purpose of consuming medical care. This terminology goes beyond the annoying and inaccurate, to the profoundly pernicious.

It objectifies our fellow citizens. The person in the airline uniform, standing at the lectern or wearing the white smock, is not a fellow worker and participant in civil society. He or she provides a commercial service on demand. We expect no social interaction between the "provider" and the "consumer." On the contrary, this would make commercialization less complete and the service less of a commodity. The education "provider" lectures, assigns and assesses, and the education consumer absorbs. The rapid expansion of off-site courses represents the logical extension. If you can listen to a CD why go to a symphony? If you study a course online, why do we need something as old-fashioned as a "university campus"?

Similarly, the health "provider" offers one or a range of treatments that the health consumer purchases or declines. We can pursue this approach further. Doctors have higher salaries than nurses or other "health professionals." It makes commercial sense to minimize what doctors do, and substitute the less expensive whenever possible. Further, because better health is a commodity for purchase, go cheaper still and diagnose illness through an automated, online system.

In this reactionary world of people as buyers, each individual seeks to buy at the lowest possible price. The transaction, for food, schooling or medical aid, involves an exchange in which the buyer views the seller as a conveyor of a commodity, not as a neighbor, even less as another member of a society of citizens. By considering the flight attendant, teacher or nurse a fellow citizen we implicitly accept him or her as an equal with basic human rights, among which includes decent remuneration for work. As a commodity conveyor, exchange objectifies the shop attendant, teacher or nurse as an agent engaged in the delivery of the commodity as cheaply as possible. It follows that the less we pay that person, the cheaper the commodity, and the happier the "consumer," because he or she can consume more of it or more of other commodities.

This ideology achieves the full destruction of citizenship by assigning to the consumer a second role, that of taxpayer. For a citizen, taxes function to fund collective, social goals. Taxation confronts the consumer as an involuntary reduction in the income available to spend in private markets. Citizens participate in government and seek their common welfare through its institutions. Consumers loathe government as an authority that denies them part of what brings them fulfillment, income to spend on commodities.

This view of society as made up of individuals whose pleasure derives from consumption, with an overwhelming interest in cheap commodities and low taxes, is so analytically vulgar that it borders on the absurd. All except the very rich must work to produce a good or service, which provides the income to obtain their basic needs. It takes no great insight to realize that obtaining commodities as cheaply as possible creates downward pressure on wages that feeds back to drive down one's own income. It is equally obvious that minimizing taxes implies minimizing those activities and functions that create a society from a collection of isolated Hobbesian individuals, "poor, nasty and brutish."

The analytical and practical absurdity of the consumer/taxpayer specification demonstrates the power of ideology to obscure reality. It overcomes the rational with the irrational, replaces reason with belief. People live in groups. Fueled by the concentration of wealth, right-wing propaganda makes us believe that we exist as isolated individuals, fated to pursue narrow self-interest. That is wrong. Democratic government serves to achieve collectively what individuals cannot do. The ideology of consumption converts us to the faith that government is a burden that through taxation robs us of the fulfillment we obtain through shopping. Over eighty years ago US Supreme Court justice Oliver Wendell Holmes saw the pernicious banality in this slander on society itself. In *Compañia General de Tabacos de Filipinas v. Collector of Internal Revenue*, he wrote, "Taxes are what we pay for civilized society."

When a news reporter on television or radio informs us that the cost of a bank bailout is "borne by the taxpayer," or improved wages for nurses "will increase our taxes," we are being fed a not-very-subtle political message: we live alone; we need feel no responsibility

How Sovereigns Rule

US household income and debt, 1960–2010 (2000 = 100 for both)

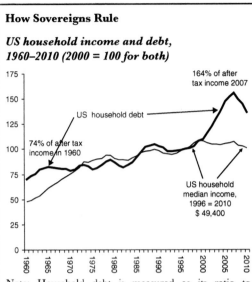

Note: Household debt is measured as its ratio to household income.

Source: *Economic Report of the President* (2011).

During the second half of the twentieth century US households had relatively low indebtedness. From the end of WWII into the 1980s the ratio of household debt to income fluctuated in the 70–80% range. In the 1980s Congress deregulated the financial sector to allow people to borrow on the value of their homes.

This "benefit" of financial deregulation coincided with stagnation of household income and rapidly rising indebtedness. The combination was no accident. The rising debt indicates that most households struggled to maintain living standards as income stagnated.

Making that struggle more difficult were falling real wages, offset by more income earners, typically through more women in paid work.

Lower pay, stagnant income and accumulating debt – consumer sovereignty in action.

for other members of society; and collective action for social improvement reduces our happiness. We are consumers, not citizens. Go out and shop.

Everyone Gains from Free Trade

Trivia pursuit

The Free Trade Hall, Manchester, UK, was constructed during 1853–1856, commemorating the repeal of the Corn Laws, a major step towards deregulation of Britain's international trade. This construction happens to be the site of the Peterloo massacre in 1819, when soldiers attacked peaceful demonstrators calling for economic and political reform.

Liberalizing trade among countries is one of the few policy issues that finds agreement across the political spectrum. Conservative commentators endorse it with gusto, centrists treat it as an article of faith, and many progressives accept it at least implicitly by their criticism of industrial country protection. If an econfaker endorses trade restrictions one day of the year, to stay in the profession he or she must spend the other 364 apologizing for it (365 for leap years).

In Wikipedia we find the free trade doctrine in semiliterate gibberish that any econfaker would endorse:

> Free trade increases the global level of output because free trade permits specialization among countries. Specialization allows nations to devote their scarce resources to the production of the particular goods and services for which that nation has a comparative advantage. The benefits of specialization, coupled with economies of scale, increase the global production possibility frontier. An increase in the global production possibility frontier indicates that the absolute quantity of goods and services produced is highest under free trade. Not only are [sic] the absolute quantity of goods and services higher, but the particular combination of goods and services actually produced will yield the highest possible utility to global consumers.

This fakeconomics jargon ("comparative advantage," "global production possibilities frontier") seeks to convey the inspirational message that liberalizing trade will increase *everyone's* welfare through a better allocation of production and consumption. It will increase domestic competition and lower prices for consumers. And it will stimulate exports and employment as the mirror of the cheaper imports. These benefits of freer trade have become globally what John Kenneth Galbraith famously designated the "conventional wisdom." For example:

> Open economies benefit from the international exchange of ideas and thus permanently experience technological progress. This in turn is the key source of long term economic growth. Greater openness also means fiercer competition. This obliges politicians to constantly improve the institutional framework and prompts companies to continually optimise their production processes and develop new products.

Even more enthusiastic, were that possible, and replete stunning examples, is the business site Go Global to Win (about as globaphile as a company moniker can be):

> Protectionism and isolation are not the right choice of action. We see the trend of freer trade and open markets having a tremendous impact on boosting innovation and creativity, sharpening the competitive spirit of companies and expanding global business… The five fastest-growing countries from 1990 to 2004…had double-digit increases in trade.

Liberalized or "freer" global trade means world trade under private regulation rather than public. Some "nervous Nellies" (to use President Lyndon Johnson's term for those predicting that the Vietnam War would prove a disaster for the US) fear this reduction in public controls will result, among other things, in production practices detrimental to the global environment. This foolishness has been insightfully dismissed by the "Nobel" laureate Jagdish Bhagwati, as reported in the magazine *Wired* (where he is described as "the world's preeminent globalization buff" and "registered Democrat"): "Trade foes argue that [freer trade] spurs the creation of cheap goods at the planet's expense. Bhagwati points out that undemocratic countries are often the worst environmental offenders. Since globalization promotes democracy, it should make the world more green, not less."

One presumes that the free-trading democracies Professor Bhagwati had in mind do not include the path-breaking neoliberal Chile under Pinochet or democratically challenged Singapore. The insight that globalization promotes democracy might be placed alongside Bhagwati's equally astute observation that the US economy in 2008 was characterized by a "*stable* venture-capital model" (emphasis added). No doubt this stability explains why the collapse of the US economy during the subsequent 6 months was the worst in 70 years; i.e., it failed to match the disaster of the 1930s.

Not only business propaganda outlets and "globalization buffs" embrace trade liberalization. The environmental organization Greenpeace, after expressing regret over the negative effects of globalization, "it usually benefits the larger, wealthier countries," moves firmly onto the free trade band wagon: "Any…'protectionist' [measure] has the effect of closing off a country's markets to goods from other countries. Many wealthy countries in Europe, as well as the US and Japan use these tactics to support their own domestic economies, making it impossible for smaller, or less developed countries to gain a foothold in the global marketplace."

While not accepting Bhagwati's optimistic view that trade fosters democracy, thus a greener world, Greenpeace is with the neoliberal view of the principle function of people in a global world: "We are calling on *consumers* to join us and demand a [genetically engineered] free world."

The argument that trade liberalization by the "wealthy" countries would be in the interest of "less-developed" countries appears less convincing in light of a World Bank report at the beginning of the millennium that concluded, "The numbers of people living on less than $2 per day has risen by almost 50% since 1980, to 2.8 billion – almost half the world's population. And this is precisely the period that has been most heavily liberalized."

This conclusion came from an in-depth study by two World Bank staff not known for antiglobalization views. The conclusions were very strong indeed: "Trade liberalization is negatively correlated with income growth among the poorest 40 per cent of the population, but positively correlated with income growth among higher income groups. In other words, it helps the rich get richer and the poor get poorer."

But, surely this cannot be right if, as the econfakers have demonstrated, the theory of international trade unambiguously *proves* that all countries must gain from freer commerce, and all experience confirms this scientific proof. If the theory were not rock solid and the evidence were not overwhelming, the near-universal endorsement of freer trade, left, right and center would not exist, would it?

If a difference exists between fact and fiction, between reality and fantasy, it is a real fact that the fakeconomics (aka mainstream, neoclassical) theory of trade consists of repeatedly recycled rubbish. All experience shows that international commerce, like all commerce, has gainers and losers, not a happy gathering of winners. We find the winners and losers not among countries, but among groups of people in countries. If a valid generalization can be made about liberalizing international commerce, it is that regardless of country, workers lose and capital gains (it is a *class* issue).

How do I propose to defend this vile heresy that denies the virtue of the commerce among countries? To do so I begin with the mythology (aka "theory") of international trade. As demonstrated over forty years ago by none other than "the preeminent globalization buff," Jagdish Bhagwati, the logic required to reach the conclusion that free trade improves human welfare is so restrictive that it should generate laughter in any intelligent person.

At this point the reader might look back at the metaphysical follies ("assumptions") necessary to construct the fantasy of "perfect competition." The "theory of international trade" requires all of those plus some outstanding idiocies of its own. These additions include: 1) continuous full employment of all resources; 2) all countries could produce all traded commodities (grow bananas in Norway, herd reindeer in Somalia); 3) the consumption pattern of all countries is the same; and my favorite, 4) every country uses the same technology to produce each commodity.

The true believer in free trade might wish to go the "preeminent buff" himself to verify these. Even if you accept all these intelligence-deadening absurdities the most that can be demonstrated is that "some trade is better than none." It cannot be demonstrated by any theoretical yardstick that more liberalization is an improvement on less.

The key concepts in this trade "theory" are not rigorously defined, and cannot be measured even in principle. Consider its central claim: countries with cheap labor will gain by specializing in labor-intensive commodities and exchanging them for capital-intensive commodities produced in countries where capital is cheap ("comparative advantage"). For example, the US should export things that use a lot of machinery and not much labor, and China should do the reverse.

This sounds reasonable. Poor countries export to rich countries things produced with a lot of labor, and rich countries... You get the idea. The problem is that this apparently reasonable proposition is gibberish, having no more cognitive coherence than a random series of words. The first problem is the word "cheap." To the person in the street, the meaning of "cheap labor" seems obvious: lower wages (converted with the appropriate exchange rate and other adjustments). If this "cheap labor" were the basis of trade, no case could be made for its benefits.

The trade imbalances in the eurozone in this century provide a case in point. The European Commission, the International Monetary Fund and the German government demand wage reduction in the trade-deficit countries. Whether or not this prescription would work (and it would not) it cannot "bring benefits to all." Lower wages by definition reduce the incomes and expenditures of the vast majority in any country. This common-sense definition of cheap labor cannot serve to propagandize free trade.

In the trade theory of fakeconomics, "cheap" is defined as "relatively abundant." For example, labor is cheap in China compared to the US if the ratio of the total labor force to the total capital stock in China is higher than the same ratio in the US. To put it simply, *for the economy as a whole*, China has lots of workers for each machine, while in the US we find lots of machines for every worker. Try to get your head around measuring that ratio.

Why on earth construct such a convoluted definition of "cheap" when we have an unambiguously straightforward definition? "Oh, the tangled web we weave when first we practice [theory] to deceive": if we use the simple definition, it implies that *absolute* costs determine trade flows. If so, as is obvious to any business person, then a big country with good infrastructure and low wages could produce almost every commodity cheaper and overwhelm all its global competitors (heard of China?). The result would be persistent trade imbalances and recurrent national and global financial instability, which may strike you as not totally improbable.

The fakeconomics ideological task is international commerce that allows, even ensures, success for every country that trades. Demonstrating this happy generalization proves impossible, though the econfakers have beavered away at it for over one hundred years. The concept of "relative abundance" of labor and capital does not leave the starting blocks, for the simple reason that we can find no sensible way to measure labor and capital in or across countries.

A simple head count for the supply of labor has little practical meaning for the potential and efficiency of production in a country because of skill differences. For measurement purposes a skilled worker counts for more than an unskilled one. But how much more? What about using wages levels to make the calculation, as in: "If a worker of skill type A receives twice the wage of an unskilled worker, then count one type A worker as two unskilled labor units." A moment's reflection shows this is no solution. To take just one difficulty, if a plumber in Texas earns $20 an hour and a plumber in Chicago $50, should we treat the latter as supplying 2.5 times as much to the US labor supply?

The problem of measuring labor pales in comparison to difficulties with calibrating the capital stock with its quality differences due to variations in age and obsolescence. Though we need not go into it, the value of the capital stock in a market economy varies with the profits it generates – a factory that cannot bring the owner profit has a value of zero.

Yet measuring the labor force and the capital stock is the necessary condition for a meaningful calculation of "relative abundance" of these inputs to production. The failure to measure even in theory implies that the "gains from trade" hypothesis consists of smoke and mirrors, a con trick that the Wizard of Oz would envy.

An excellent example of the con is found in a study purporting to show that imports into the US as well as for several other countries reduce domestic inflation. I quote: "At the heart of our argument lies the simple observation that when labour abundant nations grow, their exports tend to increase most in sectors that intensively use labour as a factor of production."

It is not necessary to be an idiot to understand this sentence, but it helps. We have no acceptable measure of "labour abundance," and no practical method of calculating whether industries "intensively use labour as a factor of production." The statement has no content.

In addition, no theoretical basis exists for the argument that freer trade stimulates domestic production and employment. It is quite impossible to produce such a theoretical conclusion, because fakeconomics trade models assume full employment. Adam Smith made the sensible argument that trade provided a demand outlet for a country's surplus production ("vent for surplus"). Econfakers reject this as naïve and simplistic. As well they would. If domestic demand were insufficient for full employment, increased public expenditure or domestic investment would resolve the problem equally well as export demand. The exception occurs if a country requires a demand stimulus when it simultaneously suffers from an unsustainable import level. In this case a demand stimulus would make the import level higher, as would trade liberalization, by facilitating more imports.

Some readers may catch an even more fundamental problem with the assertion that trade stimulates domestic employment. If more exports to Britain were to increase US employment, then by symmetry they must reduce UK employment. In order to argue that trade increases every country's employment, we need to demonstrate that international trade *in itself* increases demand in each country's domestic market. The impossibility of that task partly explains why mainstream trade theory begins, ends and never leaves full employment.

Lurking in the wings of the trade debate we always find the Greenpeace argument that "poor" countries would benefit from the elimination of "rich" country protection, especially on agricultural products. Perhaps the most surprising thing about this attempt to tug at middle-class heart strings is that anyone other than a true believer in free trade would take it seriously. The poorest countries do not produce the agricultural products protected by developed countries to any great extent. If the elimination of subsidies reduced US agricultural production, the benefiting countries could be middle-income ones (e.g., Argentina or Brazil for soy beans) where the agricultural population (and, therefore, beneficiaries) is small.

For those few products produced by both high- and low-income countries (cotton in Mauritania is invariably cited) the most likely beneficiary of a decline in production in the US or the EU would be China, not any country in Africa, with the possible exception of Egypt. And, one can ask, would not the domestic production, processing and use of cotton products while diversifying exports be a considerably better outcome for Mauritanians than exporting raw cotton to Europe and the US? To counter that Mauritanians lack the effective demand to support diversification fails to recognize that the process would be a "virtuous cycle." The diversification, by increasing domestic employment, would create the demand for the products that employment generates.

Greenpeace, Oxfam and other activist organizations are sincere, though confused, in their support for the reduction in trade regulations based on the belief that this would help the poorest countries. The defender of this position would search in vain for evidence to support it. For the econfakers this argument provokes crocodile tears of delight, allowing a flagrantly antipoor US trade policy to pluck middle-class heart strings. As Ha-Joon Chang, a Cambridge University economist (*not* one of the many Cantabrigian econfakers), sensibly argues, people in low-income countries need their governments to pursue an active industrial policy, not bet on more *laissez faire* in international commerce, which would be more accurately termed *ne laissez pas-faire* or *caveat emptor* (buyer beware).

The alleged evil of developed-country agricultural subsidies comes as a welcome cover for the devastating effect of under-regulated trade on the working class in the developed as well as the underdeveloped countries. Nowhere is this devastation more advanced than in the US, where manufacturing employment collapsed during the last two decades of the twentieth century (see Box: Free Trade and Capital Flows Create Employment [But Not in the USA]). In the new century real hourly wages dropped lower for US manufacturing workers than in the 1980s, something unimaginable in the immediate postwar decades when the American

Free Trade and Capital Flows Create Employment (But Not in the USA)

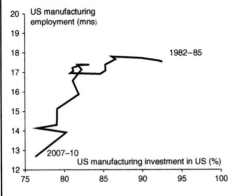

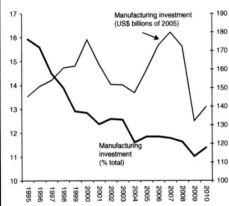

Foreign Investment Might Create Employment in the UK (If It Weren't Negative)

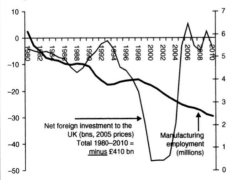

In the first half of the 1980s the manufacturing sector employed almost 18 million in the US. About 7% of manufacturing investment by US companies flowed abroad. By the second half of the 2000s employment was below 13 million, with almost a quarter of investment flowing out of the country each year.

Invest abroad, the jobs go abroad, all the more if the overall rate of investment is stagnant (see second chart).

During the "globalizing" 1990s and 2000s investment in manufacturing hardly changed when inflation is taken out ($155 billion for 1995–1999, $158 billion for 2000–2004, and $159 billion 2005–2010). The share of US domestic manufacturing investment in total investment declined, from 16% in 1995 to 11% in 2010. Not a very impressive performance, even if the recession years 2008–2010 were left out, and not close to enough to generate new jobs.

While manufacturing employment in the USA was falling from over 18 million to below 13 million, it was the same story in the UK, over five million in 1980 and approaching two million in 2010. Thirty years of neoliberal governments (Conservative and Labour) promised that foreign investment would create employment. Might have, but it was negative, minus 410 billion over the 30 years.

Dream seemed more than hot air. One of the few things that fakeconomics trade theory gets right, albeit for the wrong reason, is the prediction that freer global trade will lower real wages in the high-income countries. Their conclusion comes from so-called "factor price equalization," in which competition makes wage rates and profit rates equalize globally. If ever there were a case of reality imitating bad theory, this is it.

The free trade apologists also justify deindustrialization in middle- and low-income countries. Trade negotiators from the rich countries never fail to require that their counterparts from the developing world concede reciprocal trade liberalization. Devastation of local manufacturing comes as the consequence, as Chang shows in *Kicking Away the Ladder* (2002), with little improvement in agricultural exports.

Falling money wages will soon join the falling real wages if the "gains of free trade" continue to rain benefits upon American workers. Read all about it in the *New York Times*:

> [General Electric] is bringing home the production of water heaters as well as some refrigerators, and expanding its work force to do so. The wages for the new hires, however, are $10 to $15 an hour less than the pay scale for hourly employees already on staff – with the additional concession that the newcomers will not catch up for the foreseeable future. Such union-endorsed contracts are also showing up in the auto industry, at steel and tire companies, and at manufacturers of farm implements and other heavy equipment.

Falling wages, deteriorating working conditions and fewer benefits for those lucky enough to find work. Never mind: "For years, US consumers feasted on cheap imported goods," which makes up for lousy jobs at lousy pay. Cheaper goods are the feast, unemployment is the payback.

An alternative exists to the tyranny of the free traders: sensible economic policies that benefit the majority, not the 1%, which I elaborate in the final chapter.

Further Reading

For an impressively shallow defense of free trade

Shil1978, "Protectionism or Free Trade: Which Benefits Humanity as a Whole?" Shil1978 (blog), 29 November 2011. Online: http://shil1978.hubpages.com/ hub/Protectionism-or-Free-Trade---which-benefits-humanity-as-a-whole (accessed 16 October 2013).

A balanced treatment of the World Trade Organization

Anup Shah, "The WTO and Free Trade," Global Issues, 2 July 2007. Online: http://www.globalissues.org/article/42/the-wto-and-free-trade (accessed 16 October 2013).

The real economics of trade

Ha-Joon Chang, *Bad Samaritans: The Myth of Free Trade and the Secret History of Capitalism* (London: Bloomsbury, 2008).
Ha-Joon Chang, *Kicking Away the Ladder: Development Strategy in Historical Perspective* (London: Anthem Press, 2002).
Robert Blecker, ed., *US Trade Policy and Global Growth: New Directions in the International Economy* (New York: M. E. Sharpe, 1996).

The Chang–Bhagwati debate on trade and manufacturing

"The Economist.com Debate: Manufacturing," *Economist*, 28 June–8 July 2011. Online: http://www.columbia.edu/~jb38/papers/pdf/The_Economist_com_Debate_Manufacturing.pdf (accessed 16 October 2013).

Chapter 6

LIES ABOUT GOVERNMENT

Governments are notoriously bad at managing the money they collect. In fairness, the obstacles are many: incompetency, corruption, the sheer complexity of disbursing huge sums, the multiplicity and difficulty of the tasks at hand... The result is that the state is always in need of more money. No matter how high the taxes, there is never enough.

(Ronald Sokol)

For a long time the degree of concentration [of income and wealth] fluctuated around a fairly stable rate. But in the past two or three decades it has increased markedly, making it more difficult for supporters of capitalism to argue that a rising tide floats all boats... But for all the looming problems, it is still untrue that the nanny state knows best.

(Samuel Brittan)

Government Is a Burden

The mission statement of fakeconomics includes as its central message the inherent inefficiency and intrinsic malevolence of governments at all levels. The canons of the Society of Econfakers begin with the conviction that regulation of private economic activity brings inefficiency. This inefficiency invariably results from the malicious influence of "special interests," acting against the general welfare that free markets foster. The action of citizens in a democratic society to achieve common goals through collective action at best functions as a dictatorship of the majority. At its worst it paves the "Road to Serfdom."

The fakeconomics worldview supports the reactionary message that taxes are a burden on honest citizens just trying to make a living. Red tape, bureaucracy and regulation combine to render that burden intolerable. Or as Ronald Reagan (or a script writer) so insightfully and scatologically put it, "Government is like a baby, an alimentary canal with a big appetite at one end and no sense of responsibility at the other." Or as famously stated by Grover Norquist, author of the "Taxpayers Protection Pledge" to bind US legislators to reducing taxes, "I'm not in favor of abolishing the government. I just want to shrink it down to the size where we can drown it in the bathtub." Norquist (who himself might benefit from a bit of shrinking) has also opined that the great downhill slide of the US into socialism began with none other than Theodore Roosevelt (perhaps confusing Theodore with Franklin Delano?).

Practical problems arise for a collective fitting of the US Congress or the UK House of Commons with a diaper, as well as finding a bathtub into which even a down-sized Pentagon might comfortably fit. With these metaphorical difficulties in mind, in what sense is government a burden, and upon whom is it a burden? The last chapter took a close look at the suggestion that people are "consumers" rather than citizens. Burdensome government serves as a close companion to consumership. The concise summary of this worldview goes as follows. Oppressed consumers are "taxpayers," burdened with government levies that reduce their freedom to spend in markets, and this represents the central threat to human liberty. Or, as faux laureate Milton Friedman put it in his "Free Markets, Free Men" lecture, "you need free markets where all transactions are voluntary. That is the essence of human freedom."

Towards the end of the twentieth century the characterization of government as a burden manifested in the taxes people pay seemed an idea whose time had come with a vengeance. The burden assertion provides an excellent example of the French term *idée fixe*, usually defined as an idea that dominates the mind to the point of obsession. The media use the concept in extraordinary, indeed, nonsensical ways. The *Evening Standard* (London), for example, reported that a group of experts questioned the wisdom of "burdening taxpayers" with the cost of a high-speed rail line from the capital to Birmingham.

There could be many reasons to oppose such a scene, but burdening taxpayers would not be among them. If profitable, and there seemed little dispute that it would be to some degree, the rail project would generate the revenue to pay the interest and principle on the loan taken to finance it. Not only would it fail the burden test, it would qualify as an antiburden, generating net revenue that could be used to lower taxes or pay dividends, depending on one's ideological inclination. If the project were not profitable, it should not be done, neither by the public nor the private sector.

Any dispute over investments by the public sector implicitly or explicitly involves a debate over the appropriate function of government, not its "burden." Prior to "Iron Lady" Thatcher, the public sector in Britain owned the airports and the public utilities (telephone, electricity, gas and water). Some citizens, even a majority, may be happier to have them in private hands, but not because privatization lifted a burden. On the contrary, these were profit-making institutions that generated public income which, practically speaking, *reduced* the "tax burden."

Governments spend a majority of their resources on "current activities," not on investment. The greater part of this "current expenditure" goes to wages and salaries. Surely the taxes to pay for this type of expenditure burdens us and should be minimized. The Austerity Dogma, treated in Chapter 9, peddles that government-minimalizing argument with great zeal and startling success in the US and Western Europe. So successful has been this doctrine that any level of taxation, no matter how low, comes under attack.

The federal government of the US spends a smaller share of national income than for any developed country except Australia, and 11 percentage points below the average of the twenty-two other countries (see Box: Burden of Government). Public sector social expenditures as a share of US national income stand third from the bottom among those same countries. *Idée fixe* is an understatement in the extreme to describe the enthusiasm of Republican politicians for cutting budgets at every level because of a "burdensome government."

The neophyte might think that the UK Labour Party would have no truck with the Austerity Dogma, especially because it became the *sine qua non* of their Conservative opponents. No rational leaders of a party committed to a more humane society would endorse the Austerity Dogma. Unemployment near 10% and falling incomes of those with work, except for Tory cabinet members and top-of-the-line bankers, forced the UK population into an increased reliance on public benefits.

However, in defiance of all economic and political logic, in 2012 the Labour Party leadership led the party into this brave old austerity. Referring to the draconian reductions in social expenditures by the coalition government of Conservatives and Liberal Democrats during

2010–2011, Labour Party leader Ed Miliband less than boldly leapt
to the support of the poor and the weak: "We're not going to make
promises to reverse these [social support] cuts unless we're absolutely
sure we know where the money is coming from."

While not exactly threatening a bathtub drowning, this was a step in
the same direction (even to the invocation of the economically illiterate
"where the money is coming from"). The Labour leader thusly planted
the flag for "fiscal responsibility" alongside the many previously planted
by prime minister David Cameron and almost every reactionary
politician on both sides of the pond. Former deputy Labour leader
Harriet Harman struck a blow for irresponsible common sense: "We're
not accepting austerity cuts; we are totally opposed to them and we are
fighting them," showing why she never became leader.

Even a small injection of Harmanite common sense leaves the "burden
of government" doctrine rather threadbare. With very few exceptions
(oil-rich Norway being about the only one) governments of high-income

---

Burden of Government: Low in the USA

Total public revenue and social expenditure, in 23 high-income countries (% of GDP)

If you are looking to live in the country with the lowest tax levels (at all levels of government put together), then the place for you is either the US or Australia, where it is slightly lower (there is not much in it: 31% and 30.5% at the end of the 2000s, respectively). If you have an aversion to social expenditures, these two countries, along with Iceland, are for you, at about 15–16% of GDP.

The UK can be found in the middle for both public revenue and social expenditure (number 13 out of 23), with only one large high-income European country lower on revenue (Spain, which is slightly higher on social spending).

Source: OECD.

countries fund their expenditures overwhelmingly through taxation of their citizens and businesses. The vast majority of expenditure funded by taxation falls into two categories: 1) war-making potential and policing, and 2) social services. In the 2010 US federal budget these categories accounted for 21% and 40% of total expenditures, with the remaining going to a mixed bag, including interest on the public debt (6%).

Few would deny that the public sector has a legitimate role in national defense, except perhaps the Tea Party, the marginally respectable "libertarians" at the Adam Smith Institute in London and its ideological cousin in Washington, the Cato Institute. The first of those two "think tanks" takes its name from one of the leading figures of the Scottish Enlightenment, and the latter after Marcus Porcius Cato Uticensis, aristocrat and unyielding foe of land reform in ancient Rome. These protectors of the rights of billionaires would happily drown every agency of government at all levels – federal, state and local. The second category (social expenditures) are education, pensions and health. Is it a burden on the eponymous taxpayer to tax, then spend on pensions and education? I inspect that question in the next section.

Wasting Money on Social(ist) Spending

The "fallacy of public affordability" looms large in the attacks on public expenditure and revenue, a hyperlink on the consumer/taxpayer ideological web page. This fallacy appears virulently in the polemics over deficit reduction in the US, UK and continental Europe. The fallacy manifests itself, for example, in the argument in the UK that if university education were made available to a large portion of the population, the public sector could not afford to deliver it. Therefore, substantial fees, far from barriers to gaining a tertiary education, serve as the vehicle to broaden access to education (see Box: University Reform in the UK).

The argument goes: the public sector "cannot afford" to provide university education to the many, so ration the public contribution on the basis of need (income or "means" testing). The political Right applies the same argument in every area of social expenditure, major or minor. With an aging population, the public sector "cannot afford" to pay more than a safety net pension (see Box: Pension Reform: A Modest Proposal), cannot afford to provide all the drugs and care needed by that aging population, and so on.

A moment for serious reflection exposes the "affordability" arguments as reactionary dogma. The fallacy becomes obvious at the level of society as a whole. Consider the funding of university education. Only a tiny minority of people would argue that primary education should be a matter for individual families to decide and wholly fund themselves. Before proceeding on that premise, I feel it necessary to note that this reactionary minority may be increasing, at least in the US. On the website of the Future of Freedom Foundation, we read:

> It always shocks Americans when I inform them that free and compulsory schooling is one of the ten "planks" of the Communist Manifesto and that public schooling is a key aspect of the Soviet, Chinese, and Cuban ways of life. Yet, even after discovering these little-known facts, they continue to believe that public schooling in those countries is socialism while public schooling in the United States is free enterprise.

The author might also have mentioned that the same "plank" denounces child labor in factories and mines, and other examples of communist propaganda. But not withstanding the putative equation of Leninism with Wooldridge Elementary School (in Austin, Texas, where I attended grades four through six and which was recently torn down), the overwhelming majority in most countries hold the conviction that children have a right to be educated. This commitment is a component of the Age of Enlightenment view that an educated and informed public is essential to a democratic society. This conviction, not finance, determines the provision of primary education by the public sector, for everyone, regardless of income or status. If some wish to contract for private education, they may do so, though they must pay their taxes to help support those who do not opt out.

The social consensus on public provision of secondary education is equally broad (for everyone), but the number of years provided varies (it is lower in Britain than most developed countries); while only a far-out few on the political right wing would argue that the public sector "cannot afford" to provide primary and secondary education for all. However, in practice we find many politicians that try to minimize education expenditure and therefore the quality of provision. Very few politicians would openly declare that public primary and secondary education should be abolished, even in the US (though *père et fils* Texas congressman Ron Paul and Kentucky senator Rand Paul, might be exceptions). The governor of Texas, Rick Perry, found an effective way to defund public education while (sort of) endorsing it, making it part of "necessary austerity": "Faced with a $15 billion budget deficit this year, Texas Gov. Rick Perry signed off on $4 billion in cuts to education in the 2012 and 2013 budgets. The Texas State Teachers Association estimates that as many as 49,000 teachers may be laid off as a result of the cuts and 43,000 college students will lose all or part of their financial aid."

So what about university education that the governor would "perry" to the bone? How do we identify the appropriate coverage and to what level? Here we find no consensus. Those who believe that people have no right to higher education avoid taking that potentially damning position, seeking cover under the affordability argument: "I wish we could provide everyone with a university education, but we cannot afford it. In any case, people gain personally from higher education, so they should pay for it themselves to the extent that they can. The public sector can only afford to help the poor, and if you are poor and clever you will find funding."

One finds this line of argument frequently peddled under the moniker "equal opportunity." The result would be and is the opposite. The rich can be dumb and help themselves to a higher degree, while the poor must qualify as "clever." This approach explains why so many rich morons enroll at Harvard, with relatively few dummies from the backwoods of Arkansas or the ghettos of New York as classmates. The absurd principle would apply equally to primary and secondary education (see Box: University Reform in the UK). The essence of the affordability of higher education argument is "People have no right to higher education. If they want it, let them pay for it. If you are poor and clever you might go to university. If you are dumb and rich you are certainly university material."

Some countries have a social consensus that people have a right to a university education if they want one (as in France, Germany, the Netherlands and the Nordic countries). Reducing public expenditure and raising fees does not save society money in any country. The effects are two: 1) for those with high incomes it shifts expenditure from the public sector to households; and 2) for those on low incomes it reduces access. It "saves public money" in the same sense that not filling potholes reduces the highway budget.

14 August 1935, FDR signs the Social Security Act and American descends into socialism.

Pension Reform: A Modest Proposal

I suspect that every reader realizes the disaster humankind faces, by comparison to which the global depression and climate change are mere blips on the radar screen. People grow older. It is happening even as you read.

Liberals favor people growing older, and the inevitable result of their do-gooder policies is millions of old people. As should be immediately obvious to any rational person, the problem with the elderly is that they cost money and many if not most don't work.

The American Enterprise Institute recognizes the impending danger: "Spending on the [US] government's three main *entitlement* programs – Social Security, Medicare, and Medicaid – is projected to rise significantly in coming decades. If left unaddressed, these increases put the government's budget and *the American economy at risk.*"

The word "entitlement" is notably appropriate for pensions. Throughout the civilized world people selfishly believe they have an "entitlement" to grow old (over 70 myself, I am a shameless and repeat offender). More serious, millions of people suffer from the delusion that they have a right to grow old and stop working, *even if they are healthy* (as in, "I want to enjoy my retirement"). The source of this delusion can be traced to a nineteenth-century chancellor of Prussia, Otto von Bismarck (like Karl Marx and Adolph Hitler, a German), who introduced a state pension (*state* pension, as in nanny state, welfare state and police state). This disastrous precedent affected even the US.

In 1935 Franklin D. Roosevelt, the American Lenin, forced into law the Social Security Act, which offered parasitic idleness to *everyone* over 65 (at least those covered

Welfare faker sucking on one of 310 million tits of the US Social Security system.

by the act). The only mitigating element in this Nazi retirement law was that both male and female life expectancy were below the retirement age of 65 (60 and 64, respectively), as was the case in the UK when old-age pensions were introduced.

Offering retirement when most people would be dead may be pragmatic, but a big step to communism. Given life expectancy, at present on the largesse of the bountiful state pension a man in the US and the UK can hope to live in total idleness for 10 years and women for 15! Those who argue that these indolent oldsters paid taxes for these pensions fail to appreciate the impact on capitalist values of government endorsement of idleness. Former Wyoming senator Alan Simpson put it accurately and eloquently: "Social security is a milk cow with 310 million tits."

In the US and the UK state pension handouts keep about 40% of the over-65s out of poverty. This shows the problem starkly. Public pensions are a vicious cycle. As people grow older, they automatically receive pensions. As a result they can to continue to age to no productive purpose. The problem is pensions encourage people to live longer.

The affordability fallacy takes its most pernicious form in its application to pensions and health. In any civilized society children have a right to education and the old have a right to live their final years in decent conditions with dignity. The consensus supporting a decent life for the elderly exposes "affordability" as grotesque. The question is, in light of a country's economic development and productive resources, what level of decency can and should society provide to everyone past a certain age? Once the level is identified, it remains to decide the institutional mechanism by which society delivers it. Considerable empirical evidence indicates that provision of pensions through the public sector has the lowest resource cost (i.e., *saves money*). Unlike private insurers, the public sector need charge no risk premium. The combination of social consensus and economic growth guarantees the revenue to fund a pension system.

Even more obvious is the fallacy of the affordability argument for healthcare. The appalling power of capital in US society prevents the construction of a consensus that everyone has a right to be healthy. Franklin D. Roosevelt included healthcare in his Second Bill of Rights speech in January 1944. Every American had "the right to adequate medical care and the opportunity to achieve and enjoy good health." Every other high-income country practices this principle. When accepted, as with education and pensions, the debate focuses not on financial affordability, nor on coverage (everyone qualifies). The issue is to decide the level of society's obligation to itself on healthcare, an obligation influenced by the wealth of a country, but not by financial "affordability."

The affordability argument perpetuates a profoundly antisocial and antidemocratic fallacy. Whoever makes it asserts, as Margaret Thatcher did, that there is no society and people have no obligation to fellow human beings beyond an absolute minimum that social decency forces upon even the most reactionary troglodyte, Reaganite or Tea Partier. Reducing people's sense of social decency represents the long-term project of those

University Reform in the UK: Value for Money

Reduction of funding for universities and a trebling of admission fees are among the many blessings brought by the coalition after it formed the UK government in May 2010, in its laudable effort to privatize UK tertiary education in the US image. Because the two members of the coalition, the Liberal Democrat Party, in 2010 had a pre-election pledge to oppose university fee increases, unscrupulous opponents dubbed them "hypocrites."

Using a pedantic mendacity argument, extremists called them "liars." The party leaders defend their bold action on the argument that circumstances changed for the worse between making the pledge and gaining the power. Unprincipled opponents, such as self-seeking university students, have suggested that keeping pledges when it is difficult is a test of character.

The critics failed to realize that money spent on education is an *investment* that increases a person's earning power (excluding the social parasites that choose low-paying jobs such as school teaching and nursing). It is incentive-sapping socialism in its most degenerate manifestation for Big Government to fund education for students whose parents lack the foresight to pay for it.

We should congratulate the David Cameron–led coalition for its defense of capitalist principles at the university level. But this leaves the job considerably less than half done. It is common knowledge that research shows that the highest return to public investment in education is during early childhood. Since the return on money spent on educating the very young is so high, it is shocking that it should be done by Big Government rather than families through the private sector.

If people should pay for university education because they gain financially, why not primary school? No doubt this is why US kindergartens are rarely supported by the long-suffering taxpayer, with Britain also quite good on such nonfunding. Having clearly placed itself in support of markets for university education, the coalitionites should have the courage of their convictions and announce an end to socialism in education: abolition of all public funds for schooling at in any level.

So dramatic would be the change that it is impossible to fully appreciate the long-run benefits. Most obvious, the socialist government schools would cease their near-monopoly that crowds out the private sector at the primary and secondary levels. In the UK the portion of students at market-based educational institutions is a shockingly low 7% (lower still in the US!).

Eliminating the anticompetitive socialist sector would immediately raise the private sector share to 100%. Leftists and fellow travelers would claim that the number in school would fall once families had to pay up-front the true cost of education.

Would that be a bad outcome? It would merely indicate, as it did at the university level before the Labour government of 1945–1951, that most consumers choose to buy other commodities instead of education (food and rent are common examples). When the British Empire was powerful and great, a minority of people attended school of any type. The fundamental problem with schooling is the same as for pensions. State pensions exist because people are under the delusion that they have an entitlement to grow old. Public education exists because people are under an equally anticapitalist delusion that they have a right not to be ignorant. While the first delusion is a severe threat to the public purse, the second strikes at the very basis of the social order that the UK coalition and the US Republican Party defend.

Source: Legal Momentum and the MIT Workplace Center.

who peddle the affordability fallacy. People exist as a loose collection of isolated individuals, taxpaying consumers, in a marketized state of nature where it is each for him- or herself. Again, as Hobbes told us, in the state of nature without the social contract, life is "solitary, poor, nasty, brutish and short." Not a bad description of what the 1% would have for the rest of us.

Markets and Governments

> For my part I think that capitalism, wisely managed, can probably be made more efficient for attaining economic ends than any alternative system yet in sight, but that in itself it is in many ways extremely objectionable.
>
> (J. M. Keynes)

At its core, the ideology of "burdensome government" comes from a fundamental and intentional misrepresentation of human existence. It forms a key part of the literally egocentric worldview that people exist as individuals, and individuals create institutions which they can join or leave as they wish. The cult of the individual produces this illusion. In reality, "government" is nothing more than a word for the mechanism by which groups of human beings administer their existence. In the absence of purposeful administration, existence degenerates into chaotic violence (see Box: Somalia and the End of Government).

We find as a close familiar of this illusion the belief that "markets" and "governments" represent separate realms. This misconception results in the associated misconception that governments "intervene" in markets. If we again touch base with reality, we recognize that markets require governments as a precondition of their existence, as well as a necessary condition for their continued functioning. To put it simply, markets function because of government regulations, not despite those regulations.

Every market exchange involves a transfer of ownership. As a result, exchange always implies a prior structure or "regulation" of the definition

Somalia and the End of Government

In 1986 I spent two weeks in Somalia in a group commissioned by the International Labour Organization, contributing to an antipoverty program for that desperately poor country with a large nomadic population. Somalia was a dictatorship under Mohamed Siad Barre, who seized power in a military coup in 1969 and would rule until 1991. He ruled first with Soviet patronage, which he opportunistically replaced in the 1980s with the US in the same role. In the mid-1980s the country remained relatively peaceful, though with few personal freedoms. I could walk the streets of the ancient capital, Mogadishu, without concern about personal safety. Somalis, famous for their trading skills, boasted thriving markets throughout the country.

The regime ruled through alliances with the major nomadic "clans." As the 1980s proceeded it became increasingly authoritarian and repressive. When the dictatorship fell, competition among the major clans prevented creation of a replacement central government. For the subsequent 20 years the territory named "Somalia" on maps had no functioning government.

Are people better off with no government than a dictatorship? Somalia provides a case study. "No government" means far more than no dictatorship or no politicians. Governments provide the administrative structure for the management of markets and provision of "public goods." "Public goods" refers to those services from which people cannot be excluded. These include among their basics maintaining roads and bridges, providing a legal system to protect and defend property rights, and running a fire department. Not even in principle could private agents provide these services. Private, toll-charging roads exist throughout the world, but these must have links via feeder roads into areas of low population, or many people will have no access and commerce suffers. A private legal system would more than suffer from corruption. Purchasing justice would be its *modus operandi*. A fire service must cover every structure to prevent flames spreading (a so-called "neighborhood effect"), not just for those who pay.

The Somali government did all these things badly or not at all, so what was lost when the public administration disappeared? The alternative to bad government is reform, not "no government," because the private sector will not provide public goods. Even for services that the private sector could in practice deliver, such as schooling, exclusion is the problem, as a report on Somalia by the devoutly promarket World Bank concluded: "The private sector is currently supplying most of the basic services provided by public institutions prewar. On the negative side, they are concentrated mostly in urban areas due to commercial considerations. There is a sizable population who are unable to afford such services… A comparison with prewar socio-economic indicators reveals that most of them are still below the prewar existing levels."

The absence of a government in Somalia left the country vulnerable to invasion, and to become host to criminal and terrorist groups. For three years, 2006–2009, the Ethiopian government sent its army to occupy central Somalia, where it maintained a client government that had neither popular support nor authority. This foreign occupation helped provoke a powerful Islamic group allegedly linked to the notorious al-Qaeda network. As if this were not enough, Somalia became a haven for modern piracy, including kidnapping for ransom. The philosopher Thomas Hobbes characterized societies without governments as "solitary, poor, nasty, brutish and short." Somalia would seem to qualify for these adjectives, with the limited exception of the northern part of the country administered by the unrecognized government of "Somaliland."

and rights of ownership. An exchange as simple as purchasing an apple from a street seller requires that the buyer accept that the vender owns the apple. Similarly, prior to the exchange, the vender accepts that upon payment the ownership of the apple passes to the buyer. While it may appear that such an arrangement could arise spontaneously, reflection reveals that it cannot.

Exchange requires clear ownership rights, and with those rights go equally clear obligations. All exchanges place upon the seller the obligation not to defraud the buyer. A food seller must not poison the buyer, and claims of the qualities of the food do not constitute a defense. All countries have legal systems that enforce the obligation of the seller to adhere to basic standards without which exchange would be impossible or severely limited. Governments enforce property rights and the obligations associated with them. The regulating government cannot in most cases be local if commerce extends across national or international markets. This is why the US constitution grants the federal government control over commerce (Article 1, Section 8, Clause 3, the "commerce clause").

The idea that markets and the exchange that occurs in them arise spontaneously, and subsequently suffer government regulation motivated by self-serving interests, challenges credibility and common sense. Every successful exchange requires guarantee of property rights, enforcement of health and safety standards, legal oversight of credit and debt, and prevention of fraud, to list the most obvious. Even arriving at a market, if actually a place, requires governments to manage traffic flow, keep unsafe vehicles off the road, and monitor the qualifications of drivers. The nature and extent of regulations and management vary from place to place and from country to country, and in no meaningful sense do "governments intervene in markets." It is the equivalent of saying, "Umpires intervene in baseball games" or "Referees interfere in football matches." That is why they exist.

Further Reading

Jeff Faux, *The Servant Economy* (New York: Wiley, 2012).
Ha-Joon Chang, *Kicking Away the Ladder: Development Strategy in Historical Perspective* (London: Anthem Press, 2002).

Chapter 7

DEFICIT DISORDERS AND DEBT DELIRIUM

Peddling Nonsense

Right-wing politicians, famously the late Margaret Thatcher, preach that public finances should mimic the behavior of household budgets. There is truth in this homily, but not for the reasons that the reactionaries claim. The lesson they draw is that budgets should be balanced and debt is an evil to be avoided. They seem to take as unholy writ Benjamin Franklin's view that "the second vice is lying, the first is running in debt," and "when you run in debt, you give to another power over your liberty" (both from *Poor Richard's Almanack*). In German and Dutch the word *schuld* means both "debt" and "guilt," a double meaning that Poor Richard would no doubt endorse.

Thatcher's entreaty for governments to balance their budgets like households, and Poor Richard's equation between debt and loss of liberty represent ideology-manufactured clichés, at complete odds with how households manage their finances. A family "budget deficit" is an excess of expenditures over income for some specified time period, such as a month. The household debt consists of the value of all the loans and other liabilities (as in, "liable for them") of the family.

In the US and most of Europe households buy their homes with a mortgage; that is, they go into debt. Few people would say, "Never take a mortgage, because all debt is bad." My father did take this position, renting all his life. In his closing years on more than one occasion he told me, "My biggest mistake was not buying a house." While most would agree with the sentiment, as mistakes in life go, this qualifies as relatively benign.

For similar reasons, most people know that businesses systematically fund their investments by borrowing. Businesses do this because the size of investments means they could not be covered by current sales revenue even if it were accumulated over several years. Even more important, if an investment proves profitable, it will generate a stream of revenue more than sufficient to pay off the loan that funded it. This is the same principle as taking out a mortgage, which over the life of the loan should be cheaper to the household than renting the same property.

The vast majority of people understand that it makes no sense to save for years to purchase a house. In countries with limited mortgage markets, we find a much lower proportion of households owning their homes than in the US, Britain or Western Europe. Turkey, a place in which I have worked, stands as a clear example, as do most middle-income countries (for example, in Latin America) and almost all low-income countries. Similarly, "cash on the barrelhead" for business investment would represent bad practice in any country with the credit market to avoid it.

In contrast, when confronted with public deficits and debt, people in the US, Britain and Continental Europe prove capable of astounding gaffs due to apparent ignorance. For example, in answer to the question "Is the government debt a good thing or a bad thing?" surveys in the US and Europe show that the overwhelming majority chooses the negative reply. Substitute the words "mortgage" or 'business" for "government" and the reply changes to either positive or nuanced ("Well, it depends on…"). Asking why people treat private and public debt differently goes to the core of the ideology of public sector austerity.

The ignorance is rife in the media. In the *Guardian*, considered to be one of most progressive and "serious" of British daily newspapers, an article appeared on 27 August 2012 with the apparent purpose of informing readers about the approaching general election in the Netherlands: "[Socialist Party leader Emile] Roemer wants to preserve welfare benefits for the poor at a time when the prime minister, Mark Rutte, of the Liberals is pushing for spending cuts to bring the Netherlands' ratio of public debt to gross domestic product under 3%, in line with European rules."

By "European rules," the author must have meant the infamous Maastricht criteria (more on this in a later chapter). If the rule were indeed that the "ratio of public debt to gross domestic product" had to be no more than 3%, every government in the EU would be in very serious trouble. At the end of 2011 the public debt of the Netherlands as defined by "European rules" was *72% of GDP*. How in the world could spending cuts shift the ratio down to 3% when total public spending in the country was far less than 72% of GDP?

The question has a simple answer. The author of the article was confused about or unaware of the difference between deficits and debt. The 3% of GDP refers to the dysfunctional EU rule on the overall public sector *deficit*, not the *debt*. Were this gaff rare, it could be read as a misprint or a mistake made in haste under deadline pressure. With regret I report that this error is common in the media, derivative from an ideology preaching that public sector spending is usually wasteful, public deficits represent excessive expenditure, and public debt is a dead-weight burden on current and future generations. The ignorance of major politicians of the deficit/debt distinction should cause even greater concern, though the ignorance of the media and politicians are not unrelated. In May 2012, the deputy prime minister of the UK, Nick Clegg, made the startling announcement that his government planned to eliminate the entire public debt in six or seven years: "We have a moral duty to the next generation to wipe the slate clean for them of debt. We have set out a plan – it lasts about six or seven years – to wipe the slate clean to rid people of the deadweight of debt that has been built up over time."

Were the deputy prime minister's government to deliver on this moral duty, it would require a public sector budget surplus of about 15% of GDP over those six or seven years. In principle, achieving such an unlikely goal would require expenditure reductions and tax increases in the range of 30% of GDP. Closing the NHS and abolishing the state pension would be a step towards that end. The prime minister himself thought it necessary to point out his underling's confusion.

Public and Private: Debts and Deficits

The US is one of only two countries that legally separates the maximum level of the public debt and the legislative approval of the public budget (Denmark is the other). This separation means that if the current year's budget requires an amount of borrowing that when added to the existing debt would exceed the legislatively specified maximum for the debt, a vote to raise that ceiling is required. Congress introduced this separation in 1917.

It was a *pro forma* exercise until the last years of the century when the increasingly right-wing Republican Party used the separation as an ideological antigovernment vehicle. A Gallup poll in May 2011 hinted at the depth of misunderstanding of deficits and debt in the US. When asked whether Congress should vote to raise the ceiling in order to facilitate normal government operations, almost half of people polled opposed it, with only 19% in favor and a third unsure.

Even when politicians manage to use the correct concepts, they too frequently allege that public deficits indicate that governments are profligate and public debt is a burden. These allegations are demonstrably false, derivative from the ideology of fakeconomics. How many times when the media reports on the public debt do they tell us who owns that debt (the creditor)? Almost never. Left-of-center politicians seem as prone to this basic mistake as those on the Right. For example, in September 2012 only a few months after his victory over his right-wing opponent Nicolas Sarkozy, Socialist president François Hollande told the people of France that he would implement budget cuts because "I don't want to leave my successor and my children to pay for France's debt."

Not withstanding President Hollande's anxieties over the public sector indebtedness of France, before any intelligent comment can be made about a public debt (i.e., whether it is a "burden") we must identify the creditor. Imagine that a government pursued a policy of selling its bonds (debt) only to households, and did so randomly across the income distribution. To pay the interest on the bonds or to buy them back, the person "burdened" and the person benefiting would be the same.

This hypothetical example is not far from what occurred in the US during World War II, when the Roosevelt administration urged households to show their support for the war effort by purchasing "War Bonds" that funded the production of war materiel. The bonds were widely held throughout the population and after the war households used them as down payments toward home ownership. On a smaller scale the government sold 25-cent "war stamps" to children, which were advertised in comic books such as *Superman* and *Batman*. Britain used similar bonds for the war effort. To my knowledge no sane politician ever complained about their "burden."

My example and the actual practice with war bonds carries a major message: the potential problem with public debt is not its "burden," because interest payers and interest receivers by definition cancel out. The problems lie elsewhere; first, in the distribution of the payers and receivers. The rich save more than the nonrich, and one form that saving takes is public sector bonds. Despite much propaganda to the contrary during recent years, public bonds are about as safe an investment as one can find. As a result of income and wealth inequality, the taxes of the nonrich fund the interest payments to the rich.

This tendency strengthened from the 1980s onwards, when the income distribution in most developed countries became more unequal, especially in the UK and the US. This is not a "burden" problem. The problem is not that the debt is too large. The problem is income distribution, made worse by a reduction in progressive taxation. In practice, the excessive interest accruing to the rich could be offset by higher taxes on the rich, which was close to the case in Britain and the US during the 30 years after the end of World War II. When politicians lament about the burden of the public debt, they *de facto* complain about income and wealth inequality. Since the politicians that complain largely serve the interests of the rich, they are unlikely to acknowledge that the problem is distribution, not debt.

The second public debt problem comes from financial speculation. Speculation on government bonds is not a problem of public debt as such. Speculation results from the deregulation of financial markets over the decades after the 1970s. As demonstrated in Chapter 9 in the discussion of the crisis of the euro, the size of the public debt, absolute or relative to national income, does not fuel speculation. The government of Spain had the lowest debt-to-national-income ratio of any major European country, yet fell victim to rampant speculation. The UK debt was much larger absolutely and relatively, and suffered no speculative run after the great crisis of 2008. A frequently cited third problem, foreign ownership of public debt, I treat later.

Comparison to household finance reinforces that the absolute size of the public debt need not obsess us. When a household seeks a mortgage a central item determining its amount is the interest rate that the lender will charge. To take a numerical example, at 3% the average monthly interest on a $100,000 mortgage over 25 years would be $250 (of a total payment of $480). When the borrowing rate rises to 6%, the interest payments double (though total payments do not, going to $650).

At a low interest rate a household can carry a larger mortgage. The same applies to the public debt. In 2012 the interest rate on UK public debt varied from less than one-half of 1% for 1-month bonds to slightly less than 3% for 30-year debt paper. The same yields on US public bonds were one-tenth of 1% for the shortest maturing to 2.69% for bonds of several years. For both countries these represented the lowest peace-time rates in 200 years. To put the matter simply, never had servicing public debt been as easy in the UK and the US as after the great crisis that began in 2008.

Confusion and ignorance about debt repeat themselves for public deficits. The misunderstandings take us back to the much-misused household analogy. First, as I pointed out above, households incur debts in order to purchase homes and durables. Automobiles are an important example. Part of the monthly payments on mortgages and durables such as cars consists of the principle of the mortgage or loan. This repayment of the borrowed principle is by definition and in practice an investment, embodied in the home (for a mortgage) or the automobile (consumer credit).

In most countries government statistics recognize this principle, and treat mortgage repayments as household saving, not expenditure. Except for the very rich, this repayment accounts for the vast majority of household saving, with payments into private pension funds being the next largest category. The main reason that total personal saving turned negative in the US during 2000–2002 was that middle-class households on balance borrowed on the equity in their homes rather than paying off mortgages. This practice in the US, and less so in the UK, led to a substantial portion of the population suffering from "negative equity" not many years later.

The same behavior of households toward mortgages applies to assessing public finances. When a government borrows to finance the construction of a highway, school or hospital, this is an investment. The government could charge for the use of these, in which case their character as investments becomes obvious by generating a revenue flow to repay the loan as well as add to public sector income. If governments provide the infrastructure to the public without a direct charge, the investment character does not change. The flow of benefits remains, funded by taxing households and businesses. To the extent that total government expenditure exceeds current revenue because of public-sector investments, no "deficit" results, just as when a household contracts a mortgage it is not private "deficit finance."

This difference between investment and other public sector expenditures such as salaries, and most military equipment, provides the basis to divide government budgets into "capital" and "current" components. Rational households, businesses or governments do not fund investment through current revenue flows. What about deficits on current spending? Surely households should never practice that, nor should governments.

In practice, prudent households regularly borrow to finance current expenditure. Imagine a household in which the income earners decide to change jobs, and face a gap of several months between leaving the present employer and joining the new one. Should they cut expenditure drastically for the several months when they receive no income? Even the most obsessively frugal person recognizes that during a temporary interruption of earnings, expenditure can be maintained, either through drawing on savings or by borrowing.

The same applies to public finances. The great crisis that began in 2008 offers a case in point. Immediately prior to 2008 the governments of most developed countries operated with quite small current-account deficits or even surpluses (more on this in Chapter 9). For example, in 2007 the Spanish government could boast a budget surplus of almost 2% of GDP and Italy had a small deficit of 1.5%. The US government was a modest exception with a 3% deficit, due to tax reductions for the wealthy during the eight years of George W. Bush following his dubious ascent to the presidency in 2001. The improvement of public finances in most countries before the crisis of 2008 resulted from continuous economic growth during the decade. Tax revenue in developed countries responded positively to income growth, with the income tax being the most obvious, and this principle also applies to corporate and sales taxes.

Rising national income generates more tax revenue and vice versa. When national income fell in the US during 2008–2009 by 4%, and 5% in Britain, ratios of the deficit to GDP took a double hit. First, falling national income brought a drop in public revenue. Second, the ratio of the public sector deficit rose because the denominator (GDP) fell. Falling national income, the definition of a recession, presents the public sector with the equivalent of the household's interruption in its income flow. Because market economies experience cycles of growth and contraction, recession-generated deficits decline or turn into surpluses when the recession ends and growth resumes.

The analogy with an interruption in household income flow is not completely accurate. A household cannot increase its income by spending, but, strange as it may seem to the austerity advocates, a government can. Because they generate a relatively large portion of total demand in an economy, governments stimulate output and employment *and taxes* by increasing their expenditures. The tax increase will always be less than the expenditure increase, though the expenditure–tax balance is a very narrow view of the process. While the government has increased its deficit by spending, it has reduced the "deficits" of households by generating more employment. One household, no matter how rich, is far too small a part of the economy to have a similar effect.

Chronic Deficit Disorder

After going into remission during 2008–2009, a virulent outbreak of Chronic Deficit Disorder (CDD) erupted in the US and with equal virulence in Europe. A well-recognized but little-understood behavioral malfunction, the term is used loosely to cover a broad range of antisocial activities. Strictly speaking, CDD refers to a morbid and irrational fear of public expenditure, especially when it exceeds current revenues. We can distinguish it from Acute Deficit Disorder, a delusion that public enterprises should balance expenditures with income (e.g., the Post Office in the UK). There is also a relatively rare form, Congenital Chronic Deficit Disorder, the loathing of taxation by those with inherited wealth (e.g., Mitt Romney, David Cameron, George Osborne).

Since the global crisis of 2008, CDD swept through the Republican Party in the US and Conservative Party in the UK, where natural resistance is virtually nil. It also afflicted almost the entire UK Liberal Democrat Party and much of the Democratic Party in the US. Quite surprising was the infestation in the Labour Party. Its leader in opposition Ed Miliband promised not to reverse the draconian cuts in public services by the right-wing government.

In the US the rampant spread of CDD is extremely worrying, because it has afflicted groups previously immune: neoconservatives, neoliberals and the filthy rich. During the presidencies of Reagan, Bush I and Bush II, these groups showed not merely indifference, but enthusiasm for public sector red ink. With the arrival of a Democratic president and the possibility of spending on activities other than making war, CDD spread through the GOP with a virulence unprecedented since the Black Death.

The nonafflicted have a responsibility to take remedial action. The first step towards containing CDD requires that those who suffer from it come to recognize that they have an antisocial malady. This first step involves taking three doses of remedial rationality:

1. Recessions cause public sector deficits

Public expenditure has a tendency to increase during recessions and public revenue invariably declines. During recessions unemployment increases and wages decline for many of the employed. The former automatically generates unemployment payments, while the latter leads to increases in household support payments, such as food stamps in the US and various means-tested benefits in the UK. Recessions by definition result in declines in personal and corporate income, and taxes decline when these incomes decline. These relationships might strain the mental capacity of a preschooler.

2. Public expenditure cuts made deficits worse

Declines in household income result in declines in taxes and increases in deficits. Cuts in public expenditure reduce public sector employment and household income. Therefore, cuts in public expenditure reduce public revenue, with the result that at best a deficit does not decline and at worst it increases. If that logic has a flaw, no sane economist has found it.

3. Economic expansion reduces deficits

Economic growth increases employment and household incomes, which increase tax revenue and reduce payments to the unemployed and means-tested benefits. The fiscal deficit declines.

Try as one might, it is impossible to avoid the conclusion that endorsing expenditure cuts for deficit reduction is a behavioral disorder. Except for those afflicted by the congenital form of the malady, it is a disorder that can be treated.

In 1930, J. M. Keynes warned, "The world has been slow to realize that we are living in the shadow of one of the greatest economic catastrophes of modern history." The same warning applies over eighty years later, and the slowness to realize the impending disaster is the essence of CDD.

A few simple rules should guide sensible public financial management (see Box: "Chronic Deficit Disorder"). The problem lies not with the public debt itself, nor its absolute or relative size. Problems come from the possible income distribution effects of who holds the debt and who pays the taxes to service it, and financial speculation on the public bonds that finance borrowing. In a less reactionary period governments managed the distributional problem through progressive taxation. Much simpler is the cure for financial speculation on public debt: purposeful regulation of capital markets. As I demonstrate in Chapter 9, lower debt, whether absolutely or relatively to GDP, does not deter speculation.

To summarize the common sense of debt and deficits, debt incurred to finance investment has a balancing asset, similarly to a household mortgage. As for deficits, they tend to result from the decline in revenues due to recession. Economic recovery reduces them. Attempts to reduce them by cutting expenditure are self-defeating by generating the recessions that cause them.

Calculating Public Deficits

Even if public sector deficits are not always a bad thing, no one would deny that they can "get out of control," requiring immediate measures to "rein them in." The media told us that obvious examples of dysfunctionally large deficits were those of the US and the UK after the financial crisis of 2008. Both a middle-of-the-road Democratic president in the US and a right-wing coalition government in Britain set deficit reduction as a high priority. Surely both were not wrong.

Both were wrong. Assessing the need for deficit reduction first requires measuring it. Anyone reading and listening to the US media would have been aware that the federal government budget deficit in 2010 was more than 10% of GDP, in excess of $1.6 trillion. Or, as a Tea Party Republican might put it, *$1.6 trillion!*

Looks like a lot of money, $1.6 trillion. Before anything else, we should inspect and verify the meaning of this number. I went to the source, the statistics from the US Department of the Treasury, as reported by the Bureau of Economic Analysis of the Department of Commerce. Those who attempt to balance a checkbook (if anyone still has such a twentieth-century relic) know that sorting out a budget is not straightforward even if you get your arithmetic right. This generalization applies to public budgets.

What should we measure? The most obvious first step, total revenues minus total expenditures, measures the *overall* deficit. This deficit does not provide the guide for judging budget policy, because it includes interest on the public debt. Cutting interest expenditure would imply defaulting on part or all of the public debt, so no knowledgeable person uses it in serious analysis of deficit reduction. The US government pays about 40% of the interest to other US government agencies. These payments involve shifting money from one public pocket to another, providing a practical reason for leaving out interest payments. Exclusion of interest payments leaves you with the *primary* deficit. The International Monetary Fund (IMF), zealous enforcer of "fiscal responsibility," employs the primary deficit for all its infamous "stabilization" programs.

To repeat from the previous section, a general principle of business finance counsels that current revenue should cover current costs, and fund investment by borrowing (i.e., businesses going into debt). No successful business would spend years squirreling away funds to pay up-front for a factory expected to last 20 years. Banks exist to lend for such investment. The same principle applies to public investments.

Tedious inspection of the website of the Bureau of Economic Analysis of the Department of Commerce, plus simple arithmetic and the rule for taking percentages allow calculation of the different deficits (shown in the table below: US GDP and public finances, 2005–2010). First, notice that the bottom fell out of revenue when the financial crisis hit, going from over $2.5 trillion in 2007 to barely $2.1 trillion in 2009 (column 2). Over half of this fall came from personal income taxes, which dropped by 20%. Corporate taxes, down by half, accounted for almost all the remaining decline.

In contrast, for the same years, total expenditure rose, from $2.7 trillion to $3.5 trillion, an increase of almost $800 billion. Of the nonmilitary part, two-fifths of the increase funded unemployment benefits, social support payments, and the newly created temporary mortgage relief program. Back in the days before the economics profession converted to fakeconomics, we called items like these "automatic stabilizers."

This term describes the various automatic reactions that occur when the economy declines. They kick in to reduce the actual decline compared to what would occur without them. These stabilizing effects include a fall in personal income tax receipts greater than the fall in household income, because these tax rates are mildly progressive. In addition, personal and corporate tax exemptions do not change, so they become relatively more important as income declines. Second, and even more important, corporate income tax drops dramatically because profits initially absorb much of the fall in demand for goods and services. Back in the days when corporate tax rates were higher this stabilizer was more effective.

Third and obvious, unemployment benefits and temporary social support payments cushion the decline in household income. In 2009 the Obama government created a new automatic stabilizer: mortgage relief. Mortgage statistics attest to the need for this measure. In 2005 about 11% of the infamous "subprime" mortgages taken out by (mostly poor) Americans fell behind in payment – "delinquent" in the jargon. In 2008 the percentage rose to 20%, and higher still in 2009–2010.

In the bygone days before economists lost influence to econfakers, we treated automatic stabilizers as a good thing that prevented much of the instability inherent in a market economy. For fakeconomics the seriousness of this bygone heresy cannot be exaggerated. If you consider automatic stabilizers a good thing, then you are saying that *fiscal deficits should increase during a recession*. Even more, you allege that *increases in the deficit prevent the recession from getting worse*. As hard as it may be for the young to believe, this heretical blasphemy was the accepted wisdom as late as the 1970s.

With these shocking heresies noted, I can return to measurement of deficits. The overall deficit rose from about 1% of GDP in 2007 to almost 10% in 2009, then "improving" slightly to 9.6% in 2010. The primary deficit hung in there at 8.4% of GDP. During the previous 50 years, the primary deficit never exceeded 4%. Such was the impressive achievement of the great financial collapse that began in 2008 – the gutting of public revenue.

Serious (as opposed to casual) worriers should focus their anxieties on the current deficit. This measure calculates the part of government consumption expenditure not covered by current revenue. Whether in recession or expansion, the principle that borrowing should fund investment does not change, for businesses, households and the federal government.

Therefore, whether our government covers its noninvestment expenditure represents the key issue (leaving out interest payments, as explained earlier). The current deficit remained less than 5% of GDP in 2010, far below the "headline" 10% cited by the deficit vultures of the political Right.

Even this statistic requires interpretation, because a full percentage point of the current deficit resulted from the massive increase in unemployment in 2009 and 2010. In the US a special payroll tax funds unemployment compensation. In prosperous times the revenue from the tax exceeds payments, when unemployment remains low. During 2005–2007 the unemployment compensation fund ran an average annual *surplus* of almost $8 billion (see last column in the table: Net Unemployment Payments [NUP]).

Common sense dictates excluding unemployment payments from the deficit measure, because with recovery the net expenditure turns positive. In 2007 the taxes funding unemployment payments exceeded the benefits paid by $6 billion. By 2010 the payments exceeded tax revenue by over $140 billion. In 2007 the civilian unemployment rate finished the year at 5%, then 7.3% at the end of 2008, and 9.9% for a very unhappy holiday season in 2009. It comes as no surprise that the unemployment fund paid out almost $150 billion in 2010.

These calculations produce a straightforward conclusion. In 2010 the US public sector deficit reached a postwar high, but not as high as right-wing propaganda alleges. When appropriately measured, the deficit that represents normal expenditure reached no more than 4% of GDP. This was high by historical comparison because the recession in which we found ourselves turned extremely severe by historical comparison. End the recession, and end the deficit problem; end the recession by stimulating the economy through public spending. It really is that simple.

In 2009 the US economy required an effective fiscal stimulus, effective in the sense of achieving expansion, not merely an end to contraction. How a fiscal stimulus would bring recovery was once so generally accepted that it is astounding to need to explain it: this is a clear example of the deaccumulation of knowledge. The process is simple: public expenditure would increase demand, causing employment to increase, reducing unemployment benefits and social support payments, plus generating tax revenue. Rising household consumption expenditure would increase corporate profits, simultaneously raising corporate tax collections and stimulating productive investment.

Because of differences in institutions, practice and legal definitions, the calculation of fiscal deficits differs across countries (for the UK calculations

US GDP and public finances, 2005–2010
(billions of dollars and percentages)

Year	GDP	Revenue	Expenditure	Balance	Less: Interest	Investment	NUP
2005	12,638	2,154	2,472	–318	184	392	+7
2006	13,399	2,407	2,655	–248	219	425	+10
2007	14,078	2,568	2,729	–161	223	462	+6
2008	14,441	2,524	2,983	–459	232	496	–6
2009	14,256	2,105	3,518	–1413	169	514	–85
2010	14,660	2,256	3,661	–1405	168	540	–143

Percentages			Deficits:			Less
Year	Revenue	Expenditure	Overall	Primary	Current	Unemp.
2005	17.0	19.6	–2.5	–1.1	2.0	2.0
2006	18.0	19.8	–1.9	–0.2	3.0	2.9
2007	18.2	19.4	–1.1	0.4	3.7	3.7
2008	17.5	20.7	–3.2	–1.6	1.9	1.9
2009	14.8	24.7	–9.9	–8.7	–5.1	–4.5
2010	14.8	25.4	–9.6	–8.4	–4.8	–3.8

Notes: NUP is net unemployment revenue (unemployment payroll tax minus payments to the unemployed).
Source: US Office of Management and Budget.

see Box: UK Growth, Recessions and Deficits). The general principle that growth eliminates deficits and decline increases them does not differ, except in degrees of responsiveness. A fiscal stimulus, not a monetary stimulus ("quantitative easing"), represents the method of turning decline into growth. A monetary stimulus is passive (more in the next chapter), while a fiscal stimulus actively fosters expansion. In a recession, fiscal policy should temporarily increase deficits by spending more, and the growth that results reduces that deficit and turns it into a surplus.

"Not so fast," the econfakers shout. The US public deficit was near 10% of GDP, with default and disaster staring America in the face as the dreaded financial markets trembled and quaked. There is no alternative to austerity – cut expenditures. Cut education, health, social security payments, and unemployment benefits, too. Don't repair roads, bridges and schools.

This reactionary ideology is not merely madness. It is madness with a purpose. It uses recession and misrepresentations of public deficits

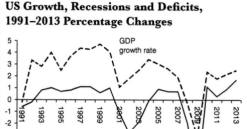

US Growth, Recessions and Deficits, 1991–2013 Percentage Changes

Source: *Economic Report of the President* (2013), 2013 figures estimates.

If recessions are the basic cause of the public sector deficits since 2008, we should be able to show this concretely. And we can.

The chart to the left shows the deficit–growth interaction for the US from 1991 to 2013. The dashed line is the annual rate of growth of the economy (GDP). The solid line is the year-to-year *change* in the overall fiscal balance, not the budget balance itself (total revenues minus total outlays by the federal government).

For example, in 2000, the economy expanded at 4%, and the federal budget balance increased (improved) by one percentage point, from a surplus of 1% of GDP to a surplus of 2%. By contrast, in 2009 the economy contracted by 2.6% and the budget balance went from –3.2% to –9.9% of GDP. Growth reduces deficits by generating more tax revenue and reducing unemployment payments. Recessions increase deficits by reducing revenue and increasing unemployment payments. Simple as that.

as weapons to further strengthen the power of capital over social and political life in the US. The forces of reaction are following the advice of Rahm Emanuel, President Obama's first chief of staff and subsequently mayor of Chicago: "A good crisis should not be wasted."

Calculating Public Debt

After the financial crisis of 2008 the public debt of almost every advanced country expanded substantially, as the global contraction undermined revenue and generated recession-linked expenditures, support for the unemployed being the most important. Politicians of almost all ideological inclinations deplored the growth of public indebtedness as dangerous, threatening to "unsettle financial markets." For those who harbor these anxieties it may come as a surprise that the public debt of very few developed countries increased to a level worthy of mild concern, much less anxiety.

Demonstrating this apparent heresy requires a branch of advanced mathematics, known as basic arithmetic. To make the task even more

UK Growth, Recessions and Deficits

Measures of the UK deficit, percent of GDP,
2010

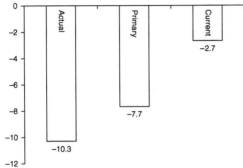

All Deficits Are Not the Same

There are 3 important budget balance categories: the overall, the primary and the current. The primary balance omits interest payments on public debt, payments which cannot be reduced without defaulting on debt. The IMF stresses that "responsible budget management" always refers to the primary balance.

UK growth, recessions and deficits, 1996–
2012

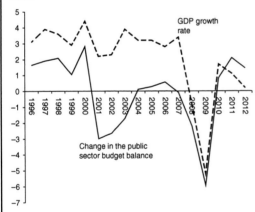

In 2010 when the Conservative Party and Liberal Democrat Party formed a coalition government and peddled the propaganda of deficit hysteria, the overall UK fiscal balance reached its deepest point, about −10% of GDP, very similar to the same measure for the US. Interest payments on the debt were 2.6% of GDP, so the *primary* deficit was below 8% at 7.7%.

In that year the UK government *invested* a substantial 5% of GDP. Businesses never fund investments from current income. If we apply the same sound business principle to budget management, the public sector deficit requiring action becomes less than 3%. This was a problem to correct, but no cause for hysteria or even "hard choices."

While I am on this topic, check the second diagram. As for the US (and every other market economy), the UK fiscal balance moves with the growth rate, as shown clearly in the second chart.

difficult, assessing the danger of indebtedness requires common sense. The common sense consists of three general rules.

First, a debt is a potential problem when owed to someone else. I could be so bold as to assert that a debt owed to oneself is not a debt.

Second, and to repeat a basic principle already explained, there is a difference between a debt contracted to create an asset and one contracted for consumption, whether for a household, business or government. The former creates wealth. To labor the household example yet again, when a family borrows to purchase a home, the debt (mortgage) corresponds to an asset whose value in normal times exceeds the debt. The *net* debt of a person or household equals that owed to others, minus the assets of the household or person.

Third, and again reiterating an earlier general rule, the cost or burden of a debt results from what a person or household must pay to others in interest and to reduce the original value of the debt. To keep to the mortgage example, its running cost is not the amount of it, but the periodic interest and repayment of principle ("debt service").

Apply this same common sense to the US debt in the table below (US public debt, end of 2010). At the end of 2010 the federal public debt of the US rose to just over $14 trillion. This amount represented about 96% of GNP for that year. This seems a very large debt, until we inspect it.

The federal government owed 40% of this debt *to itself or to institutions under its control*. To repeat, 40% of the $14 trillion represented debt owed by the federal government to the federal government. It follows that the interest payments involved nothing more than a shift of funds from one pocket to another. Even more, much of this shift funded social security benefits, which few Americans would criticize (especially if over retirement age, as I am). The US debt held by the Social Security Trust Fund represents the *assets* of the beneficiaries of the system, generating their (my) retirement income.

Next, we need to subtract from the total ("gross") debt the liquid assets of the US government, gold reserves, holdings of foreign currencies, bonds, etc., to net actual liabilities – the net debt. By the international standard methodology of the Organisation for Economic Co-operation and Development (OECD), the net debt of the US reached just over $6 trillion at the end of 2010. This number was less than half of the nominal debt total of $14 trillion. Take out what the government owes itself, take out government's liquid assets, and the debt was just over 40% of GDP, not even close to 100%.

That's not the end of the debt story. The media and politicians carry on about the debt because of a terror of the merciless "financial markets." So, how much of the debt (gross or net) do these gnomes of finance hold? This is difficult to estimate precisely, but obvious candidates for exclusion present themselves, beginning with state and local governments.

This portion of the federal debt, which includes public employee pension funds, represented 5% of the total in 2010. Excluding this government-to-government debt brings the maximum possible "financial market debt" down to about $7.5 trillion gross, barely $6 trillion net.

What about that debt owed to China, $1.1 trillion at the end of 2010? Whatever nefarious plans the Chinese government may or may not have for its debt holdings, they do not include financial speculation. Nor is there a safer form in which the Chinese government could hold its massive foreign exchange reserves, as explained not very graciously by the director-general of the China Banking Regulatory Commission: "Except for U.S. Treasuries, what can you hold? Gold? You don't hold Japanese government bonds or UK bonds. U.S. Treasuries are the safe haven. For everyone, including China, it is the only option... We know the dollar is going to depreciate, so we hate you guys, but there is nothing much we can do."

When we make the reasonable subtraction of the Chinese debt from the total, the maximum gross debt potentially vulnerable to private speculation falls to $6.5 trillion, considerably less than half of GDP. The net equivalent drops to less than a third of GDP.

When we take out what the federal government owes itself, the US public debt is a smaller proportion of GDP than the same debt measure for any other major developed country. When other obvious calculations are made (net instead of gross, public bonds held by local and state governments), you have to think, *where is the problem?*

US public debt, end of 2010

Ownership categories	US$ bns	% of total	% of GDP
Total federal public debt	14,206	100.0	95.7
owed to itself	5,656	40.3	38.6
owed to others	8,370	59.7	57.1
Net debt to others	6,017	42.9	41.1
Non-financial owners			
State & local gov'ts	706	5.0	4.8
China	1,160	8.2	7.9
Everyone else,* **gross**	6,504	46.4	44.4
Everyone else,* **net**	4,677	33.3	31.9

*Maximum possible value for debt entering "financial markets."
Sources: Gross: *Economic Report of the President* (2011); net: OECD.

"Ah, but the problem lies not in the size of the debt," say the econfakers and the austerity hawks whose policies they justify. We face the problem of *servicing* it – paying the interest. Not much a problem for the US, I fear, as the table below (Interest payments on public debt) shows. Of the five largest developed countries, payments on the gross debt as a percentage of GDP (the "debt burden") remained lower in the US than for any of the others except Japan. By contrast, the allegedly frugal German government paid out considerably more than the US Treasury, and France and the UK also weighed in well above the US in their interest/GDP ratio. Interest on the net debt of the US federal government in 2010 barely reached one percent of GDP, not "nothing," but "next-to-nothing."

"Not so fast," argue the fakeconomics-inspired "deficit hawks," now down to their last argument. If "financial markets" take fright, they will drive up interest rates and that little 1% or 1.6% will go through the unsustainable roof. But wait. How can "financial markets" drive up interest rates when at most they have access to less than half of gross debt? And how would they do it when any new borrowing by the US government can be from itself (e.g., the Social Security Trust Fund) or the Chinese government? The answer is obvious and requires no expertise in economics: "financial markets" cannot drive up US interest rates.

Quite the contrary, and the threat to "downgrade" US public debt by the rating agency Moody's in September 2012 bordered on the surreal. As Mark Weisbrot of the Center for Economic and Policy Research in Washington observed, "If you had to pick any sovereign bond in the world that has the least risk of default, it would have to be a US Treasury bond. Anyone who is holding bonds issued by the US government can be pretty sure that they will get their full interest payments and principal, if they hold it to maturity, unless there is some calamity as gigantic as a nuclear war."

The US government has always met its debt obligations. In contrast, it flagrantly fails to meet its obligations to provide for the education and health of its population, repairing the country's public infrastructure, and preventing state and local governments from going bankrupt. The false claims of federal default serve the rich and powerful, aided by the rating agencies, and would increase real default on social and economic justice for people in the US.

Interest payments on public debt,
percentage of GDP, 2010

UK	2.6	
France	2.3	
Germany	2.0	Net
US	1.6	1.0
Japan	1.4	

Source: OECD.

Further Reading

Paul Krugman, *End This Depression Now!* (London: W. W. Norton, 2012).
David Graeber, *Debt: The First 5000 years* (Brooklyn: Melville House, 2011).

Chapter 8

GOVERNMENTS CAUSE INFLATION?

Fears of Inflation

"Government causes inflation" probably stands first among the favorite refrains of the econfakers. Allegedly based on sound economic theory, the argument provides great benefit to the rich and powerful, repeatedly used against public spending. As a practical matter, except for fears of alien invasion, few anxieties are less relevant early in the twenty-first century than those about dangers of inflation.

In 2010 the rate of inflation in the US was less than 2%, and negative the year before. During those two years unemployment in the US rose to over 14 million, close to 10% of the labor force. A US Gallup poll in May of 2010 demonstrated the power of the inflation ideology by reporting that 59% of those surveyed described themselves as "very concerned" about the rate of inflation, with another 29% "somewhat concerned," and only 15% "not very or not at all concerned."

In 2012 in the UK, with its unemployment rate of 8% and falling household incomes for three consecutive years, inflation fears allegedly gripped the public: "The Bank of England's dilemma over whether to stimulate the recession-hit UK economy was sharpened further yesterday by a survey showing that the public's inflation expectations have risen in recent months, despite falls in the headline rate [to less than 3%]."

Why should inflation at 2% and 3% grip the public with such angst that its makes rampant unemployment and declining earnings secondary concerns? And why attribute inflation to governments ("the Bank of England's dilemma")? These unlikely beliefs result from the hard and diligent work of econfakers in faithful service to those who benefit from fostering free market myths – the rich, especially those rich from financial speculation.

As a first step to deconstructing inflation fears I ask: if people fear inflation, why do they think that governments cause it? This leads to an obviously related question: if governments cause it, can governments turn inflation on and off? We find the faux answer to these in a simple storyline: prices go up because too much money chases too few goods, and governments are the source of money.

As appealing as it might be, as often as repeated, this story is false. It stands out as perhaps the single most important ideological scam of fakeconomics. Close inspection of the government–money–inflation triad reveals a complete lack of content. On inspection nothing is there. The absence places this story alongside the much-cherished "supply and demand," analytically and empirically vacuous. To understand why this story contains nothing but hot air, we must begin at first principles: what is money, what is inflation and why do prices change?

What Is Money?

The clearest and most simplistic statement of the government–money–inflation hypothesis comes from twentieth-century ideologue Milton Friedman, who among his many other faux Nobel–worthy contributions, asserted that "inflation is always and everywhere a monetary phenomenon."

Under what conditions would this be true? Friedman's oft-quoted cliché implies far more than "money chases prices." It asserts that increases in prices have no other cause than monetary expansion, and that expansion always comes from public, never private, behavior. Making any sense of this assertion requires an understanding of the nature of money and its relationship to government policy.

In day-to-day conversation we use the word "money" rather broadly and without great precision. For example, someone might say, "My family did not have much money when I was growing up." Such a statement does not literally refer to the dollars, pounds, marks, etc. that parents kept in a cookie jar or elsewhere. It usually means "income," as in, "My parents did not earn much when I was growing up."

By contrast, econfakers, as well as economists, mean something very specific by "money." For them the word means the vehicle for buying and selling, as in "means of circulation," or "medium of exchange." I buy something and what I use to pay for it is by definition money except in those rare cases of direct barter of goods. All analysis that attributes inflation to how much "money" is in circulation uses this definition. If people carried out exchanges with something other than money, then no necessary link between prices and money would exist. In addition to the requirement that money be one side of every exchange, the money-determines-prices argument also requires that the quantity of money exists independently and prior to exchanges. In addition, this causality requires that people do not hold money idle, or, if they do, the desire to hold money is stable. If this were not the case, the overall supply of government created money would differ from the amount in circulation.

We can identify these three requirements as the "universality principle" (all exchanges occur with money), the "autonomy principle" (money exists separate from the exchanges it facilitates), and the "nonhoarding principle." If these principles hold, then they tell a simple story about money and prices. All exchanges occur with money and the number of exchanges people wish to make has no impact on the quantity of this money. Production of goods and services determines the maximum number of exchanges at any moment, and the amount of money determines their prices.

Increases and decreases in the quantity of money must result in increases and decreases in the value of total exchanges. If the quantity of money goes down, either the prices of goods and services fall, or people buy and sell smaller amounts of them. If the quantity of money goes up, either people buy and sell more, or prices rise. If production of goods and services does not or cannot go up, increases in money cause prices to rise. To finish the story, because governments have a monopoly over printing money, variations in the total value of exchanges result from the government increasing or decreasing the quantity of money.

Therefore, inflation is always the result of governments increasing the quantity of money when the supply of goods and services cannot increase or increases slower than the quantity of money. It all seems quite sensible and simple. On the one hand we have the great pile of society's production, and, on the other, a pile of money. If the money pile grows larger and the production pile does not, prices must rise.

This apparently sensible story shares the central characteristic of the supply and demand stories (see Chapter 4). It is false. It is a fakeconomics fairytale in which the central character in the story, "autonomous money," has no real-world counterpart. In order to develop a truly sensible view of prices and inflation, we must start all over.

The first and central building block is the universality principle. If all exchanges occur with "money," then we confront the real-world fact that the vast majority of "money" lies outside the direct control of governments. Consider the transactions that a person in an advanced country might carry out in the course of a day. Among the frequent and typical means of exchange will be cash and coins, checks drawn on a commercial bank account, credit cards, mobile phone credits, and various mechanisms of deferred payment, such as department store charge accounts.

If all of these do not qualify as "money," then the money-determines-inflation hypothesis finds itself in deep trouble. The hypothesis would require a complete reformulation without the universality principle, in which two types of exchanges occur – those with "money" and those with "nonmoney." If everything used for transactions falls under the term "money," then the same analytical problem presents itself in a different form. To link to government policy, the universality principle that all exchanges occur with money requires a credible mechanism for how what governments control links to other forms of money. To put it simply, the money-determines-prices story requires the econfakers to demonstrate beyond reasonable doubt that the quantity of "government money" determines the quantity of total money, government and private. To be specific, the autonomy principle requires that somehow government monetary policy determines the day-to-day use of PayPal.

Establishing the autonomy principle presents both empirical and theoretical issues. Standard terminology, accepted by both economists and econfakers, facilitates the empirical discussion. The jargon term in economics (or fakeconomics) for what I have named "government money" is "the monetary base," aka "narrow money," "money base," or "high-powered money." My favorite euphemism, because of its singularly appropriate double entendre, is "base money." Even this, the simplest money concept, cannot be defined without reference to specific social institutions: the "central bank" and "commercial banks." A "central bank" is the institution responsible for overseeing the monetary system of a country (or group of countries in the case of the European Central Bank or ECB). A commercial bank is an institution that holds the deposits of households and companies, using these deposits as the basis for issuing loans.

Legislation determines the governance, functions and tasks of a central bank, and these vary considerably among countries. In the US the Federal Reserve System, created in 1913, performs the functions of a central bank. The commercial banks in each geographic area formally own the 12 regional branches. The president of the US appoints the Board of Governors of the Federal Reserve System, subject to approval by the Senate. Its legal mandate includes fostering full employment, maintaining "moderate" long-term interest rates and price stability. By contrast, the Bank of England, second in age only to the Bank of Sweden (giver of those faux Nobel prizes), remained privately owned from 1694 until being nationalized in 1946. These country-specific characteristics demonstrate the impossibility of a general theory of money that makes no reference to social institutions, though the econfakers do their best to cut and paste one together.

Defining central banks and commercial banks allows an empirical identification of the monetary base in the US: coins, currency and commercial bank "reserves" held by the central bank. These "reserves" are deposits that commercial banks are required to hold in their accounts with the Federal Reserve, much like the deposits of households in the same commercial banks. Wading into the tedious detail of the monetary system allows understanding of links between the money governments control and the money used in transactions.

The important thing to know about national governments and private finance is that far from facilitating, governments restrain and limit banks from generating money. Banks create money by making loans, which take the form of balances in accounts of the bank customers, usually called "demand deposits." In the absence of government intervention, nothing except fear of borrower default limits the credit banks create. Banks profit from loans. Making loans creates money. Governments created or took control of the Federal Reserve System, Bank of England and every other public monetary authority to reduce the inherent danger of banks making too many loans, creating too much money, leading to a financial collapse.

More than a few econfakers have proposed an end to central banks, arguing that the "discipline of markets" would be sufficient to prevent excessive credit creation. Friedrich Hayek, a great favorite of Margaret Thatcher alongside Milton Friedman, famously developed this argument into a dogma that called for abolishing central banks. In a statement so astoundingly off the wall that it is beyond parody, Hayek asserted that "the past instability of the market economy is the consequence of the exclusion of the most important regulator of the market mechanism, money, from itself being regulated by the market process." True to his right-wing principles, US congressman Ron Paul endorses Hayek's monetary nihilism with a gusto: "The purpose of a central bank is to deceive and defraud the public," unlike the squeaky-clean private bankers who brought us the Great Recession of the twenty-first century.

In a remarkable marriage of the ridiculous with the sublime, Hayek shared the faux Nobel Prize of 1974 with the great Swedish progressive and social democrat Gunnar Myrdal. Perhaps their general political and economic orientation is best summarized by two books published in 1944. Hayek's *The Road to Serfdom* polemically attacked the role of the public sector and social protection as the source of totalitarianism, while

Myrdal's *The American Dilemma, the Negro Problem and Modern Democracy* was one of the first serious academic studies of the racism endemic in the US.

Hayek and Paul not withstanding, it falls to governments to constrain private credit, through "reserve requirements" (or "cash reserves"). This requirement sets the legal relationship between the funds that banks hold idle (in reserve) and how much they can lend. For all but the smallest banks, the legal reserve requirement at the end of 2011 in the US was 10%, implying that US banks could extend loans of $10 for every $1 "in reserve." Some governments set no direct reserve requirement, using other regulatory instruments to rein in the credit creation by private finance (e.g., Britain and its former dominions, Canada, Australia and New Zealand).

The US "Money Supply," 2000–2011 ($ billions)

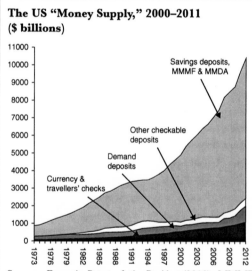

Source: *Economic Report of the President* (2013). MMMF is money market mutual funds and MMDA is money market deposit accounts.

By standard international definition, a national "money supply" has two major components. First, the "monetary base," designated M1, consists of currency and coins plus funds in bank accounts on which checks can be drawn. Until the late 1970s, banking regulations restricted access to other types of accounts ("savings" accounts). M1 was the "base" or basis of the rest of the money supply (sometimes called "base money").

After deregulation of financial institutions, households' and businesses' access to other accounts became no different from the access to checking accounts (equally "liquid"). The "base" lost much of its basicness and the definition of the money supply became less simple.

Deregulation rendered M1 out of date, prompting creation of M2, which is M1 plus almost all accounts held in financial institutions: "saving," "money market mutual funds," and "money market deposit accounts." From 2000 through 2011, currency and coin represented barely over one dollar in ten of the money supply, and the checking accounts just over one in five.

Blaming governments for excessive creation of money is rather like blaming fire departments when buildings burn down. Whether a fire department does a good or a bad job of fighting fires, it stands between the public and a raging inferno. Similarly, central banks attempt to stand between the public and the consequences of intemperate behavior in private finance. In other words, do governments "print money"? No, banks do.

Too Much Money Causes Inflation?

Wherever it comes from, what could possibly cause inflation other than too much money? Well, consider the 1960s and 1970s. During 1960–1969, when international petroleum prices remained almost constant, manufacturing prices in the US rose by about 1% a year, 11% for the decade. Not by chance this increase equaled the change in wages minus the change in output per worker (i.e., prices rose in step with unit labor costs).

During the next ten years international petroleum prices increased from about $3 to over $20 per barrel, rising by 115% in the US. Almost every country experienced similar fuel inflation. These price increases spread through national economies because petroleum represented a major item in household expenditure and industrial costs.

Was this a "monetary phenomenon"? To be more specific, did prices in the US and elsewhere rise in the 1970s because governments directly or indirectly "printed money"? Training people to answer "yes" to this question when the truth is so obviously "no" represents one of the greatest ideological scams of fakeconomics. The econfakers achieve the scam with a faux-theoretical construction they call the "quantity theory of money." As with supply and demand, the quantity theory holds under such restricted conditions that its practical significance is virtually nil. Also like supply and demand, its simplistic logic rules the thoughts of even sensible people.

I continue the analysis as the econfakers never do, with what we observe. In market economies people and businesses buy and sell thousands and thousands of commodities and services. Some of these things we produce domestically, some we import or export, some are both produced domestically and imported, as well as both imported and exported. The buying and selling of these many commodities and services occurs using many different means of exchange, as pointed out previously. Most of the purchases by households occur with what might be called nonmoney instruments (such as a credit card). For businesses

US Inflation, 1992–2010: Too Much Money Chasing?

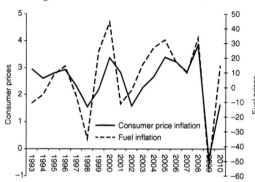

Source: *Economic Report of the President* (2013).

Actual Inflation and Fuel-Only Effect, 1993–2010

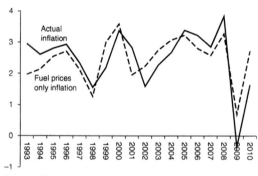

Source: *Economic Report of the President* (2013).

From 1992 through 2010 the average annual rate of consumer price increase in the US was 2.5% and fuel prices on global markets increased at 6.7% (oil, gas and coal).

These average changes hide differences in annual variation. US consumer prices varied relatively little, from a low of −0.4% (2009) to a high of 3.8% (2008). In contrast, fuel prices fluctuated between a low of minus 54% (again, 2009) to a high of 44% (in 2000).

With one average more than double the other plus a massive difference in variation, they would not seem closely related. But they were, and very closely as the chart above shows. The graphic technique to show this assigns each of the two price series to its own appropriate scale. On the left the chart measures US consumer prices, on the right global fuel prices. Seeing the obvious link between global fuel prices and US inflation requires no expertise in economics or statistics.

The second chart shows just how close they were. The solid line is actual consumer inflation (as in the other chart) and the dashed line is the same inflation rate if consumer inflation moved in response with changes in global fuel prices.

The US government does not control global fuel prices to any significant degree. Therefore, the extremely close relationship, in which fuel explains well over half the consumer price index, casts considerable doubt on the idea that inflation in the US is the work of, and/or under the influence of, the government or the Federal Reserve.

cash purchases are rare as hens' teeth, commonly made through promises to pay on a future date.

The econfakers face the problem of constructing a simple story, government–money–inflation, out of this great complexity. The reality that governments provide only the monetary base compounds their problem. In order that the simple quantity-theory story appear credible, it must directly link all means of payment to what governments control. This link proves extremely difficult to demonstrate even for the relatively simple case of bank credit.

Governments through their central banks cannot "control" the lending done by any private institution. At most, central banks can use specific monetary instruments in an attempt to nudge private lending. The two most important instruments are the interest rate at which central banks lend to private banks and "open market operations." To take a simple example, when the US Federal Reserve lowers the rate at which it lends to private banks, it hopes that the banks will pass this decrease onto *their* lending rate to businesses and households. The central bank further hopes that the lower lending rate will increase client borrowing and expenditure. Alternatively, the central bank can try to increase and decrease the reserves of banks on which the capacity to lend is legally based. Central banks do this by buying or selling the banks government bonds (claims on the dreaded public debt).

When the global financial crisis struck in 2008, central banks in most countries used both instruments in what proved an unsuccessful attempt to induce private banks to lend and stimulate the investment that might bring recovery. Use of the central bank rate in Britain and the US reached its limit when it fell below 1%, lower even than the rate of inflation. Even with credit better than free, investment did not recover. Directly increasing private bank lending reserves through "quantitative easing" (open market operations under a different name) proved equally ineffective.

Establishing a direct and effective link between what central banks can do and private bank credit proves theoretically and practically difficult. Extending the link to the increasingly arcane and exotic creations of unregulated finance approaches the hopeless. To the other analytical problems I can add that the money markets in which banks operate are global. As a result, national regulations only weakly limit the actions of financial institutions. It is difficult for any open-minded person to avoid the conclusion that governments at best have little ability to "control the money supply."

These analytical and practical problems lead many economists, but certainly no econfakers, to abandon the idea of the autonomy principle. In place of the quantity theory of causality running from independent money to the value of exchanges, the reverse is proposed, that the exchanges businesses and households initiate bring forth the means by which they can be circulated. For example, this occurs when banks lend from idle credit reserves or on the basis of no reserves in countries that permit such behavior. In the early 2010s banks throughout the world held enormous amounts of idle cash (violating the no-hoarding principle), but this prompted little lending. The cash lay idle because private production remained too sluggish to call it out of its hoards.

The econfakers must refute this interpretation of money at all costs. The money-to-inflation mechanism requires the autonomy principle, that all exchanges occur with "money" that is independent of the exchanges themselves. To put it another way, "money" must exist as a definitive amount before the transactions occur. As in the case of the omniscient auctioneer clearing markets (see Chapter 1), fakeconomics solves this potentially intractable problem *deus ex machina*. All transactions occur with homogenous money, over which the "monetary authorities" hold effective control. How do we know? The same way we know God is Good – blind faith.

This patently absurd approach to money is justified on the basis of moving from the simple to the complex. While "everyone knows" that buying and selling does not occur with a homogenous means of circulation, the conclusions arising from this simplification will not be contradicted when we consider the increasingly complex situations of real economies. By analogy, consider the simple rule that on the Earth falling objects accelerate at 9.8 meters per second, reaching a speed of 9.8 after one second, 19.6 after two, etc.. This refers to a vacuum without air resistance. Observed acceleration will be less depending on the shape of the object and the density of the air. These complications of reality do not alter the validity of the acceleration principle. The same argument holds for money, the econfakers tell us.

However, while the falling object and the earth exist with or without a vacuum, all-inclusive homogenous money with an existence independent of economic activity does not exist in the real world. The real-world "money supply" consists of a heterogeneous collection of components with no common source through which "monetary authorities" could regulate it. Like the auctioneer, fakeconomics money classifies as purely a mental creation (i.e., made up out of nothing and explaining nothing).

What Is Inflation?

Sorting out the "money supply" is not the only problem undermining fakeconomics inflation. The heterogeneity of goods and services generates the next big problem for the quantity theory. The difference between those things traded internationally and those exchanged domestically represents a basic distinction in every economy. Changes in the price of olive oil in Northern Europe and the US must in part result from cost changes in producing countries and world demand, to which Northern Europeans and Americans contribute only a part (though a large part).

Many products are both imported and produced domestically. Petroleum is an obvious case. In the twenty-first century the US remained the world's third largest producer of crude oil, and first among importing countries (imports about double production). Anyone who claims that the "money supply," however defined, determines the prices of pineapples and petroleum does not live in the real world.

Some goods and services, mostly the latter, do not enter international trade. For example, the process of travelling from New York to San Francisco cannot be imported, though the vehicle and the fuel for that vehicle can. The price of such services depends overwhelmingly on factors internal to the US: workers' wages and owners' profits. However, at an increasing rate, we observe an internationalization of goods and services, call centers, online education, even medical care via the computer and telephone. No credible explanation of price changes can treat them as independent of international prices and reflecting only changes in something as analytically and practically flawed as the "quantity of money" or the "money supply."

At the risk of tedium I point out a third, totally practical problem with fakeconomics inflation. Market economies require increases in prices to bring about the reallocation of productive resources from less profitable to more profitable activities. This process embodies the dynamism of capitalist economies. Changes in technology and the expenditures of households generate the development of new products and the decline of old ones. To take an example, the production of typewriters disappeared with the development of computers. New sectors of an economy must attract workers and other productive inputs from stagnant and declining sectors. In a market economy this reallocation occurs through rising wages and prices in expanding sectors. Dynamic market economies have an inherent if mild inflationary tendency.

Similar inflationary pressure results from new products replacing older ones, and quality improvements in existing products. The price of an automobile in 2010 was considerably higher than in 1980. How much of the increase reflected inflation and how much quality improvement (whether or not desired by purchasers)? The task of separating higher prices when a product improves, paying more because market conditions allow the producer to raise prices, and some "pure inflation" effect has taxed the expertise of statisticians for decades. Perhaps with this in mind, the ECB, as dedicated to fighting inflation as it is possible to be, defines a 2% rate of aggregate price increase as "price stability." Anyone can verify this by viewing its more than slightly alarmist video cartoon dedicated to fuelling inflation fears: "Have you seen the inflation monster?"

In the mid-1990s identifying the quality change component in inflation sufficiently concerned the US Congress that it funded an expert group to investigate. The Boskin Commission (Advisory Commission to Study the Consumer Price Index) concluded that about 1.2 percentage points in the standard measures of inflation represented quality change. That is, price increases of 1.2% were *not* inflation. If to this we add price increases arising from market pressures to reallocate productive resources, the result is close to that of the ECB. The ECB "inflation" target is zero inflation.

So what? Whatever the origin of price increases, they must lower the purchasing power of households, which is what people complain about, right? No, interpreting complaints about falling purchasing power as fear of inflation is ideological. A loss of purchasing power can result from stagnant or falling nominal earnings as well as rising prices. Since the 1970s in the US the purchasing power of the vast majority of households stagnated because wages stagnated, not because of rising prices (see Box: Demand and Incomes, in Chapter 10).

These analytical and practical objections leave the government–money–inflation story without content. The hypothesis of an independent quantity of money that chases after goods and services fails its basic tests, analytical and operational. The "price level" is a complex concept including goods and services whose prices and quantities are determined through different mechanisms. Market economies require increases in the "price level" in order to achieve their dynamism. And some price increases reflect quality change, not inflation. As employed by the econfakers, the two key terms, "money supply" and "inflation," are vacuous. As a result of this vacuousness, a large portion of economists treat money as driven by transactions, "endogenous" in the jargon.

But prices go up and sometimes do so at extremely alarming rates. Don't tell me governments are not responsible for rapid inflation. When governments spend more than their revenue, they have to pay for the excess spending by creating money, and the increase of money in circulation generates inflation. How else do we explain runaway inflation as occurred in Germany in the early 1920s, Latin America in the 1980s and Zimbabwe in this century? This I address in the next section.

Why Do Prices Go Up?

Further progress in understanding inflation requires the dispelling of yet another misconception fostered by fakeconomics: low inflation can transubstantiate into hyperinflation. The more-or-less respectable version of this argument maintains that any level of inflation creates in people expectations of further inflation, so inflation feeds on itself. This scare tactic (that inflation always threatens to spin out of control into hyperinflation) is equivalent to arguing that conventional war always leads to thermonuclear holocaust.

Hyperinflation, usually and arbitrarily defined as a *monthly* rate in excess of 50%, comes with its own specific causes that have almost no relevance beyond the specific circumstances in which it occurs. With few exceptions high inflation rates carry no policy lessons for countries with rates in single and low double digits.

The US has never experienced hyperinflation, though during the Civil War something close to it occurred in the states of the Confederacy. The Confederate inflation provides a useful analytical beginning. While the weak central government and the state governments of the Confederacy issued increasing amounts of currency during 1961–65, the hyperinflation resulted from the anticipated victory by the Union army, which would and did render the southern currency worthless. Political events, not too much money, caused the runaway inflation of the Confederate dollar. The twentieth century provides several examples of politically driven hyperinflation. The value of the "Straits dollar," the currency used in Japanese-occupied Southeast Asia, collapsed when Manila fell to the US Army in May 1945.

Sudden and severe declines in production represent a second major cause of hyperinflation. Here the examples are many, including the most infamous inflation of them all, 1923 in Germany. Routinely presented as the result of a feckless government running the printing presses, the German hyperinflation had a clear political cause. In 1922 J. M. Keynes issued a prophetic warning about the reparations forced upon the German government by the Treaty of Versailles:

> If we aim deliberately at the impoverishment of Central Europe, vengeance, I dare predict, will not limp. Nothing can then delay for very long that final civil war between the forces of Reaction and the despairing convulsions of Revolution, before which the horrors of the late German war will fade into nothing, and which will destroy, whoever is victor, the civilization and the progress of our generation.

The evocative phrase, "vengeance will not limp," conjures up the iconic photograph of Adolf Hitler dancing an impromptu jig following the signing of the French surrender in May 1940, in the same railway car where in 1918 the Germans signed their surrender to France. In 1922 the German government failed to make the reparations required of it by the treaty, which resulted in occupation by France and Belgium of the Ruhr Valley, Germany's industrial heartland. The political and economic consequences of the occupation, including loss of a substantial portion of national output and fiscal revenue, generated a massive shortage of goods. Imports could not satisfy the excess demand because of the diversion of export earnings into reparations.

High but not hyperinflation swept Latin America in the 1980s, not because of printing money, but due to a different form of reparations, servicing private bank debts during the infamous Latin American debt crisis. During the 1970s when a fierce debate raged over the reason why Latin American, especially South American, countries seemed especially prone to inflation, the annual rate of price increases across the major countries was a bit less than 30%. While 30% may strike one as high (prices doubling in 33 months), in the 1980s with the debt crisis in full gallop the average for the same countries rose to near 400% per year (prices doubling every 5 months), then "moderated" to 200% in the 1990s. In the twenty-first century with the debt burdens declining, these countries rarely experienced annual rates above 10%.

Why should debt payments, either in Germany in the 1920s or in Latin America in the 1980s and 1990s generate "runaway" inflation?

The answer is not "money," but total demand compared to total supply of goods and services. To simplify, consider a country that produces 100 units of output. This output generates 100 units of income for those involved in its production (wages plus profits in this simple case). The income generated in production provides the real demand for the goods and services the production creates.

This simple example demonstrates the inherently inflationary impact of payments on foreign debts. In effect, the interest and principle sent abroad to service a debt represents an export for which there can be no compensating import. In the 1920s the victorious powers required reparation payments from Germany of 3% of national income. Using my simplified framework, these payments reduced goods and services available domestically to 97 units without reducing the income generated by production of those goods and services. The debt service created an excess expenditure of 3% of national income.

During the debt crisis of the 1980s, Latin American countries confronted excess demand effects considerably larger, over 5% of national production, reaching almost 6% for Peru and 8% for Bolivia, with both countries hit by hyperinflation. In the 1990s average debt service across Latin America declined below 4%, falling further in the 2000s.

The case of debt service does not represent too much money chasing too few goods. If by some policy instrument a government making debt service payments could reduce the amount of money in circulation, this would have almost no impact on price changes. The problem lies with real demand, not money or "nominal" demand. Production generates incomes, but the goods and services available do not match the incomes. The only way to eliminate this type of inflationary pressure would be for the government to tax people and corporations by an amount equal to the debt service payments. This would bring real demand for goods into equality with the real supply of goods.

Along with conflict and debt service, severe imbalance between exports and imports represents a third cause of high inflation. Frequently associated with one or both of the other two, a severe trade deficit provokes a weakening of the national currency. As a currency's value declines compared to the currencies of the countries from which it imports, price increases first hit the imports themselves, then domestic products similar to the imports, then all domestic production that uses imports. When the trade deficit continues to devalue the currency and increase prices, pressures for wage adjustment generalize the inflationary effect throughout the economy.

None of these causes of hyperinflation has relevance for the US or any high-income country. Even trade deficits are noninflationary for high-income countries because foreign exchange from various types of services (such as transport and insurance) and capital flows cover them. Why, then, do people in high-income countries experience any inflation above the 2% or 3% that comes from quality change and reallocation of labor and capital?

To answer this question it helps to look at the inflation scorecard for high-income countries since the early 1970s. Before that decade, from the end of World War II until 1971, the US government guaranteed a gold price of $35 an ounce. Almost all currencies in the capitalist world had a fixed exchange rate with the dollar (the so-called Bretton Woods system). After the end of the Korean War in 1953, the US experienced low inflation for almost twenty years. Inflation in other high-income countries also remained low except when provoked by exchange rate depreciation relative to the dollar.

In August 1971 the US government, with Richard Nixon as president, ended the dollar link to gold, setting loose a free-for-all among the major world currencies. Two periods of sudden and large increases in petroleum prices exacerbated the instability created by the absence of the US gold price guarantee. By the late 1980s this global price instability had passed. Across the 20 largest high-income countries the average inflation rate was 10% in the 1970s, 7% in the 1980s, below 3% in the 1990s, and barely 2% in the 2000s.

By any technically respectable measure, inflation disappeared from the high-income countries after about 1995. The 2 to 2.5 average percentage point increases in prices during the subsequent years resulted from quality change, new products and market-driven price changes among industries to facilitate the shift of resources from less to more profitable activities. No inflation there.

To return to the question raised at the outset, when there is inflation, do governments cause it? No. Markets cause inflation and governments try to control it. Markets induce private banks to create credit, a process over which governments have limited control. But this credit creation is not the basic cause of inflation. Upward pressure on prices has two sources. The more common one occurs when primary commodities increase in price due to temporary shortages domestically or in global markets. The impact of the volatile movements in prices of hydrocarbons on manufacturing costs represents the best known of these. Few production processes do not rely on petroleum, natural gas or coal either as a fuel or a processed input.

Producers of hydrocarbons manipulate the supply side of markets, so that price volatility generates immediate inflationary pressure in importing countries. Copper provides another (albeit lower-impact) example, experiencing shortages and price booms during the 2000s.

Before the replacement of fakeconomics for common sense and analytical rigor, economists named this inflationary pressure "cost push." While accurately evocative of a bottom-up process of price inflation, the term invited attack by suggesting that it arose purely from the supply side. In practice, upward cost pressures result from a temporary excess demand for a critical input, involving a transmission of that excess demand to the production process (supply side) in the form of high input prices.

Fear of Inflation

Inflation across 18 high-income countries, 1972–2012

- - - Average inflation rate, percent
—□— No. of countries, > 3%
—■— No. of countries, > 10%

Included are the US, Canada, 14 Western European countries, New Zealand and Japan.

Over the four decades of 1971–2012, the person in the street could be forgiven for believing that inflation posed the greatest economic threat to civilization, because this was the propaganda focus of those years.

A look at the numbers tells a different story, as the diagram to the left shows in two ways. First, over the 41 years for 18 high-income countries, the rate of inflation reached 10% or more 77 times (out of 18 × 41 = 738 cases, about 10%). The last double-digit inflation episode occurred in 1991 (Sweden, 10.7%). The last time it occurred in more than two countries was in 1982 (in six).

Countries with 3% inflation and above had the same downward trend, occurring only six times after 1996. Half of these happened in 2001, in response to the 45% increase in international petroleum prices the year before. Fuel prices qualify as the usual inflation suspect (see Box: US Inflation, 1992–2010: Too Much Money Chasing?).

People in high-income countries who fret over inflation might more appropriately focus their anxieties on reducing the consumption and imports of hydrocarbons.

In the greatest economics book of the twentieth century, *The General Theory of Employment, Interest and Money* (1936), J. M. Keynes called this phenomenon of specific input shortages a "bottleneck." These can occur at any level of unemployment, but happen with increasing frequency as unemployment declines. When even unskilled labor becomes short and wages rise, the "bottlenecks" generate economy-wide price increases. This should not in itself be considered a problem. From a functional point of view, the wage increases serve to redistribute workers from less profitable to more profitable sectors of the economy, which is what capitalist dynamism is all about.

Inflation Fears: A Class Act

The experience of the high-income countries, especially the US, provides no basis for inflation fears. Most of what the media calls inflation they should identify as quality change and allocative effects. So why the anguished inflation concern across the political spectrum and different classes? The answer lies in the obfuscation of the class impact of the gains and losses from the maladies of markets – unemployment, inequality and inflation. Fakeconomics dedicates itself to maintaining this obfuscation.

As part of the obfuscation, one frequently encounters the statement that the burden of unemployment falls on those who lose jobs, and not the vast majority that stays in employment. In contrast, inflation hurts everyone, the rich, the poor and those in the middle, because things become more expensive for everyone. This "plague on all houses" allegedly makes inflation the only economic malady uniquely general in its impact. This is false; like inequality and unemployment, inflation creates winners and losers, and the distribution of gains and losses has a class character.

It is obvious that inequality has a class impact. For the losers, increased inequality reduces the benefits from general prosperity, shifting those benefits disproportionately to the rich. A defense of growing inequality requires the belief that in a capitalist society the rich are paid too little and the poor too much (to paraphrase John Kenneth Galbraith).

Unemployment is also strictly class linked. Low unemployment and rising wages mean that households find employment and their incomes rise. This is exactly why low unemployment offends business and especially the "malefactors of great wealth" (Theodore Roosevelt), and most of those who gain riches through financial speculation. An enlightened capitalist in the manufacturing sector would realize that full employment brings him or her benefits by putting more spending power into the pockets of households to buy what the capitalist produces. The same cannot be said of the lords of finance, producers of nothing but instability.

While true, it is simplistic to argue that finance loathes inflation because it erodes the value of the debt held by banks and other lenders. However, the disastrous deregulation of finance in the US and parts of Europe that began in the late 1970s shifted the major source of financial profits from lending to speculation. Inflation can facilitate speculation. The opposition of financial interests to inflation has a more subtle and less obvious motivation than concern over the real value of debt. The anti-inflation ideology serves as a central argument against the public sector as a whole. Beginning with the premise that governments cause inflation and inflation is the worst villain because it harms everyone, the argument reaches the conclusion that a smaller, less active government provides the route to prosperity for all.

Fear of inflation also strikes a blow in the class struggle, against wage increases. Along with the feckless money printing of governments, reckless demands for better pay drive inflation. In one of those triumphs of nonsense that only the economics equivalent of alchemy could defend, a higher standard of living for the vast majority, achieved through its only possible route (higher wages) is redefined as the source of general misery by its alleged inflationary impact. "Wage restraint," the vehicle for impoverishment of the majority, becomes a social virtue for its benign effect on prices. In reality wage restraint leads to falling incomes and growing household indebtedness.

Low inflation is the ideology of the rich. Full employment is the ideology of the vast majority (or should be). Inflation properly defined and measured occurs in high-income countries under very unusual circumstances. A market economy creates much more serious concerns: unemployment, inequality and environmental degradation. These, however, are not the concerns of the rich and powerful. Over one hundred years ago Theodore Roosevelt recognized this fundamental class division and called it by name: "These men [of wealth] are equally careless of the working men, whom they oppress, and of the State, whose existence they imperil. There are not very many of them, but there is a very great number of men who approach more or less closely to the type, and, just in so far as they do so approach, they are curses to the country."

Chapter 9

INSTITUTIONALIZED MISERY: AUSTERITY IN PRACTICE

Balanced Budget Ideology

With the US presidential election of 2012 in the rearview mirror, a so-called fiscal cliff allegedly threatened the country with disaster. The time is long overdue to drive a stake through the heart of the budget-cut ideology manifested in the "fiscal cliff" propaganda, not only in the US but also Europe. This ideology draws great support from the coup that replaced economics with nonsense as the true guide to public policy.

In the politically reactionary period that we find ourselves, all but a few politicians and most of the media present as self-evident and needing no defense the proposition that governments should continuously balance their budgets and not accumulate debt. Lack of an economic or even accounting justification for balancing the budget has not stopped this fiscal foolishness from justifying appallingly antisocial policies under the umbrella of "austerity." In the US the power of this venal ideology convinced a substantial portion of the public of the necessity for reductions in Medicare and Social Security benefits, previously judged as politically untouchable.

The "austerity doctrine" maintains that *current* public revenues should cover *all* government expenditures. If they do not, tax increases and/or spending reductions must quickly correct the deficit. Part of this ideology is the fantasy that "fiscal correction" will have little or no impact on total output or growth because expansion of the private sector automatically compensates for the contraction of the public sector.

Though shamelessly simplistic, the balanced budgets doctrine captures hearts and minds of much of the public. Once its respectability fades like the Cheshire Cat, the antisocial measures it advocates as necessary prove totally unnecessary, as a misapplication of reactionary ideology to public policy. When not presented in full form like a rabbit from a magician's hat, the antideficit argument would seem to find faux respectability in two separate but complementary arguments.

The "impersonal forces of markets" argument posits that financial "investors" continuously evaluate the ability of governments to meet their debt obligations and "punish" them if the financial marketeers think they cannot ("punish" is frequently used in this context). Stated crudely, the growth of debt *ipso facto* reduces the faith that "markets" have in the ability of governments to meet those obligations.

Public debt grows when governments run fiscal deficits, so it follows that deficits increase "market fears" of nonpayment. These fears induce "investors" to demand higher interest rates to lend to governments, which further increases the perception of future debt default by raising the cost of debt service. To prevent this unhappy ("vicious") cycle governments should not run fiscal deficits. If a deficit exists, the government must eliminate it either through increased taxes or reduced expenditures. Because "everyone knows" that the public rejects tax increases, "there is no alternative" (TINA) to budget cuts. Objective forces that no one can change make eliminating deficits unavoidable.

The market forces argument runs parallel with the "crowding out" critique of deficits. Governments finance deficits by borrowing and selling bonds in financial markets. At any moment intelligent and rational "investors" must be happy with the amount of government bonds they hold at the prevailing interest rate, or they would buy more (catch the tautology?). Therefore, to sell more bonds the government must increase their return, which means raising the interest rate. Because private companies borrow in the same financial markets as the government, when the interest rate on public bonds rises, the private sector must also pay more to borrow. At higher borrowing rates, the private sector, quite naturally, will borrow less, meaning less investment. Through its own borrowing, the government "crowds" out private investment. The process is rather like a person forcing him or herself into a crowded elevator, thus expelling someone else, because the elevator has just so much room.

Put the two arguments together and they seem to make a tidy little package against all deficit finance. It has a very pleasing corollary for those opposed to public spending. The allegation that public borrowing crowds out private borrowing can be generalized. What if the government has a surplus and spends more? No borrowing is required, but the private sector will still suffer from government "crowding." Why? Because credit is not the only resource required by both government and business. Both hire people, consume inputs such as electricity, perhaps even compete over use of land. Therefore, any public expenditure reduces private spending, by both businesses and households, by pushing up input costs, including wages.

It just gets worse when you believe this argument, because the government can create money and the private sector cannot (see Chapter 8). In other words, the private sector has no defense against the pernicious ability of government to grab scarce resources. He who said, "The best government is that which governs least" didn't know the half of it. The full right-wing version is "The best government is that which spends least."

This tidy, all-purpose critique of public expenditure suffers from a fundamental flaw. It is false. The entire logic, if one can call it that, rests on the presumption that the economy continuously operates at its full potential (see Chapter 4). If the doors open to a half-empty elevator, no one need exit to let a new person in. The analogy is appropriate for public and private spending, and most emphatically appropriate when deficits increase.

When resources are fully employed, governments, businesses or households can each spend more only if one or two of the others were to spend less. When resources are idle, governments, businesses and households can all spend more. In the experience of the advanced countries over the last several decades resources have been idle much more often than society has fully employed them.

After 2007 idle resources in almost every advanced country reached scandalous levels. The suggestion that public expenditure might crowd out private investment and consumption has little foundation most of the time, and none since the global financial collapse of 2008. As for public borrowing driving up interest rates, this depends entirely on the specific circumstances of each country, as I pursue below.

Deficit Disorder in the Land of the Free

From the end of World War II until the election of Ronald Reagan, the politics of public spending at the federal level followed a consistent pattern. Most Democratic Party national politicians supported a broadening of social support programs to cover more people and services. Most Republican Party politicians opposed this broadening, but did not seek to alter the programs drastically. Though an oversimplification, I can characterize US domestic politics during 1945–1980 as incorporating a consensus that the public and private sectors complemented each other, each having its legitimate role.

The election of 1964 provides clear evidence of this truly centrist coalition. The Republican Party convention rejected several moderate candidates, most notably Nelson Rockefeller (ultramillionaire and governor of New York), in favor of a right-wing senator from Arizona, Barry Goldwater. In a 1960 ghostwritten statement of his convictions, Goldwater told the faithful, "I have little interest in streamlining government or in making it more efficient, for I mean to reduce its size. I do not undertake to promote welfare, for I propose to extend freedom. My aim is not to pass laws, but to repeal them."

Offered a straight-up choice between this promise to dismantle the public sector and the last New Deal Democrat, Lyndon Johnson, the latter won the largest popular majority in the history of US presidential elections, 61% (Franklin D. Roosevelt took 60.8% in 1936, and Richard Nixon would win 60.7% in 1972). Other than his own state of Arizona, Goldwater won five in the Deep South, as a direct result of Johnson's championing of the Civil Rights Act passed a few months before the election.

The defeat of the incipiently neoliberal Jimmy Carter in 1980 by the right-wing Ronald Reagan formally and definitively ended the postwar political consensus. Very much in the Goldwater tradition, Reagan would say in his January 1981 inaugural address, "In this crisis, government is not the solution to our problems; government is the problem." This antisocial doctrine would manifest itself a decade later in the first of an unbroken series of bitter conflicts over not merely the level but the legitimacy of public spending. Certainly in Britain and to a lesser extent in the eurozone countries mainstream politicians of the Right might secretly harbor the same reactionary dream of a direct assault on the public sector. However, until very recently political circumstances in Europe dictated that politicians show a façade of regret for the putative necessity of destroying the public sector.

Not so in the US, where debate over the legitimacy of "Government" (the capital G is essential) makes fiscal austerity a derivative issue. The approach of the far-right extremists of the Republican Party in the twenty-first century to the public sector renders logic unnecessary and irrelevant. These extremists require no justification for their loathing of the public sector at all levels, just as a Christian fanatic requires no justification for adherence to the Bible. Nonetheless, the right wing of the economics profession (i.e., almost all of it) aided and abetted this antisocial ultraindividualism, and eagerly supported its wild allegations.

I am not the only economist who has denounced these ultra-right troglodytes, and far from the most prominent. To take perhaps the most famous, as part of what he called the "Dark Ages" of economics, faux Nobel laureate Paul Krugman observed that "one of the many unpleasant things we've learned in this crisis [financial collapse of 2008] is that there was plenty of intellectual corruption in the economics profession from the get-go."

A rather banal economic manifesto for presidential candidate Mitt Romney provided an excellent and appalling example of this "intellectual corruption." In "The Romney Program for Economic Recovery, Growth, and Jobs," four putatively respectable economists, three of whom could claim widely used undergraduate textbooks, urged Americans to vote for the megamillionaire in order to "stop runaway federal spending and debt." To this end the manifesto called for reduction of tax rates for the wealthy, slow growth of publicly funded retirement and medical benefits, and to "remove regulatory impediments to energy production and innovation."

The reactionary politics found in this document ("a concerned effort by three economists…to destroy their own reputations," wrote Krugman) pales alongside the thought that at least a generation of university students suffer from the reactionary rubbish in their introductory textbooks. In yet another reactionary twist no progressive would dare make up, one of those destroying his reputation would in 2013 pen a journal article (and have it published!) with the title "Defending the One Percent" (N. Gregory Mankiw, chair of the Harvard economics department). In the concluding paragraph of this affront to the intellect, we read, "Using the force of government to seize…a large share of the fruits of someone else's labor is unjust, even if the taking is sanctioned by a majority of the citizenry." On the other hand, if you can seize "a large share of the fruits of someone else's labor" through financial speculation, go for it.

The fact is, if the entertainment of facts were allowed in US budget debates, public spending and taxes in the US fall well below almost any high-income country, and below most middle-income countries. The media and right-wing economists consistently misrepresent statistics on public finances. They are motivated by the intention to present public deficits and debt as irresponsible and dangerous. The truth is quite the contrary. Except in rare circumstances, deficits and debt are responsible and safe. Deficits and debt are *good things*, contributing to social welfare, and public sector surpluses and the absence of debt usually signal public sector dysfunction, *bad things* for the well-being of households and businesses.

Many if not most people would judge absurd this heretical characterization of deficits and debt. Having this skepticism in mind, I begin with an analysis of the US deficit. The discussion by necessity repeats arguments found in Chapter 7. In most cases public deficits do not result from excessive spending. They result from recessions. This happens in a simple way.

As countries develop, taxes on expenditures and incomes of both households and businesses increase to the point of overwhelming all other sources of revenue, such as tariffs and fees charged by governments. Income and sales taxes have two very useful characteristics. First, governments find them easy to collect and, second, they increase as the economy grows. Their ease of collection results from their concentration in businesses, either as profit or as payments to employees and suppliers. In practice, businesses themselves collect both types of taxes, paying governments sales taxes and "withholding" taxes of employees, and governments monitor business adherence to the tax laws. Sales and income taxes "collect themselves."

When the economy grows, that growth consists of business revenue, the value of commercialized output. Therefore, public revenue from taxes on business revenue increases as the economy grows. This may seem so obvious that it needs no explaining, much less explaining in tedious detail. Simple and obvious as it may be, it has major implications for our assessments of public sector deficits.

By contrast to revenue sources, no important category of public expenditure increases automatically due to economic growth alone. Expenditures fall into two general categories: those determined by specific legislation and those linked to unemployment and poverty. The first category is by far the larger, including expenditures on health, education, the military, and public sector pensions. Legislatures allocate the funds for each of these to a great extent independently of the immediate state of the economy (or, if not, they should).

The expenditures linked to unemployment and poverty change opposite to the changes in the health of the economy. Unemployment declines as the economy grows, which reduces compensation payments. In some countries, and the US is an example, an ear-marked tax funds payments to the unemployed. When the economy grows, the unemployment fund moves into surplus and vice versa. Similarly, though not so tightly linked to the pace of the economy, support payments to those households defined as being in poverty tend to decrease as the economy grows.

These expenditures act "countercyclically" in two senses. First, by definition they go up when the economy goes down, and vice versa, moving against the "cycle" of the economy. Second, and more important, they make a contribution to reducing the extremes of the economic cycle. When the economy declines, people lose their jobs and with them all or part of their current income. As a result, household consumption declines, reinforcing the initial contraction of the economy. Unemployment benefits reduce the income decline and, therefore, the fall in consumption provoked by growing unemployment.

In this way countercyclical expenditures reduce the strength of the process in which contraction leads to more contraction. By their nature countercyclical expenditures contribute to deficits. We should be very glad that they do. They also work the other way, reducing deficits and helping to turn them into surpluses when the economy expands.

There is more to the countercyclical story. When a country has a progressive revenue system it means that the percentage of income paid in tax increases as households move onto higher marginal tax rates. Therefore, when the economy contracts, the average tax share for households declines. As a result, household income after tax ("disposable income") falls less than total income, and household consumption falls less than household income.

Even in the US after all of the Reagan and Bush tax breaks for the rich the public revenue system retains a small progressive element. This results in great part from "deductions" that households can claim for dependents. As income falls, the part of household income that is subject to tax also falls. The contraction-reducing effect of the revenue system in most cases demonstrates why a strictly proportional tax rate (i.e., not progressive), much loved by reactionaries everywhere, qualifies as bad economics (though great fakeconomics) as well as grossly unfair.

Three processes stand out that link the health of the economy to public sector finances. First, government revenue comes from taxes on the economy's output. Second, in the aggregate taxes have a progressive structure, so they decline more than incomes decline and vice versa. Third, a portion of public expenditure acts countercyclically, kicking in when the economy contracts and switching off as it expands.

These three processes lead to a very important conclusion. The public sector goes into deficit just when we need it to. Deficits serve a good purpose, and we should welcome them. If a government attempted always to maintain a balanced budget, this attempt would make recessions longer and deeper by reinforcing economic contractions. As a result, proposals in the US and elsewhere for a legal requirement to continuously balance the public budget qualifies as self-destructive insanity.

Public sector deficits are the automatic byproduct of countercyclical processes that act to reduce recessions. How then should we assess the

Deficit Fallacies in the US

Fallacy 1: Public sector competes for scarce resources

Fiscal balance (% of GDP) and the unemployment rate, 1955–2011

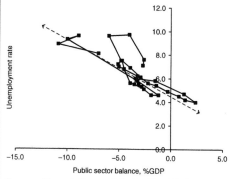

Source: *Economic Report of the President* (2012).

Right-wingers accuse public sector deficits of undermining the private sector growth. This allegedly occurs when public sector borrowing pushes up interest rates through competition over credit.

This argument is fallacious. If deficits occur with idle resources, both private and public borrowing can increase without raising the cost of borrowing. Credit is not scarce because the things businesses and governments use credit to buy are not scarce.

The chart shows the most obvious measure of idle resources, the US unemployment rate (measured vertically), and on the horizontal axis the US federal fiscal balance, over six decades, 1955–2011.

The relationship between the two is obvious and summarized by the dotted line with arrows at each end. Deficits almost always increase when resources are idle. Idle resources occur during recessions. Recessions cause tax revenue to fall and social support expenditures to rise, which reduces a public sector surplus or increases a deficit.

Fallacy 2: Inflation Rorschach test; or, what do you see?

Inflation rate and the public sector balance, 1960–2012

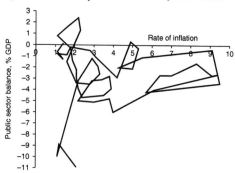

Source: *Economic Report of the President* (2013).

"Deficits cause inflation" is a perennial favorite of the Right, aided and abetted by the econfakers. The analytical errors of this assertion are sufficiently numerous to make it nonsense, as explained in this and the previous chapter.

As we should expect, we find no empirical support for the deficit-inflation allegation. The linked-up scatter points mapping deficits and inflation show a virtually flat tangle. This is what to expect with Fallacy 1 in mind. Deficits increase when the economy suffers from unemployment and other idle resources.

Inflation results from excess demand compared to available resources. The econfakers and right-wing politicians have it backwards. Inflation becomes more likely as the economy expands and deficits turn into surpluses.

Fallacy 3: Deficits raise interest rates

Federal bonds interest rate and public sector balance (% GDP), 1980–2012

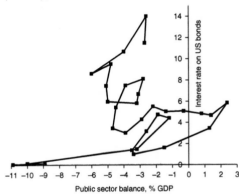

Public sector balance, % GDP

Source: *Economic Report of the President* (2013).

The antigovernment crowd never tires of listing the abuses public spending brings to private enterprise. Prominent among these offenses against capital we find the "deficits raise interest rates" complaint.

It supposedly happens like this: Big Government borrows to spend and get bigger. This reduces what private capital can borrow. When the much-abused capitalist tries to borrow, the interest rate (cost of credit) goes up and investment down.

The evidence contradicts this Tall Tale. If the interest rates and deficits chart suggests anything systematic, it is that a larger deficit goes with *lower* interest rates on public bonds.

The antigovernment crowd and the econfakers get it wrong because they live in a fantasy world in which resources are scarce, not in the real world of unemployment and idle capacity. Deficits grow when unemployment rises (see Fallacy 1). Resources fall idle because of lack of overall demand. Facing falling demand, businesses have no motivation to borrow, so commercial interest rates fall and the cost of borrowing for the public sector falls. In 2012 this debilitating process allowed the federal government to borrow at less than 1%.

uncontrollable enthusiasm of almost every Republican Party politician, and the lukewarm acquiescence of the vast majority of Democrats, for expenditure cuts to balance the federal budget? It shows the triumph of ideology over rational policy, the imposition of fantasy upon reality, achieved through the propaganda funded by the 1%.

Fear and Financial Market Loathing in the UK

The same fallacies that plague debate over economic policy in the US afflict Britain with equal force. The refutation of the assertions about the impact of deficits on private investment and inflation is the same story for the UK and the US (see Box: Deficit Fallacies in Britain).

The major fallacies of public finances in the US, reckless spending, inflation and crowding out, refer to allegedly direct and concrete consequences of deficits. The dominant fallacy in Britain and Continental Europe focused on "expectations," or what Paul Krugman named the "confidence fairy." The argument goes that deficits provoke fears in "financial markets" that the offending government will find itself unable to repay its debt at some time in the future. The date when this putative default will occur usually goes unspecified, which might be seen as a strength of the argument – "It could happen any time."

Assessing the real danger that the "financial markets strike back" requires a clear specification of the links from deficit to default. The full process must unfold as follows. A government finds that it must borrow in money markets in order to finance the excess of expenditure over revenue. The potential bond buyers assess the probability that the bond-issuing government might not honor its debt obligation. This failure to honor debts might take several forms: 1) refusal to repurchase a bond when it reaches its maturity date; 2) refusal to service fully a debt prior to maturity; or 3) refusal to pay now or at any time in the future (complete default).

Of these the last is the least likely, but not unknown. During the 1930s and 1940s several Latin American governments repudiated their foreign debts. These unambiguous defaults resulted either from the collapse of export prices during the Great Depression, physical disruption of international trade during World War II, or seizing the opportunity to abandon external debt when the creditors lacked the means to prevent it. More recently, the government of Argentina repudiated much of its debt in the early 2000s. The repudiation was part of a conscious strategy to eliminate the country's enormous debt burden in order to rejuvenate the economy after a disastrous collapse in 2000–2002 caused by faithful adherence to fakeconomic exchange rate policies. The debt default strategy proved extremely successful until the global financial crisis, when all Latin American countries suffered from the contraction of global demand.

No government of a developed country, in North America or Europe, would adopt such a strategy except under extreme duress. Perhaps the most important obstacle would be national integration into international financial markets, and the associated political power of financiers. In the developed countries the "riskiness" of public bonds arises from the alleged fear in "financial markets" that governments will borrow themselves into a debt position that reduces their ability to service that debt. To be explicit, the risk, thus the "fear in financial markets," would come from the expectation that a government would have no choice but to renege on debt payment obligations.

Under what circumstances might expectations of default be realized? I begin by specifying the circumstances that make it unlikely. The first and most obvious is that the country in question has its own currency. When it has its own currency, and almost every country outside the eurozone does, the government can fund expenditures by borrowing in its national money. This process requires a bit of elaboration to make its implications clear.

Governments borrow to finance expenditures in excess of revenues. Like businesses they borrow by selling bonds. When a government finances expenditures by sale of bonds to the private sector, the amount of money in the private economy does not change. The decrease that results from the sale (private sector money in exchange for public sector bonds) exactly equals the increase from the expenditures (government spending goes into private hands).

Government borrowing and spending without changing the amount of money in the private sector has its advantages and disadvantages. If the economy is near full capacity, the government may think that an increase in privately held money might generate inflationary pressures. If so, borrowing that leaves the amount of money unchanged is a plus. However, as frequently alleged and occurred in eurozone countries after 2010, bonds sales to private buyers could result in speculators pushing up interest rates.

As an alternative, the government can sell its bonds to the central bank, the Bank of England in the British case. This is called "monetization," because it both increases expenditure and puts an equal amount of money directly into circulation. Selling bonds in financial markets results in the former but not the latter. Critics attack monetization of all or part of deficit spending as equivalent to "running the printing presses." Not withstanding this simplistic propaganda, monetization has possible advantages. First, it avoids the potential problem of private buyers bidding up interest rates because the bonds do not go into financial markets. Second, when the economy is depressed, as in Britain after 2008, putting more expenditure and more money into the private

Deficit Fallacies in Britain

Fallacy 1: Deficits result from too much spending

GDP growth and changes in the UK deficit, 1992–2010

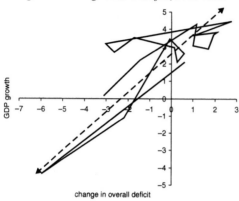

change in overall deficit

Line with arrowheads summarizes the overall relationship.
Source: UK Office of National Statistics.

As in the US, changes in the UK public sector deficit are closely linked to the economy's growth rate.

The relationship between the two is even closer for Britain than in the US because of the broader and more inclusive social support system. The simple two-way relationship is almost one-to-one. A percentage point increase in the growth rate causes a percentage point decrease in the deficit, and vice versa.

When the economy grows slower, the unemployment rate increases, and support payments increase, while tax revenue declines.

The increase in the UK deficit after 2007 resulted from recession reducing tax revenue and welfare expenditures linked to higher unemployment. QED.

Fallacy 2: Deficits raise interest rates and undermine the currency

UK government borrowing, interest rate on borrowing and the $/£ exchange rate

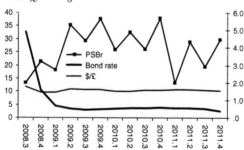

PSBr is public sector borrowing by month (left vertical axis, billions). The bond rate is the interest rate (percentage) on that borrowing and $/£ is the dollar–pound exchange rate (ratio), the last two on the right vertical axis.

Do deficits invoke the wraith of financial markets, causing fears of government default, which increase the cost of public borrowing? So claimed the UK coalition government in the early 2010s. The prime minister himself pointed to crisis-ravaged Greece as Britain's certain future unless the government cut expenditures.

Unluckily for the coalition argument, facts

> exist to test the accuracy of this prediction. The second chart shows the monthly borrowing of the UK government in billions of pounds from the beginning of the financial crisis until the end of 2011.
>
> The message from the numbers is simple and clear: no relationship. For over three years public sector monthly borrowing fell below £20 billion only once (January 2011), with large month-to-month changes. Through all of that borrowing, the public sector borrowing rate remained constant at about 0.5%, and the pound exchange rate to the US dollar hardly changed.

economy makes good sense. In effect, monetization represents a more effective form of stimulating demand than the famous "quantitative easing," in which a central bank transfers funds to the private sector without public expenditure.

What does all this have to do with whether and when public bonds are risky? The answer should be obvious. When a country has its own currency, the government has the option of funding any expenditure, including debt service, by monetization. Because it can borrow from itself, the UK government need never default on debt denominated in pounds. The same applies to any other country with a national currency.

But wait. Surely this self-borrowing would itself raise the hackles of "financial markets," pushing interest rates on privately held debt through the roof. Perhaps, but the likelihood of this happening depends on a second characteristic of countries – the size of the economy. For example, the net UK public debt at the end of 2011 had reached 77% of GNP, which was £1,250 billion. By contrast, the Irish public debt, a substantially higher 96% of GDP, weighed in at only £121 billion.

A degree from the Harvard or London Business Schools is unnecessary to infer that speculating on Irish bonds is likely to be more effective than speculating on UK debt. A *New York Times* article of 3 August 2012 reported that one speculator with the Royal Bank of Scotland traded £3 billion of eurobonds every day. If launched against the Emerald Isle this daily amount would hit almost 2.5% of Ireland's gross debt and over 20% of its new borrowing for 2012.

With all this in mind, a national currency and size of the economy, no one should suffer surprise that the public bond rates of the US, UK and Japan showed no increase during 2010–2012, when bond speculation ravaged the eurozone countries. The absence of noticeable speculators' attack against the bonds of these three countries had a further cause. A speculator must hold his or her attack cash in some relatively secure form, which represents the mirror image of the asset under attack. In the 2010s the leading candidates for holding speculative caches were US dollars, UK pounds and Japanese yen. A speculator cannot hold his or her currency and speculate on it too.

A bit of common sense and real economics, not fakeconomics, allows a simple assessment of UK public finances. First, the post-2008 deficits resulted from recession, not reckless or feckless spending. Second, the deficits did not and would not provoke speculative attack either on public bonds or the UK pound. Third, no expenditure cuts were necessary for "sound public finance." On the contrary, rational policy would bring more expenditure, to stimulate the private economy to recover.

An informed, objective person could not fail to be shocked by the ignorance and/or duplicity of UK politicians and the media in their presentation of a faux crisis of public finances in the "green and pleasant land." And the worst manifestation of this ignorance is yet to come, in the madness into which the eurozone politicians descended after 2008.

Great Euro Scam

The crisis of the euro currency zone provides an excellent example of the successful conversion of flagrant misrepresentation into accepted wisdom. Almost every generalization about the crisis found in the mainstream media was false. As a result of successful sale of these falsehoods, the alleged need for "austerity" entrenched itself in the public mind throughout Europe, bringing unprecedented peacetime misery to the 99%.

The mainstream narrative told a simple story. Unlike the fiscally sound government of Germany, several EU governments, most of them on the southern periphery of the EU, for years grossly mismanaged their finances. Excessive social expenditures represented the typical form of this mismanagement, far beyond what these countries could afford. The weight of the welfare state left these countries uncompetitive in global markets due to artificially high labor costs. In addition to salaries artificially inflated by unions and minimum wages, labor costs escalated because of short working hours, generous unemployment benefits and early retirement. The phrase "labor market rigidities" summarizes these excesses.

To state it in a right-wing nutshell, the welfare state caused the euro crisis. Overcoming the crisis required drastic reduction of public provision throughout the EU, especially in the so-called periphery. The skeptic could allegedly find proof of the urgent need for spending cuts in the excessive debts and deficits of the countries suffering from speculative attack on their bonds (Portugal, Ireland, Italy, Greece and Spain – the

"PIIGS"). We could find the mirror image of the PIIGS misbehavior in the fiscal virtue of the few countries not under attack, most notably Germany, but also Austria and Finland. According to the mainstream narrative, in the European South people were paid too much, worked too little, received excessive public benefits and retired too young.

The culprits in approximate ordering of their "crises" measured by when their cost of borrowing substantially increased were Greece (May 2010), Ireland and Portugal (July 2010), Spain (November 2010), and Italy (mid-2011). The enforcement of fiscal propriety upon these miscreants fell to a coalition of the virtuously willing consisting of the he European Commission, European Central Bank and the IMF, the so-called Troika (with the Deutsche Bundesbank making it Troika-plus-one).

For those not familiar with the byzantine intricacies of the EU, I should explain that the original members created the "Commission" half a century ago to function as the executive branch of the country grouping. Despite being unelected, some of the 27 "commissioners," one for each member country, enjoyed extraordinary powers, including the enforcement of governments to a set of ill-conceived fiscal guidelines established in a 1992 agreement. These misguidelines are commonly known as the Maastricht Treaty after the rather small city in the Netherlands where negotiations and the signing occurred.

Two of the Maastrichtian (as in "Faustian") guidelines stand out. First, that no EU member should have an overall fiscal deficit in excess of 3% of GNP, and no gross public debt more than 60% of GNP. The technically incompetent use of the overall deficit instead of primary, and the gross debt instead of the net, resulted from the insistence of the central bank of Germany, Deutsche Bundesbank. The preference of Bundesbank officials for these dysfunctional measures arose from the conviction that no government other than a German one could be trusted in matters of fiscal and monetary policy.

The primer on calculating deficits and debt in Chapter 7 showed the dysfunctional nature of such guidelines. Simple arithmetic demonstrates that a deficit of 3% implies for most countries a very small negative or near-zero primary balance (overall deficit minus interest on the public debt). This means funding public investment out of current expenditure. Funding any investment from current expenditure makes sense only if you believe that the investment has a zero rate of return, in which case it should not be funded at all.

As for the public debt rule, Spain demonstrates the absurdity of using the gross measure. In 2010, Spain breached the 60% limit, with its public debt weighing in at 67% of GDP. However, the government's liquid assets, such as foreign currencies held by the central bank, reduced the true or net debt to barely 40%, better than Germany could claim. Nevertheless, the Triad demanded draconian budget cuts of the Spanish government, not the German.

No matter how foolish these fiscal rules of the European Union are, after so many culprits fell into crisis mode the possibility of a system-wide problem might have occurred to the austerity enforcers. On the contrary, with each new casualty of the crisis, the Triad became more convinced of its own virtue and obligation to oversee the redemption of the fiscal sinners, even as crises continued to appear with alarming regularity.

Reference to reality revealed the central problem with this diagnosis and austerian remedy for the euro crisis. It was false on all counts, left, right and center. To begin with the most obvious fallacy, the crisis-hit countries did not have excessive social protection or high social expenditure. For example, in the early 2010s the retirement age for the state pension was the same for men in Germany, France and each of the PIIGS, 65, though in Italy and Greece women could take their pensions at 60. As for short working hours in the crisis-hit countries, the opposite was true. In 2007, the last year before the global crisis hit and depressed employment, the average number of annual working hours per employee in Germany was less than 1500 (about 30 a week). Average annual hours in every crisis-hit country stood well above this, from 15% more in Ireland to over 40% for Greek workers (see Box: Euro fallacy 1).

If social expenditure explained the fiscal deficits in the eurozone countries, German public finances would be on life support. At 25% of national product, German social spending exceeds that of all the putatively spendthrift PIIGS (see Box: Euro fallacy 2). If the peripheral PIIGS were not guilty of lack of competitiveness due to excessive social expenditure or short working hours, how do we explain their excessive public debts and unmanageable fiscal deficits?

The answer is simple. The debts were not excessive and the deficits were not unmanageable. An essential element in the mainstream narrative was German government fiscal prudence, and, by implication, of Germans in general. Were this prudence true, we would expect to find Germany with the smallest public debt of the eurozone, or, at the very least, smaller than the debts of the five misbehaving PIIGS.

The facts show it larger than that of Ireland and Spain, and the same as for Portugal until 2005 (see Box: Euro fallacy 3).

Those who know German might recall that the word *schuld* means both "debt" and "guilt." With this in mind, Germans would feel *schuldiger* (more guilty) than the Spanish in all years after 2001, than the Irish until 2010, and the same as for the Portuguese until 2006. The German government's debt management looked relatively better than that of the PIIGS because the German economy suffered less from the global economic crisis at the end of the 2000s, not Teutonic self-discipline. Why the German economy did better will soon become clear.

Much the same analysis holds for public sector balances. Again, two governments, of Ireland and Spain, could claim fiscal balances considerably "better" than Germany's until the crisis hit (see Box: Euro fallacy 4). Even more shocking to Northern European self-respect, the allegedly free-spending Italians consistently matched the deficit of the German government, before, during and after the crisis (and the Portuguese government gave the Germans a serious challenge until 2009).

What happened around 2007 to make the German government a winner with its finances and the PIIGS a bunch of losers? The answer resides in what I have argued for several chapters. Growth reduces deficits, not "fiscal prudence." In 2008 the five PIIGS and Germany had the same severe recession. Germany and Italy suffered the largest contractions, with their national products a full 7% lower in the first quarter of 2009 than 12 months earlier. After the beginning of 2009, one country suffered drastic decline (Greece), others contracted but considerably less than Greece (Ireland, Italy, Portugal and Spain), and Germany *grew*. Germany was the only country of the six with a national income higher at the end of 2011 than it was at the beginning of 2009. Germany grew and its deficit declined. The others contracted and their deficits increased. Grow and the deficit declines – not rocket science but first-year economics (rather than first-year fakeconomics).

Why did the German economy grow and the others contract? The answer clearly presents itself, except to the austerity enthusiasts. The German government had for over a decade implemented a beggar-thy-neighbor, export-led growth policy. In the last years of the 1990s, the Social Democratic government of Chancellor Gerhard Schroder struck an unsavory deal with the large German trade unions to freeze real wages. This freeze continued through the 2000s under the right-wing

Euro fallacy 1: Lazy PIIGS

Annual working hours in six EU countries, 2007 (private sector)

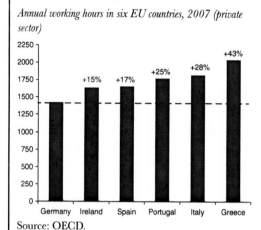

Source: OECD.

Whatever its original intent, the frequently used "PIIGS" for the five most crisis-hit eurozone countries carried an unambiguously negative connotation. It suggests more than a hint of feckless behavior, as well as absence of the Germanic work ethic.

In terms of hard facts, the PIIGS scored considerably better for dedication to work that any Northern European country. Employed Germans worked about 1500 hours a year, or about 30 hours a week. Closest to the German working year were Ireland and Spain, 15–17% higher, then Portugal and Italy more than 25% greater.

The long working hours award went to Greece, with an average of 2038 a year, more than 40 hours a week. In the EU only 3 of the other 26 countries came close to this: Estonia at 1999, Hungary at 1983 hours, and Poland with 1976 hours. Aversion to work was not a Greek malady.

Euro fallacy 2: High social spending in the PIIGS

Public sector social spending in six EU countries, 2007 (% of GNP)

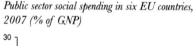
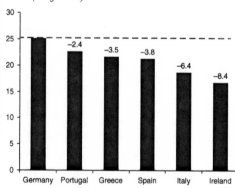

Source: OECD.

The suggestion that the fiscal sins of the PIIGS might include excessive social expenditures betrayed impressive ignorance. None of the five came close to qualifying as a "welfare state." This distinction applies to Northern Europe, not Southern.

Just before the onset of the global crisis, the ranking in descending order of EU countries by the share of social expenditure in GDP was France, Sweden, Denmark, Austria, Belgium and Germany (number 6 of 27). The average for the 27 EU countries was 22%. Only one of the five PIIGS was higher than the average (Italy).

Euro fallacy 3: Germany, the paragon of prudence

Gross public debt of the PIIGS minus that of Germany, 1998–2011 (debt/GDP)

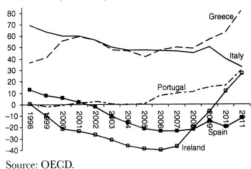

Source: OECD.

In German the same word means "guilt" and "debt" (*schuld*). The public debt chart shows that until 2010, the economy of Germany carried more *schuld*, perhaps in both senses, than either Spain or Ireland, and about the same as Portugal until 2006. Even during the crisis the Spanish debt remained considerably lower.

The sudden increase in the Irish debt had a simple explanation: bank bailout, not feckless spending on welfare. As for Italy, its debt declined continuously relatively to Germany's. The *schuld* was not limited to the PIIGS.

Euro fallacy 4: Low deficits in Germany

Overall fiscal balances of the PIIGS minus the German balance, 1994–2011 (percentage of GDP)

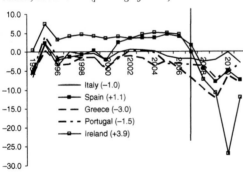

Source: OECD.

The deficit story follows the script for public debt. During 1998–2007, both Ireland and Spain showed greater "fiscal prudence" than Germany, and Italy's balance closely tracked Germany's.

So, did the Spanish, Irish and Portuguese governments throw caution to the wind and let spending go wild? Yes, they did, spending on bank bailouts. As for Italy, the government stubbornly refused to live up to its feckless reputation, maintaining a deficit close to Germany's for all the years.

As for infamously irresponsible Greece, through 2007 it was within 3 percentage points of Germany.

We have a simple story, but beyond the comprehension of the IMF, the European Commission, and the German government. Recessions cause deficits to increase, and increasing deficits cause increasing debt, all the more if the governments bailout the private sector.

Christian Democrat government led by Angela Merkel. To enhance that zero-sum strategy for the eurozone, in the mid-2000s the Merkel government changed tax policy with the *de facto* result of subsidizing exports.

As a result of a real wage freeze and tax changes, real wage costs rose in the other eurozone countries, but not in Germany. The consequence of the growth of German productivity faster than wages proved both dramatic and quick. In 2000–2001 Germany, France and the PIIGS all had small trade surpluses or small deficits, approximately converging. An extraordinary change occurred after 2001. Germany began to accumulate enormous surpluses, acquiring the world's largest net trade balances in some years and second largest in the others (behind China). During 2002–2007, Germany piled up a cumulative six-year surplus of $867 billion, while the PIIGS accumulated a collective deficit of $411 billion. The only one of the five PIIGS with a positive balance for the six years was Ireland (see Box: Beggar Thy Neighbor in the Eurozone). Leaving out Ireland, the remaining PIGS accumulated a deficit of $555 billion. During the three years after the global financial crisis, 2008–2010, Germany kept piling on the surplus ($523 billion), and the PIIGS kept going south (minus $623 billion).

The fakeconomics narrative tells us that inefficiencies generated by the welfare state caused the euro crisis, and the solution required public sector spending cuts. In reality German trade policies caused the euro crisis. German mercantilism provided the "backstory" of the euro crisis, a beggar-thy-neighbor trade policy. Through tight monetary and fiscal policy combined with wage restraint, the German government successfully achieved export-led growth. No need to be an expert in economics to know that success in export-led growth by one country will result in import-led recessions for the trading partners when global demand declines, as it did after 2007.

Even if the eurozone story were one of excessive fiscal deficits driving countries into ruin, the solution would be growth, not expenditure cuts. But deficits and debt were not the correct story. The eurozone sank into economic quicksand because of the aggressive and self-serving policies of the government of its largest member. Until that member changed to a cooperative trade policy, willingly or dragged kicking and screaming, the eurozone would be a disaster foretold.

But, didn't the Germans deserve their growth success, generated by sacrifice and self-discipline? No. It was the 99% in Germany that sacrificed and the 1% that gained, growth by freezing living standards of the vast majority. Would you want to run the global economy that way? The 1% wants to and has been doing so for decades.

99% in Thrall to the 1%

Complexity typically characterizes social and economic problems, and simple solutions are elusive. The Great Recession of the 2010s and the global financial crisis of 2008 that caused it are exceptions. The abandonment of public sector restrictions on private finance provides the simple answer for the financial crisis. This regulatory surrender resulted in the inexorable rise of the economic and political power of financial interests. In the economic sphere, financial capital asserted domination over industrial capital, speculation over production, the unproductive over the productive.

The disasters resulting from deregulation of finance, striking first in the US and soon to follow in Europe, did not, strictly speaking, involve the law of unintended consequences. Hopes of facilitating speculation and other unproductive activities motivated banking deregulation, hopes realized beyond the wildest dreams of the lords of finance. From a relatively dull and not very profitable activity in the 1960s, banking transformed itself by legal means into a disastrously parasitic and viral vehicle for profit taking and global instability.

The liberation of finance from its cage of regulatory bars might be likened to setting a greedy wolf loose in a pasture of sheep. Had strict regulation continued, the financial crisis of 2008 would remain in the realm of airport novels, fun for those who enjoy horror stories. It would have been as technically impossible as the storm in the 2004 film *Day after Tomorrow* that in a matter of days brings on a new Ice Age. Thanks to deregulation, we find ourselves in a Financial Ice Age, which perverts the profit drive into speculation rather than production.

Without financial deregulation I doubt that anyone, even an imaginative novelist, would have conjured up a story remotely as disaster-laden as the eurozone crisis. In 1970 German chancellor Willy Brandt made the first concrete plan for a common currency among the countries of the then European Community, the Werner Plan (named after Pierre Werner, prime minister of Luxembourg). Brandt proposed 1980 for its realization. Had its creation come then, with the Western European financial restrictions of the time, we

Beggar-thy-Neighbor in the Eurozone

Two images of the same thing: Mercantilism

Trade balances of Germany and PIIGS, US$ bns, 2000–2011

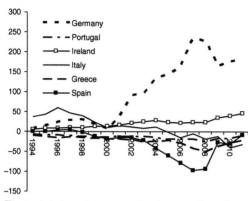

The trade balance is exports minus imports of goods and services.
Source: OECD.

Mirror image: Trade balances of Germany and PIIGS, US$ bns, 2000–2011

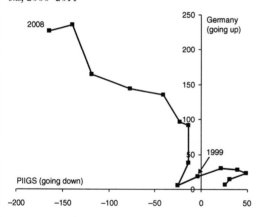

The balance for Germany is the vertical axis and for the five PIIGS the horizontal axis.

Adam Smith and David Ricardo, the two great founders of English political economy, dedicated themselves to attacking the policy of governments seeking trade surpluses.

Here we are 200 years later, and German governments have yet to get the message. At the beginning of the 2000s, the German trade balance was close to zero. In 2008 it reached $227 billion. The balance for the PIIGS went the other way, from a tiny minus $4 billion in 1999, to minus $164 billion in 2008.

The secret of German "success"? Freeze wages and reduce taxes on exports, among other things. Both of these contradict the spirit and/or the regulations of the EU.

A glance at the trade balance chart shows another "success," Ireland, with a constantly increasing trade balance. On closer inspection, Ireland-the-trade-success becomes Ireland-the-human-welfare-disaster. In 2007 Ireland's trade balance was 5% of national income. In 2011 with national income 10% *lower*, the trade surplus had risen to over 20% of GDP. What the Irish exported they could not eat, wear or otherwise use themselves. These two numbers, GDP down 10% and the trade surplus up to 22% of GDP, means that in 2011 the goods and services available to people in Ireland was 30% lower than in 2007. That's success?

A "beggar-thy-neighbor" policy involves a government subsidizing exports and restricting imports. A wage freeze helps achieve this. In other countries workers benefit from increasing productivity with rising living standards. Not in the wage freeze country. There companies export the benefits of rising productivity to be more "competitive," until the other country sinks into recession due to its trade deficit.

A wage freeze limits the demand for imports, thus "improving" the trade balance both ways.

Does it work? Have a look at the chart showing the rapid rise of the German trade balance after 1999, and, at the same time, the PIIGS trade turning negative with a vengeance. It works.

---

could dismiss the suggestion of a continent-wide debt crisis, remote as a life-ending asteroid striking the earth – conceivable but of miniscule probability.

The power of finance changed the low probability into a near-certainty. Complementary to the speculation-driven crisis in Europe, the Great Recession created fiscal deficits in both Europe and North America. Financial capital had redesigned the political landscape in its own image. Once liberated, the wolf replaced both the sheepdog and the shepherd, to ensure that regulation would not return.

During the first half of the twentieth century two great European conflicts and a depression in-between racked Europe and North America. Out of these disasters came a postwar consensus, politically dominant in Western Europe and strong in the US. Peace and stability required strict regulation to prevent the excesses of capitalism that substantially contributed to those conflicts and the interwar depression. Christian Democrats and Social Democrats in Europe, Labour and the Conservatives in the UK, and Democrats and many Republicans in the US formed this consensus. Central to this consensus were severe limitations on financial capital.

Writing in the foremost economic publication of the time, the *Economic Journal*, in 1946 the British economist K. W. Rothschild summarized the consensus succinctly:

When we enter the field of rivalry between [corporate] giants, the traditional separation of the political from the economic can no longer be maintained. Once we have recognised that the desire for a strong position ranks equally with the desire for immediate maximum profits we must follow this new dual approach to its logical end.

Fascism…has been largely brought into power by this very struggle in an attempt of the most powerful oligopolists to strengthen, through political action, their position in the labour market and vis-à-vis their smaller competitors, and finally to strike out in order to change the world market situation in their favour.

The deregulation of financial capital brings us full circle, and even more so, into a downward spiral. We have entered a time when financial giants have the power not only to change the world market situation in their favor, but the world itself, and they have done it with amazing speed to the detriment of the 99%.

Chapter 10

ECONOMICS OF THE 99%

Wealth Accumulates and Democracy Decays

Ill fares the land, to hastening ills a prey,
Where wealth accumulates, and men decay:
Princes and lords may flourish, or may fade;
A breath can make them, as a breath has made;
But a bold peasantry, their country's pride,
When once destroyed can never be supplied.

...

But times are altered; trade's unfeeling train
Usurp the land and dispossess the swain;
(Oliver Goldsmith, *The Deserted Village*, 1770)

The enforcement of fiscal austerity qualifies as the single most important public policy consequence of the abandonment of economics in favor of fakeconomics. Acceptance of austerity by the public in almost every major advanced country is even more perversely impressive than the austerity itself. Anyone born after 1960 must find it hard to believe that once, long ago it seems, the belief in balanced budgets did not drive public finances, nor did governments agonize over and quake in breathless anticipation of the "verdict of financial markets" on their policy decisions.

The overthrow of rigor and common sense in what we once called the economics profession did not cause this seismic shift in the ideology of public policy. We can trace the chronology of causality quite clearly, especially in Britain and the US. The cause lies in the secular decline of trade union influence and the parallel rise in the power of capital. Aneurin ("Nye") Bevan, tireless Welsh campaigner for the rights of working people, stated the danger succinctly. Unless the working majority organizes to prevent it, "it is an axiom, enforced by the experience of the ages, that they who rule industrially will rule politically." In the twenty-first century we can replace "industrially" with "financially."

The influence of trade unions declined, beginning in the 1970s in the US and in the 1980s in Britain, as a direct result of concerted attacks by employers. These attacks came most obviously in legislation to make organizing more difficult and bargaining rights harder to obtain and defend. In 2012 the UK journalist Polly Toynbee, who had left the Labour Party in the early 1980s in part due to anxieties about excessive union strength, accurately captured the consequences of union decline:

> The late 70s saw the most equal time in British history, but since then the rich have got richer and the poor poorer. The City [of London, the world's largest financial center] burst its bounds in the 1980s, its hubris still unabashed by scandal, far mightier than mere politicians. Strong unionism had its dysfunctions, but unions prevented the explosion in unfair pay that followed their abrupt decline.

But perhaps the clearest and most powerful contemporary statement of the consequences of declining unionism in the US comes from Jeff Faux, former director of one of the only progressive think tanks in the US (the Economic Policy Institute).

> With [union and New Deal] protections gone or greatly diminished, class lines will harden and social mobility in America – already below that of many other advanced nations – will decrease further. The humiliations of working life under raw capitalism before the New Deal will return. Bosses will be more arrogant and demanding. Overworked bureaucrats at shrunken government agencies will be less responsive. The distinction between service and servitude will blur.

The decline of trade union membership and the associated increase in the wealth of the 1% brought on a malady even more serious than income stagnation: the decline of democracy itself. As John F. Kennedy said while president, "Those who would destroy or further limit the rights of organized labor – those who cripple collective bargaining or prevent organization of the unorganized – do a disservice to the cause of democracy."

The unregulated rise of markets undermines democracy through two interrelated processes enabled by the deregulation of capital. First, so-called free markets result in rising inequality in income and wealth. This increasing inequality itself leads to fusion of political power with economic power, leaving the vast majority of the population without effective political voice as elections and politicians become commodities bought and sold.

"Free markets" themselves render it impossible to organize society in the interests of the many. The liberation of market forces establishes an antisocial tyranny that enforces its own version of Hobbes' "state of nature." Imagine that a foreign power attempted to convert the US or Britain into a political dependency in which that foreign power demanded the right to veto decisions of the democratically elected governments.

We require no strain of the imagination to conjure up such a nightmarish world. We live in it. In Britain and the US, politicians are told that the economic policies they would implement must receive the prior endorsement of "markets," a euphemism for financial capitalists. Far more powerful than any foreign country, these men and women (most of them the former) demand and receive the unlimited right to restrict the choices that both the electorate and the politicians can consider, much less implement. Not since the era of divine right of monarchs have populations suffered under the tyranny of such unaccountable power.

An example demonstrates the unrestrained dictatorship of finance, as well as the arrogance of those who wield its power. In 2008 almost all major banks in the US and the UK, and many in Continental Europe, teetered on the verge of collapse. Only the intervention of governments rescued these speculating utensils of the megarich from their own feckless behavior. For some of the most important of these miscreants, the US or UK government acquired majority ownership in the process of bailing them out.

In 1991 a similar banking crisis struck Sweden. With the support of the opposition Social Democrats, the conservative ("Moderate Party") government nationalized the Swedish banking sector and created the Banking Support Authority to bring financial decision making under public authority. Neither the UK nor the US government took any serious step towards asserting the obviously needed public control over the banks they *de facto* owned. The banks almost collapsed due to their own reckless speculation. Governments rescued them but took no serious step towards controlling their obviously unreliable behavior. In addition, neither the UK or the US government prosecuted anyone for these financial crimes.

In Spain the failure to take control of the financial sector descended into farce, albeit a farce that devastated the 99%. True to their inner nature as houses of speculation, major Spanish banks entered the US "subprime" mortgage market with gusto. When the global financial crisis brought them to the brink of bankruptcy, the social democratic government of Spain saved them through recapitalizing their asset base. As in the UK and the US, the Spanish government did not assume control, which resulted in a textbook case of "no good deed goes unpunished." The refunding of the banks switched the Spanish fiscal balance from surplus to deficit in 2008. The bankers used the their gift from the Spanish public to speculate on the bonds that had saved them. This speculation brought down the socialist government and was the direct cause of the rising interest rates that prompted the new, right-wing government's austerity policies.

Whether the financiers themselves designed these betrayals of the public, or the governments created and implemented it themselves, is of little importance. If the former, some limited hope exists for change. But more likely is that the president and Congress in the US, the prime minister and Parliament in Britain, and the allegedly left-of-center Spanish socialists did it on their own, needing little prompting. An institution's power approaches hegemony when it no longer need issue orders, but can rest assured that its underlings voluntarily act as expected of them. We have reached that point in most of the advanced world where all major politicians know their place and function under the rule of finance.

Democracy in the advanced countries remains alive, but severely restricted. From the last years of the twentieth century onwards, the troglodyte Right in the US labored hard to restrict the right to vote in hope that this would bring electoral victories to the overwhelmingly Caucasian Republican Party. Venal as this antidemocratic strategy may be, it pales to the point of the ludicrous alongside the success of financial interests in reducing democracy to a sham. For the bankers voting serves as no more than a sideshow. Elections are marginal events that they can buy and sell with their massive riches. Will Rogers, perhaps the greatest American political comedian quipped, "A fool and his money are soon elected," which in the twenty-first century might be enhanced as "a fool and his financial sector backers are sure of election."

Strikes, Unions and Earnings, USA 1964–2010

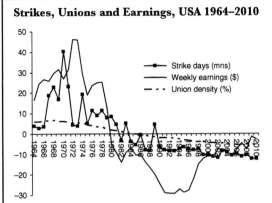

People must fight to protect their incomes. If you need convincing, look at the chart. Inflation-adjusted average weekly earnings of all US employees hit their peak in 1972. They have been below their 50-year average since 1980 (30 consecutive years). The association between the continuous fall until 1993 and the equally continuous decline of strikes is obvious.

Guide: Each line is the year's value minus the average for all years as a percentage of the average. For example, weekly earnings equaled their average for all years in 1980. Earnings are measured in prices of 1982–84.
Source: *Economic Report of the President* (2012) and Bureau of Labor Statistics, US Department of Labor.

After 1993 earnings began a slow recovery as the decline in strikes slowed down. But in 2010 earnings still remained below the average for the 46 years, and almost 20% below their peak in 1972 (over *forty* years ago!).

Inflation-adjusted earnings reached $342 per week in 1972, with an average for the 46 years of $296. Days lost to strikes hit a maximum of 52.8 *million* working days in 1970, falling to 302 *thousand* in 2010, less than 1% of the peak value. Meanwhile, the proportion of private and public workers in trade unions ("union density") declined from its high of 23% in 1968, to barely 10% in 2010.

Fakeconomics and Class Struggle

> The institution of a leisure class has emerged gradually during the transition from primitive savagery to barbarism; or more precisely, during the transition from a peaceable to a consistently warlike habit of life.
>
> (Thorstein Veblen)

The current mainstream of the economics profession, what I call fakeconomics, faithfully serves the rich and the powerful. Even those among the econfakers of good will and good intentions do so. Perhaps even more than self interest, the theoretical method of fakeconomics dictates an antisocial worldview. Frequently the political Right accuses progressives of preaching and advocating class struggle. This is false. The Right advocates class struggle, and fakeconomics carries class conflict as a central, distinguishing characteristic.

Fakeconomics, the current mainstream, carries a simple message: dog eat dog, and the 1% hound far outweighs the 99% mutt. The analytical dismantling of the Law of Supply and Demand reveals that message. All fakeconomics generalizations derive from the assumption of "scarcity," the generalization that resources are fully employed. From this assumption it necessarily follows that one person can have more of a good or service only by accepting less of another.

Transubstantiated from products to people, this means that the economy operates as a zero-sum game. At any moment, one person can enjoy a higher income only by someone else suffering a lower income. As I explained in an early chapter, introductory textbooks define the "economic problem" as the attempt by people to satisfy unlimited wants with scarce resources. This definition of economics carries a simple message: "Grab what you can before someone else does, because there is only so much to go around."

The word "individual" functions as a central element to disguise the class message in fakeconomics. The textbooks, the professional commentators on economic events and the media in all its forms tell us that markets provide for individual choice, for the individual to pursue his or her personal ambitions and dreams, and that a great body of theory supports this benign interaction between individuals and markets.

The common belief that current mainstream economics provides a theory of individual behavior is wrong. No individuals exist in this theory. All "microeconomics," the study of markets, proceeds analytically by use of stereotyped and uniform behavior, captured in the term "representative agents." The theory creates the "representative consumer," the "representative worker" and the "representative firm."

How do we encapsulate a theory in which a homogenous collection of workers faces a homogenous collection of employers? If this does not qualify as a theory of class struggle, what would? The trick is to disguise this theory of confrontation as harmony. Fakeconomics creates the disguise by adding to the faux individual its flexible and duplicitous use of the word "competition."

As I showed way back in Chapter 2, the reality of the famous saying from Welsh rugby sums up competition in markets: "Get your retaliation in first." In reality, as opposed to fakeconomics fantasy, unregulated competition disintegrates society into alienated and mutually suspicious individuals, and *de facto* divides these individuals along class lines. The degeneration of society into competitive individualism results not from human nature. It emerges slowly, as the 1% destroys the basis of social cooperation, through the ideology of the "individual" and the reality of a stagnant or declining standard of living.

In the 1980s British right-wing prime minister Margaret Thatcher showed great fondness for accusing those favoring greater income equality as practicing the "politics of envy." Fakeconomics contains the "politics of envy" in its purest form. Resources are scarce. Grab your share. Trust no one. And grab before the others do.

If, indeed, we face no alternative to a brutal world of unregulated markets in a world ruled by the lords of finance, the economy would without doubt function as a zero-sum game. In such a world the only choice is that found in the famous union song by Florence Reece, "Which Side Are You On?":

> You go to Harlan County
> There is no neutral there
> You'll either be a union man
> Or a thug for J. H. Blair.

To put it simply, fakeconomics offers the choice between its procapital version of the class struggle or the Marxian prolabor version. But another possibility exists. Human life need not follow the dictates of unregulated markets, "solitary, poor, nasty, brutish, and short."

Open Debate in Economics

Economics need not be the servant of the 1%. It has not always served the narrow interest of the rich and powerful and need not in the future. The conversion of 1% economics to the economics of the majority begins with the most fundamental premise: resources lie idle and economics has the task of explaining that idleness, then proposing public policies to end the waste of human skill and productive wealth.

Recognition of reality, that unemployment characterizes market societies except in rare moments, transforms economic analysis as profoundly as the replacement of alchemy with chemistry, of geocentric astronomy with heliocentric. This does not involve a choice between competing theories. Alchemy does not compete with chemistry to explain the composition and properties of matter. We do not need to produce an alternative to the current mainstream, but to rid ourselves of its pernicious dogma.

A reader might think me dogmatic and intolerant of alternative opinions. I hope this book has shown the contrary. In all fields differences of analysis emerge through intellectual inquiry. For example, some cosmologists continue to defend the steady state theory of the universe against the mainstream Big Bang framework. However, no cosmologist argues that the earth stands at the center of the universe and the stars hold stationary positions in the firmament. Analogously, historians debate fiercely the nature of New World slavery, but none any longer attributes it to the natural inferiority of the non-Caucasian races. On the contrary, most would reject the concept of "race" as a legitimate analytical category.

These examples indicate that over time both the physical and social sciences advance by discarding the demonstrably wrong, though we should not view this process as a purely intellectual one (as famously argued in Thomas Kuhn, *The Structure of Scientific Revolutions*, 1962). After eliminating the demonstrably wrong, debate should dissect and challenge what remains in a never-ending process. Maintaining and defending the demonstratively wrong is not tolerance, it embraces ignorance as equivalent to knowledge.

The current mainstream in economics proudly claims the astounding characteristic of holding to the same analytical framework for 150 years. The principle elements of this framework are scarcity (full employment), unlimited wants (hedonism) and rational behavior of individuals (atomized society), all achieving unchallengeable status by the end of the nineteenth century. Many economists, conservative, progressive and radical, sought to modernize and transform this anachronistic framework and render it relevant for industrial societies. A short list of progressives and radicals includes the Europeans Karl Marx, J. A. Hobson, J. M. Keynes, Michał Kalecki, Gunnar Myrdal and Joan Robinson; and the Americans Thorstein Veblen, John R. Commons and John Kenneth Galbraith. An equally short list of non-European progressives must include Raul Prebisch (Argentine), Makot Itoh (Japanese) and W. Arthur Lewis (Saint Lucian). At the top of the list of conservative modernizers is Joseph Schumpeter.

All these major thinkers shared an implicit or explicit rejection of the assumption of full employment as appropriate to market societies. Abandoning the full employment assumption and with it mainstream fakeconomics does not limit debate. On the contrary, it opens debate to progress, with progress now almost totally constrained by the full

"Keynesian" Economics and "Copernican" Astronomy

In the third century BC Aristarchus from the island Samos proposed that the earth circled the sun, rather than the other way around. Plutarch, writing 300 years later, tells us that contemporaries demanded he be charged with impiety for such heresy. While other ancient writers also proposed a heliocentric solar system, the view of Aristarchus made no headway. In the second century AD Claudius Ptolemy elaborated an internally consistent, though extremely complex, version of the geocentric system in his still-extant work the *Almagest* ("Treatise"). This model remained the basis of astronomy for over a thousand years. In 1543 Nicolaus Copernicus revived the heliocentric hypothesis and by the end of the following century no serious astronomer defended the Ptolemaic system.

The early economists Adam Smith ("invisible hand"), Thomas Malthus (population growth leads to general impoverishment) and David Ricardo (of "comparative advantage" fame) constructed their arguments in the context of idle resources. Karl Marx continued this approach, as did his contemporaries. However, in 1871 a book by William Stanley Jevons, *The Theory of Political Economy*, set the profession firmly on the full-employment analytical road. By the end of the century full employment gained ideological (if not intellectual) hegemony among those calling themselves "economists."

After World War I, as Britain and several other European countries suffered severe unemployment, with the US to follow in 1929, many in the economics profession sensed that the full-employment approach contradicted reality. Prominent among these were several Swedes (e.g., Knut Wicksell), Americans (e.g., John Maurice Clark), and the much neglected Michał Kalecki. The formal return to reality came in the famous book by J. M. Keynes, *The General Theory of Employment, Interest and Money* (1936), in which the word "general" refers specifically to the construction of theory beyond the special case of full employment.

The "Keynesian Revolution" proved short, over by the 1970s and virtually purged from the mainstream by a full-employment counterrevolution in the 1980s. Subsequently, those making analytical arguments within the context of idle resources would earn the designation "Keynesian economists." To my knowledge no astronomer refers to him- or herself, or anyone else, as a "Copernican."

The Copernican revolution in astronomy and the Keynesian revolution in economics, one victorious, the other defeated by counterrevolution.

employment straightjacket. When I and others advocate that economics jettison the dead weight of fakeconomics, this is little different from chemistry leaving the alchemists behind, the astronomers abandoning horoscopes, and genetics rejecting creationism.

When the econfakers fade to the margins, like astrologers buried in the newspapers next to the crossword puzzle and agony aunt columns, economics for the majority becomes possible. The econfakers found themselves on the margin of the profession throughout the world in the 1950s and 1960s. We can build on the scientific advances in economics during that brief period, plus the subsequent work of the outcasts and exiles, from narrowly technical "Keynesians" to radical Marxians.

I place "Keynesians" in quotation marks because the term is invariably misused by the econfakers and the media to refer to those who explain idle resources by the level of aggregate demand. This identification of all who address the problem of inadequate demand as "Keynesian" is the equivalent of identifying heliocentric astronomy as "Copernican."

Economics in a Decent Society

I begin the ending of this book with the appropriate definition of economics: "the study of the causes of the underutilization of resources in a market society, and the policies to eliminate that resource waste for the general welfare." Many ways to pursue that study present themselves. I shall focus on 1) the cause of unemployment, 2) the source of inequalities, and 3) policies to minimize these maladies consistent with the institutional and ownership structure of a market (capitalist) society.

In every advanced country many factors influence the composition of the unemployed, requiring a country-specific analysis. For example, in the US three important characteristics determine who is or is not unemployed: ethnicity, age and gender. In 2010 the civilian unemployment rate reached its highest level since the end of World War II, 9.8%. For those 16 to 19 years old unemployment climbed to an appalling 26%. Unemployment for the statistical category "white" stood slightly below the overall average, at 8.7%, compared to 16% for "black or African American."

At first glance the statistics indicate a lower unemployment rate for women than men, 8.6% compared to 10.5%. Here we have a clear case in which averages deceive, because the rate for married men with a spouse was only 6.8%, while for women heads of households the rate almost doubled, to 12.3%. In one of those ironies that thrives in market economies, the Great Recession actually compressed the inequalities in unemployment rates. For example, in the low unemployment year 2000, female household heads had suffered at a rate three times greater than that of males.

A clear message comes from America: if you are black, young and female with a family, the chances of unemployment are very high. Analogous unemployment inequality appears in the European countries, with different compositions of those suffering because of ethnic discrimination.

Whatever the composition of the unemployed at any moment, what determines the aggregate rate? Once we abandon the full-employment framework, the answer jumps off the page: the level of aggregate spending in the economy. In every economy spending has four sources, each with its own specific terminology. Households consume, businesses invest, exports respond to demand from other countries, and governments spend to provide public services, administration and defense. Each source has its specific motivations for spending and specific source of funding.

Household consumption is the largest component of aggregate demand, varying from 60% to 75% across countries. All but the richest households spend for consumption primarily from their current incomes, which come from their employment or public sector transfers when they are unemployed or retired. The great majority of the expenditure goes to day-to-day costs of food, transport and housing. In brief, household expenditures cover immediate necessities with current income.

The rest of aggregate demand consists of three components. Businesses spend on buildings and equipment, defined as "investment." Businesses fund this investment from their profits, through borrowing or by selling new equity shares. Anticipated profits provide the motivation for this spending. In contrast to households, businesses spend to create the capacity for future production, and go into debt to do so. Foreign demand derives from causes and motivations outside the influence of domestic households and businesses. Finally, public sector expenditure results from legislation – current and past.

I repeat these well-known relationships because they have important analytical and practical implications. Households with members holding jobs in the private sector receive their incomes when businesses successfully sell the goods and services the employees work to produce; i.e., household incomes derive from the revenue of businesses except for those households with members in public employment. The taxes paid by businesses and private sector employees also come from business revenue via wages and salaries. Over the medium term the growth of public revenue determines the growth of public employment.

Businesses, in turn, receive their revenue from sales to households, other businesses, overseas buyers and the public sector. First take on these relationships suggests that we have a loop. Most household expenditures, "consumption," come from business-generated income, but business revenue comes in great part from sales to households, consumption. How can household consumption serve as both a cause and a result of business sales revenue? The answer is quite simple. The spending outside this business-household-business loop determines the business revenue that generates the wages and salaries that make up most of household income.

To be more specific, export demand (coming from outside our economy), business investment (based on predictions about future sales) and public expenditure (set by legislation) via businesses determine household incomes and, therefore, household consumption (see Box: Demand and Incomes). Put the four together, the three independent sources of demand plus the dependent one, and we have total expenditure in our economy.

A simple way to understand the relationship between consumption and the other components of aggregate demand is that the former is *dependent* on current income while the latter are *independent* of current income. The vast majority of households, the 99%, has little choice but to tailor its current expenditure to its current income, except for large expenditures such as purchasing a house or an automobile. Even these purchases link closely to current income, as anyone who has sought a mortgage knows. The infamous subprime crisis arose because unscrupulous lenders weakened or abandoned the income link.

No rational businesses invest on the basis of their current incomes. An investment will have a productive life of many years or it would not be undertaken. Therefore, its motivation comes from anticipated future sales and profits. Exports are sold abroad with no link to domestic demand. As I explained in Chapter 7, public expenditure can be less (budget surplus) or more (budget deficit) than current public revenue. The balance between expenditure and revenue is a political decision guided by economic circumstances.

The relationship between the independent and the dependent shows that the idea of a "consumer-led growth" involves fundamental confusion. For example, on a BBC website we could read, "Because goods could be produced in greater numbers and at much lower prices, more people were able to afford them. This led to huge increases in the sales of products such as cars, refrigerators, radios and cookers."

People buying more goods because those goods are cheaper is, quite literally, impossible. Lower prices mean lower business income, lower business income means lower wages and salaries, lower wages and salaries result in lower consumption. No less nonsensical is the suggestion that an exit from the Great Recession could come from a "consumer-led recovery." From where would this net increase in household spending come?

It would not come from saving by households. Of the four largest advanced country economies in 2011 in only one, Germany, was the ratio of saving to household income after tax in double digits (10.4%). For the other three countries the saving rates were considerably lower, US (4.2%), Japan (2.9%) and the UK (6.0%). And these numbers use disposable income as the denominator, meaning that the ratio of household saving to GDP was lower still. For example, it falls to barely 3% for the US. When you add to this that the rich account for almost all household saving, the suggestion that any advanced economy would receive a substantial boost from "consumers" qualifies as fanciful.

However, could the "consumer-led recovery" come from borrowing? Indeed, it could, and that bit of neoliberal magic helped plunge us into the Great Recession. In 1990, with the US economy in recession (it lost George Bush I the election of 1992), household debt was about 90% of household income. It rose to over 160% in 2007 (look back at the Box: How Sovereigns Rule, in Chapter 5). We should hope that this version of a "consumer boom" has little chance of recurring.

What about an export-led recovery? When a country increases its exports, some other country or countries must increase imports. It takes no specialist knowledge to understand that every country could not successfully pursue an export-led growth strategy. More important than this obvious limit to the strategy, when a large country follows this strategy catastrophe follows in its wake. Germany presents an infamous and appalling example of what happens when a large country takes this route to growth, as demonstrated in Chapter 9. The euro crisis of the 2010s resulted directly from Germany's export-led growth.

In 2011 the US trade deficit weighed in at almost $750 billion, and the combined deficits of France and the UK totaled $265 billion. To put these numbers in perspective, the trade deficits of these three countries, all in recession in 2011, represented over 15% of the exports of all other countries in the world combined. An attempt by these three advanced countries to recover through exporting without importing would drive many other countries from a trade surplus into deficit, or deeper into deficit. The net-importing countries would fall into recession as they

---

Demand and Incomes: How the Private Economy Works (or Doesn't)

Spending prompts the production of goods and services. For households, the reverse is also true, but not for businesses. A market economy has three sources of demand that do not result from the current level of domestic income: foreign demand (obvious), domestic investment (based on future profits) and public spending (legislatively mandated).

Together, these determine simultaneously business revenue (sales), household income and household expenditure (consumption). In addition (and not shown in the diagram), a large portion of public expenditure goes directly to households that are employees of governments, retired and receiving pension payments, or unemployed and receiving unemployment insurance benefits. The two independent sources of domestic demand, public spending and private investment, are closely linked. Governments pay businesses to construct social and economic infrastructure, as well as to conduct research (military and health sector research are major examples).

More important, because its spending can compensate for declines in exports and investment within the private sector, governments have the ability to determine the overall level of prosperity. Expectations by businesses about the future are a major determinant of private investment demand. When governments successfully foster current prosperity, they give business expectations a boost.

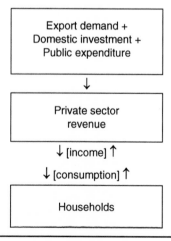

sought to reverse their own unsustainable trade balances. Exactly this happened in the eurozone in the 2000s. When economics talked sense instead of nonsense, we used the term "fallacy of composition" to describe export-led growth, or more forcefully, "exporting unemployment" and "beggar-thy-neighbor growth."

If "consumers" and foreign demand cannot extract us from recession, all we have left are business investment and public expenditure. If an increase in business investment offered a viable option we would never have dropped off the "growth cliff" into recession in the first place. By definition recessions occur when business optimism and investment plans collapse.

When export expansion brings false hope and the domestic private sector fails to generate growth, only the public sector remains. That is the economics of the 99%.

Implementing Economics for the 99%

At the level of the entire economy the public sector should function as the social institution responsible for maintaining full employment, so that everyone who wants a job can find one. A government that fails in this task qualifies for Roosevelt's description of Republican administrations during 1920–1932: "For twelve years this Nation was afflicted with hear-nothing, see-nothing, do-nothing Government. Powerful influences strive today to restore that kind of government with its doctrine that that government is best which is most indifferent."

Exactly this type of government held sway in most of the advanced countries at the end of the twentieth century and into the twenty-first, whatever the political parties in power called themselves. Keeping the economy close to full employment involves well-known policies practiced in the US by all presidents, Democrat or Republican, for 25 years, 1945–1970. The same was true for the UK and the countries of Western Europe, for considerably longer.

Public sector implementation of full employment needs no innovation, just an adaption of principles and practices well-known long before J. M. Keynes. The public sector increases its expenditure to achieve the level of aggregate spending that reduces unemployment to its practical minimum. As the economy recovers, the public sector scales back its spending to match the private sector increases.

The policy package is technically simple, easily implemented and as feasible in the twenty-first century as during the immediate post–World War II decades of the twentieth century. Governments stopped applying these policies because they abandoned the commitment to full employment, not because implementation became any harder or the need declined. As radical a change as it would appear in the twenty-first century, maintaining full employment only begins with the task of a government responding to the needs of the 99%.

A fully employed workforce with a large portion receiving wages inadequate to meet basic human and social needs does not serve the interest of the vast majority of working people. On the contrary, a low-wage, fully employed labor force might better meet the interests of the 1% than the scandal of unemployment in the advanced countries since the Great Recession. A society whose economic institutions function for the many, not the few, requires the public sector to design and implement policies for an equitable distribution of income with no person and no household below the poverty line.

Achieving equity without poverty involves more complicated design and imaginative implementation than reaching and maintaining full employment because of institutional and demographic differences among countries. Despite these differences and complexities a few generalizations stand out clearly. First and foremost, poverty *reduction* differs fundamentally from poverty *alleviation*. The latter involves reducing ("alleviating") the misery of the poor, while the former seeks to eliminate poverty itself.

The US "food stamp" program, later named the Electronic Benefit Transfer, which provides people with the means to purchase food and nonalcoholic drinks in supermarkets and fast food outlets, falls into the "alleviation" category. The British system of housing benefit also fits this category. At least two characteristics of these programs identify them as "alleviating": 1) they were income ("means") tested, so only those defined as poor receive them, and 2) they do not directly enhance the income-earning potential of the recipient.

Successful poverty-reduction programs enhance earning capacity and protect people against falling into poverty once out of it. For neoliberals education serves as the most important, sometimes their only, poverty-reduction mechanism. While educating people to enhance skills should occur in any decent society, it does not in itself reduce poverty. The newly skilled person must find a job with take-home pay above the poverty level, as well as enjoy protection against difficulties large and small that would provoke a return to destitution. Improving people's education may contribute substantially to poverty reduction in a society that provides healthcare for all, ensures a living wage and adequately supports workers when they fall into unemployment. Without full employment, a national health system, minimum wages and unemployment protection, more education only results in a more highly skilled population in poverty.

With very few exceptions, discrimination in its many forms presents a formidable barrier to poverty reduction even in a society with a national health system, wage floors and unemployment insurance. Ethnic and gender discrimination prevent people from full participation, resulting in inequalities that can and do include social banishment to poverty. Experience indicates that "market forces," however they are ideologically packaged, do not eliminate or even substantially reduce the economic effects of discrimination against ethnic groups. Obvious examples are African Americans in the US and the Romani in Europe. Because if anything "markets" make such discrimination worse, societies face no alternative to combating discrimination through direct legal imperatives (e.g., "affirmative action").

Discrimination against women in their work and throughout society characterizes all countries. Few people may realize how recently women achieved formally equal rights in the advanced countries. In Britain it was not until the Labour governments of 1945–1951 that women approached equal treatment under inheritance laws, as a result of the Married Women (Restraint upon Anticipation) Act of 1949.

While as severe as ethnic discrimination, simpler methods exist to reduce the denial of equal opportunities to women. These include a range of measures to make the care of children more gender balanced. In the Scandinavian countries work release for child rearing applies to both men and women. Parts of the Swedish Left argue for mandated equal distribution between father and mother of the guaranteed sixteen months "parental leave." In few other countries do the laws even approach this degree of antidiscrimination. In the US and Britain public sector provision of child care remains appallingly inadequate.

Antidiscrimination laws and restrictions themselves fall far short of ensuring equal access to the benefits of economic prosperity. As Jeff Faux, quoted above on the US trade union movement, once said to me, "In the United States your employer cannot fire you for being an African American, for being gay or for being too old, but can fire you for no reason at all." Effective pursuit of full employment and work place rights represents the necessary condition to reduce all forms of economic discrimination.

Eliminating ethnic and sex discrimination requires clarity in language in order not to implicitly endorse anachronistic stereotypes. We find a clear example of such implicit endorsement in the use by progressives of the term "working families," especially in the US. Whatever the user may mean by this term, many listeners would conjure up an image of two heterosexual parents with children. Even if the more tolerantly inclined included gay or lesbian parents in the image, the term remains inaccurate. Many people in the US and Europe do not live in "families" by any common interpretation of the word. But more important, what of the "nonworking families," the unemployed, pensioners and those unable to work due to physical and mental maladies?

In practice "working families" serves as a euphemism for "working class," and a potentially reactionary one. For example, David Cameron, the right-wing prime minister of Britain, has frequently referred to "hard-working families" who "do the right thing." He has sought to convey the not-so-subtle message that in contrast to "working families," out there lurk shirkers and slackers in dysfunctional "not-working families" that live on welfare, "doing the wrong thing," parasites on "hard-working families." This terminology has no place in a decent society.

Along with "working families" my fellow progressives in the US should abandon the term "people of color." This term is only a preposition and word transformation away from how Southern segregationists referred to African Americans when I grew up in Texas in the 1950s – the loathsome term "colored people." Society is not divided between the "normal," "colorless" European descendants and vast masses of "others" of "color." The implementation of the economics for the 99% requires an end to social categories that implicitly divide us between insiders and outsiders.

Discrimination represents but one of the many transgressions of fakeconomics against the welfare of society. Among its worst obfuscations for the future of humanity is its mistreatment of the gathering environmental disaster. Its method of analysis compares the cost of restrictions to protect our planet against the benefits of those restrictions. Many books devote themselves to demonstrating how this approach misleads and misinforms decision making in general. For the environment this so-called cost–benefit approach is completely inappropriate and pernicious.

"Cost–benefit" claims to calculate the "trade-off" between costs and benefits on the assumption that these apply to the entire range of possible outcomes. As a necessary condition, this type of calculation requires that the balance between costs and benefits remain constant for future changes small and large. This approach contradicts the scientific analysis and evidence on environmental change. For our climate, oceans and quality of the air itself, changes are not "marginal"; they do not involve "more of the same."

These are chaotic systems, in which repeated small changes, previously having no noticeable effect, suddenly produce a chaotic or catastrophic outcome. A frequently invoked example of a nonmarginal process is the common ocean wave. As the tide comes in, the surface of the water first produces increasing swells. The swells do not recede as they expand, but suddenly "break." The environment in general has this characteristic, such that the faux-scientific calculations of the econfakers not only suffer from irrelevance, they actively mislead us. The next little bit of pollution may not have the same social cost as the previous. It could bring catastrophe.

In a decent society people look after and protect their environment to render it sustainable. Economists, much less econfakers, provide little technical expertise for the protection of a sustainable environment. The same applies to the allocation of resources for different elements of healthcare, and levels and types of education. In a decent society allocation of these human necessities requires technical expertise to inform the public and its representatives in making these decisions.

It is unlikely that economists have much to contribute to that expertise. We should take seriously the suggestion of the greatest economist of the twentieth century: "If economists could manage to get themselves thought of as humble, competent people on a level with dentists, that would be splendid." We should consult doctors about medical care, not management of the economy. Substitute "economists" for "doctors" and reverse "medical care" and "the economy."

"Our Future Lies before Us"

> Let us never forget that government is ourselves and not an alien power over us. The ultimate rulers of our democracy are not a President and senators and congressmen and government officials, but the voters of this country.
>
> (Franklin D. Roosevelt)

In the early 1990s I suffered the unfortunate experience of attending a graduation ceremony at a small US college in New England.

The "commencement" speaker, typically enough for such institutions, was a businessman that college officialdom hoped would feel sufficiently flattered to become a generous donor. In the course of his not terribly notable keynote address, the speaker informed his young audience of eager graduates that "your future lies before you." Since our future is unlikely to lie behind us, it struck me that this phrase could qualify high on the league table of the banally vacuous.

Now, older if not wiser and attuned to my own banalities, I realize that I misjudged this minor robber baron ("robber baronet"?). In the important sense that we can to varying degrees design and affect things to come, our future does lie before us. A bright future for the vast majority would bring a society with no need of "safety nets" because the economic institutions would provide income, health and education for all.

My mother, born in 1905, with a grandfather who was a minor slave owner in Alabama before the Civil War, would hark nostalgically back to an allegedly genteel antebellum South, despite (or because of) laboring as a "shop girl" in a clothing store in segregated Austin, Texas. In these moments of reactionary nostalgia, she was wont to advise me as we sat in our rented house, "Making money does not befit a gentleman." Within this rather quaint and slightly absurd phrase lay a deep message, stated more eloquently by Keynes in his 1931 book, *Essays in Persuasion*:

> When the accumulation of wealth is no longer of high social importance, there will be great changes in the code of morals... The love of money...will be recognised for what it is, a somewhat disgusting morbidity, one of those semi-criminal, semi-pathological propensities which one hands over with a shudder to the specialists in mental disease.

The economics of the 99% can take us there.

NOTES

Preface

xi   **"they don't need a priest to read the Bible"**: See the Texas State Historical Association biography of Robert Hargrove Montgomery, available online at http://www.tshaonline.org/handbook/online/articles/fmodd (accessed 22 November 2013).

Introduction

xiii   **"to move in the opposite direction"**: Albert Einstein, quoted in *British Medical Journal* 319 (1999): 1102.

xiv   **"managed to survive"**: John Kenneth Galbraith, *A History of Economics: The Past as the Present* (New York: Penguin, 1989), 260.

xv   **"cut $1.3tn"**: Heidi Moore and Dominic Rush, "The Fiscal Cliff Explained: What to Know about the Biggest Story in Washington," *Guardian*, 27 November 2013. Online: http://www.theguardian.com/world/2012/nov/27/fiscal-cliff-explained-spending-cuts-tax-hikes (accessed 10 October 2013).

Chapter 1

1   **"This paper, then, is a serious analysis of a ridiculous subject"**: Paul Krugman, "Theory of Interstellar Trade," (1978). Online: http://www.princeton.edu/~pkrugman/interstellar.pdf (accessed 10 October 2013).

1   **"Do not be alarmed by simplification"**: John Kenneth Galbraith, *The Age of Uncertainty* (New York: Andre Deutsch, 1977), 8.

2   **"forms that have been tried"**: *Parliamentary Debates*, Commons, 11 November 1947, vol. 444, col. 207.

3   **"truck, barter and exchange"**: Adam Smith, *An Inquiry into the Nature and Causes of the Wealth of Nations* (New York: Cosimo, 2010, first published in 1776), bk 1, ch. 2, par. 1. Online: http://www.econlib.org/library/Smith/smWN.html (accessed 12 November 2013).

3   **"Oh wait, I guess I just did"**: Paul Krugman, "A Dark Age of Macroeconomics (Wonkish)," *New York Times*, 27 January 2009. Online: http://krugman.blogs.nytimes.com/2009/01/27/a-dark-age-of-macroeconomics-wonkish (accessed 10 October 2013).

4   **"The difficulty lies, not in the new ideas, but in escaping from the old ones"**: J. M. Keynes, *The General Theory of Employment, Interest and Money* (London: Macmillan, 1935), preface.

9   **"higher income neighbourhoods"**: Phillip R. Kaufman, James M. MacDonald, Steve M. Lutz and David M. Smallwood, *Do the Poor Pay More for Food? Item Selection and Price Differences Affect Low-Income Household Food Costs* (Washington: USDA, 1997). Online: http://www.ers.usda.gov/Publications/AER759/ (accessed 13 November 2013).

14 **"That's some catch, that Catch-22"**: Joseph Heller, *Catch-22* (New York: Simon & Schuster, 1961).

15 **"what I tell you three times is true"**: Lewis Carroll, *The Hunting of the Snark: An Agony in Eight Fits* (London: Macmillan, 1876).

15 **"crier" would announce prices**: Scarlett History of Economic Theory and Thought, "Leon Walras Biography – (1834–1910) General Equilibrium Model," June 2008. Online: http://www.economictheories.org/2008/06/leon-walras-biography-general.html (accessed 10 October 2013).

15 **"interest of the society"**: Adam Smith, *The Theory of Moral Sentiments* (1759), pt. 4, ch. 1. Online: http://www.econlib.org/library/Smith/smMS.html (accessed 13 November 2013).

16 **"different times in their lives"**: Barbara Bergmann, "Abolish the Nobel Prize for Economics," *Challenge* 42, 2 (1999): 52–3.

16 **"cheeringly optimal processes"**: Ibid., 55–6.

17 **"While they prate of economic laws, men and women are starving"**: Democratic Party Convention, Chicago, 2 July 1932.

Chapter 2

19 **"People of the same trade seldom meet together"**: Adam Smith, *An Inquiry into the Origin and Causes of the Wealth of Nations* (New York: Cosimo, 2010), bk 1, ch. 10, par. 82. Online: http://www.econlib.org/library/Smith/smWN.html (accessed 12 November 2013).

19 **"Competition has been shown to be useful up to a certain point"**: Speech at the People's Forum in Troy, New York, 3 March 1912.

20 **"pure competition"**: "Perfect Competition," BusinessDirectory.com. Online: http://www.businessdictionary.com/definition/perfect-competition.html (accessed 13 October 2013).

21 **"private and social costs and benefits"**: "Perfect Competition: The Economics of Competitive Markets," tutor2u (emphasis added). Online: http://tutor2u.net/economics/content/topics/competition/competition.htm (accessed 13 October 2013). An "externality" is a word used to make a simple idea complex, and maintain the mysteries of the profession. An example of an "externality in production" is if a company producing an

input such as steel has its unit cost of production decline as output increases. This results in a fall in the costs of all steel users though no action of their own. Thus, it is "externalized" to other companies. Pollution generated by production is another "externality," in this case a negative cost to society as a whole.

22   **"Road haulage"**: "Perfect Competition: Introduction," tutor2u. Online: http://tutor2u.net/economics/content/topics/monopoly/perfect_ competition.htm (accessed 13 October 2013).

23   **over half of adult Americans do, which is not encouraging**: Online: http://www.newspolls.org/articles/19620 9 accessed 15 December 2013).

23   **"he is everywhere in chains"**: Thomas Hobbes, *Leviathan*, ch. 13, par. 8. http://www.gutenberg.org/files/3207/3207-h/3207-h.htm (accessed 13 November 2013).

23   **"Once it is realized that business monopoly in America paralyzes"**: "Message to Congress on Curbing Monopolies," 29 April 1938.

24   **"over 20% of these institutions"**: FDIC, "The S&L Crisis: A Chrono-Bibliography," 20 December 2002. Online: http://www.fdic.gov/bank/ historical/s%26l/ (accessed 13 November 2013).

25   **"Good supervision and regulation have contributed to that"**: Robert Wade and Silla Sigurgeirsdóttir, "How to Discredit a Financial Regulator: The Strange Case of Iceland," Triple Crisis (blog), 27 March 2012. Online: http://triplecrisis.com/the-strange-case-of-iceland (accessed 13 October 2013).

29   **Donald Duck on Capitalism**: Taken from a Walt Disney Sunday cartoon strip in the *Washington Post* in the early 1980s, which it appears is no longer extant.

30   **"join a union"**: 1936. The entire speech can be heard here: http://www. dailykos.com/story/2010/06/13/875519/-FDR-I-would-join-a-union (accessed 13 November 2013).

31   ***prima facie* rubbish**: Paul Krugman, "Does Economics Still Progress?" *New York Times,* 27 September 2011. Online: http:// http://krugman.blogs. nytimes.com/2011/09/27/does-economics-still-progress/ (accessed 13 October 2013).

33   **well over 20%**: See http://stats.oecd.org/index.aspx?queryid=21760 for the standardized measure (accessed 13 November 2013).

33   **"new industrial dictatorship"**: Speech to the Democratic National Convention, Philadelphia, PA, 27 June 1936.

34   **Figure: Average and median income, adjusted for inflation**: Council of Economic Advisers, *Economic Report of the President* (Washington, DC, February 2011). Online: http://www.gpoaccess.gov/eop/tables11.html (accessed 13 October 2013).

35   **"bevy of camp-following whores"**: James M. Buchanan, *Wall Street Journal*, 25 April 1996, A20.

35   **"civil societies in the United States and throughout the world"**: See http://www.iop.harvard.edu/cato-institute (accessed 22 November 2013).

36   **"maximize the role of private economy"**: *National Journal*, 16 May
      1992.
36   **"new cases confirming its results keep coming in"**: Paul Krugman,
      Conscience of a Liberal (New York: W. W. Norton, 2007), 261.
38   **"masters can hold out much longer"**: Adam Smith, *Wealth of Nations*,
      bk 1, ch. 8, par. 11.

Chapter 3

40   **Box: Financial Fiascos in Our Times:** To Samuel Clemens (aka Mark
      Twain) is attributed the quip "History never repeats itself, but it can rhyme."
      To hear history rhyme, listen to Roosevelt's 1933 "fireside chat," as he
      explains the to Americans the need for the Emergency Banking Act: http://
      en.wikipedia.org/wiki/File:Fireside_Chat_1_On_the_Banking_Crisis_
      (March_12,_1933)_Franklin_Delano_Roosevelt.ogg (accessed 15 October
      2013).
41   **about $90 billion, or $150 billion at 2012 prices**: Online: http://
      useconomy.about.com/od/grossdomesticproduct/p/89_Bank_Crisis.htm
      (accessed 15 December 2013).
42   **almost 65% in the 2000s:** Find these numbers in: Council of Economic
      Advisers, *Economic Report of the President* (Washington, DC, February 2012). Online:
      http://www.gpoaccess.gov/eop/tables11.html (accessed 13 October 2013).
46   **(5.6% lower)**: *Economic Report of the President* (2013), annex table B 45.
46   **average daily turnover in currency markets in 2010 was about
      $4 trillion**: Bank for International Settlements, "Derivatives Statistics," 8
      May 2013. Online: http://www.bis.org/statistics/derstats.htm (accessed 15
      October 2013).
47   **"markets and instruments succumb to globalization"**: https://
      docs.google.com/a/wpcpress.com/document/d/1gUw5AR6ZbdEuZbtu71
      G1K-n79qxxWD_Bly6CbDJnt74/edit (accessed 15 December 2013).
47   **"history of markets"**: James O'Toole, "Explaining the Libor Interest
      Rate Mess," *CNN Money*, 10 July 2012. Online: http://money.cnn.
      com/2012/07/03/investing/libor-interest-rate-faq/index.htm (accessed 15
      October 2013).
47   **"some contrivance to raise prices"**: Adam Smith, *An Inquiry into
      the Nature and Causes of the Wealth of Nations*, bk 1, ch. 10, par. 82. Online:
      http://www.econlib.org/library/Smith/smWN.html (accessed 12 November
      2013).
47   **For no trade is that truer than finance**: I discussed this on video for
      therealnews.com. Search: John Weeks, "It's about Wall St. but It's Not All
      about Speculation," at http://therealnews.com (accessed 15 October 2013).
47   **"But the banks are made of marble"**: Hear Pete Seeger sing it in a
      video: http://www.oldielyrics.com/lyrics/pete_seeger/banks_are_made_of_
      marble.html (accessed 15 October 2013).
48   **"Hurricane Irene"**: "Hurricane Irene Seen as Ranking among Top Ten,"
      New York Times, 31 August 2011, 1.

48   **below the peak of mid-2008**: *Economic Report of the President* (2013), annex table B 45.

48   **actual level of $14.9 trillion**: Ibid.

49   **Figure: Actual US GDP during 2000–2013**: Calculated using statistics from the *Economic Report of the President* (2013).

50   **the count went from two to six**: *Economic Report of the President* (2013), annex table B 45.

50   **"rising standard of living"**: Franklin D. Roosevelt, 1941 State of the Union Address ("The Four Freedoms") (Washington, DC, 6 January 1941).

51   **rewards of over 30%**: Read it and weep (or cheer) at http://www.federalreserve.gov/releases/z1/20121206/accessible/f7.htm (accessed 13 November 2013).

51   **"The thief or swindler who has gained great wealth"**: Thorstein Veblen, *Theory of the Leisure Class* (1899) (New York: Modern Library, 2001), 117.

51   **"corporations are people"**: You can find the speech on YouTube: http://www.youtube.com/watch?v=E2h8ujX6T0A (accessed 15 October 2013).

52   **"it has got what it takes to save the currency"**: Timothy Heritage, "EU Struggles to Convince Markets in Euro Crisis," Reuters, 28 May 2010. Online: http://uk.reuters.com/article/2010/05/28/uk-eurozone-politics-idUKTRE64R24S20100528 (accessed 13 November 2013).

52   **"higher interest payments on debt"**: Toby A. A. Heaps, "Can Bond Markets Save the World?" *Corporate Knights*, 13 July 2011. Online: http://www.corporateknights.com/article/can-bond-markets-save-world (accessed 15 October 2013).

52   **"shall we not revenge?"**: William Shakespeare, *Merchant of Venice*, act III, scene 1.

53   **20-year low**: See Alexander Eichler "Federal Prosecution of Financial Fraud Falls to 20-Year Low, New Report Shows," Huffington Post, 15 November 2011. Online: http://www.huffingtonpost.com/2011/11/15/financial-fraud-prosecution_n_1095933.html (accessed 15 October 2013).

53   **"the many are governed by the few"**: David Hume, *First Principles of Government* (1742), part 1, essay 4, par. 1. Online: http://www.econlib.org/library/LFBooks/Hume/hmMPL4.html

Chapter 4

55   **"The first man"**: Jean-Jacques Rousseau, *Discourse on Inequality* (1754). Online: http://www.philosophyparadise.com/quotes/rousseau.html (accessed 16 October 2013).

55   **"People will believe a big lie"**: Walter C. Langer, *A Psychological Analysis of Adolph Hitler: His Life and Legend* (Washington, DC: OSS, 1943).

56   **we should not take such polls too seriously**: "Do We Trust Our Government? See How Your Country Compares," *Guardian*, 24 January 2012. Online: http://www.theguardian.com/news/datablog/2012/jan/24/trust-in-government-country-edelman (accessed 14 November 2013).

56   **"Big Business"**: Elizabeth Mendes, "In U.S., Fear of Big Government at Near-Record Level," Gallup, 12 December 2011. Online: http://www.gallup. com/poll/151490/fear-big-government-near-record-level.aspx (accessed 14 November 2013).

56   **"champions the free market as a matter of faith"**: Justin Rorlich, "One in Five Americans Thinks God Controls the Stock Market," Minyanville, 20 September 2011. Online: http://www.minyanville.com/ dailyfeed/2011/09/20/one-in-five-americans-thinks/

59   **"The market prices"**: I. M. Kizner, "Mises and His Understanding of the Capitalist System," *Cato Journal* 19, 2 (Fall 1999): 26. Online: http://www.cato. org/pubs/journal/cj19n2/cj19n2-2.pdf (accessed 16 October 2013).

59   **"The simplest case"**: P. Lewin, *Capital in Disequilibrium: The Role of Capital in a Changing World* (1999), 26.

60   **"Economics is the science which studies human behaviour"**: Lionel Robbins, *An Essay on the Nature and Significance of Economic Science* (London: Macmillan, 1932), 68.

61   **"common to all men"**: Adam Smith, *An Inquiry into the Nature and Causes of the Wealth of Nations*, bk 1, ch. 2, par. 1. Online: http://www.econlib.org/ library/Smith/smWN.html (accessed 12 November 2013).

63   **"the laws of supply and demand that I learned in my formative years still hold true"**: "Supply and Demand Rules Still Hold True," *Farmer's Guardian*, 30 March 2007. Online: http://www.farmersguardian. com/supply-and-demand-rules-still-hold-true/7849.article (accessed 16 October 2013).

63   **"lead to price volatility"**: Toni Johnson, "Oil Market Volatility," *Council on Foreign Relations*, 6 May 2011. Online: http://www.cfr.org/energy/oil-market-volatility/p15017 (accessed 16 October 2013).

63   **"the fundamental laws of supply and demand, and naked fear"**: "The Price of Fear," *Economist*, 3 May 2011. http://www.economist.com/ node/18285768 (accessed 16 October 2013).

69   **"It plays a central role in production theory"**: Wikipedia, "Diminishing Returns." http://en.wikipedia.org/wiki/Diminishing_returns (accessed 16 October 2013).

70   **"high priests of this ethic"**: Axel Leijonhufvud, *Keynesian Economics and the Economics of Keynes* (Oxford: Oxford University Press, 1968), 102.

70   **"the best of all worlds"**: Karl Marx, *Capital: A Critique of Political Economy* (Moscow: Progress Publishers, 1970), vol. 1, ch. 1, footnote 33.

70   **"For idle factories and idle workers profit no man"**: Franklin D. Roosevelt, "Message to Congress on Curbing Monopolies," 29 April 1938. Online: http://www.presidency.ucsb.edu/ws/?pid=15637 (accessed 14 November 2013).

72   **Figure: Spot the trend: 50 years of factory idleness in the US, 1960–2012**: Council of Economic Advisers, *Economic Report of the President* (Washington, DC, February 2010; 2013), annex tables B 45 and B 54. Online: http://www.gpoaccess.gov/eop/tables11.html (accessed 13 October 2013).

74   **"one in four of the working-age population in Splott is on some form of benefit"**: *The Future State of Welfare*, BBC2, 27 October 2011.

Online: http://www.bbc.co.uk/programmes/b016ltsh (accessed 16 October 2013).

74   **"there was a 'healthy supply of jobs'"**: "BBC Too Right Wing?" Biased BBC, 30 July 2013. Online: http://biasedbbc.org/blog/2013/07/30/bbc-too-right-wing (accessed 16 October 2013).

75   **"a temporary rise of a quarter of a million is not unusual"**: "Huge Increase in Unemployment," *Guardian*, 7 January 1931. Online: http://century.guardian.co.uk/1930-1939/Story/0,,126796,00.html (accessed 16 October 2013).

75   **"The *market*, in its majestic equality, forbids the rich"**: Anatole France, *Le Lys Rouge* (1894) (New York: Barnes & Noble, 1998), ch. 7.

76   **"presence of free markets makes free men"**: Quoted in Sanjeev Sabhlok, "Free Markets and Free Men," India I Dare You to Be Rich! (blog), 16 December 2010. Online: http://sabhlokcity.com/2010/12/free-markets-and-free-men-by-milton-friedman (accessed 16 October 2013).

76   **"the stuff of which dictatorships are made"**: Franklin D. Roosevelt, State of the Union address, 11 January 1944. The words in quotation marks are from Robert Henley, Lord Chancellor of Great Britain, in a law case, *Vernon v. Bethell*, in 1762.

77   **"the relative luxuries of healthcare and schooling"**: See "Hunger in America: 2013 United States Hunger and Poverty Facts," *Hunger Notes*, 22 November 2011. Online: http://www.worldhunger.org/articles/Learn/us_hunger_facts.htm (accessed 16 October 2013).

77   **"free at the source"**: See "Key Facts," The Poverty Site. Online: http://www.poverty.org.uk/summary/key%20facts.shtml (accessed 16 October 2013).

78   **"carried into practice for all our citizens"**: Roosevelt, State of the Union address. Hear it from FDR himself, at http://www.youtube.com/watch?v=UwUL9tJmypI (accessed 16 October 2013).

78   **"if it is bought at the cost of idleness and misery for millions"**: "Let Us Face the Future: A Declaration of Labour Policy for the Consideration of the Nation," Labour Party manifesto (1945). Online: http://www.labour-party.org.uk/manifestos/1945/1945-labour-manifesto.shtml (accessed 16 October 2013).

Chapter 5

81   **"Two elderly women are at a Catskill mountain resort"**: From *Annie Hall*, directed by Woody Allen (1977).

81   **Sendero Luminoso**: Sendero Luminoso was the nom de guerre of a Peruvian Maoist insurgency.

82   **Figure: Growth in after tax constant price household income by quintiles, 1979–2007**: Congressional Budget Office, "Trends in the Distribution of Household Income Between 1979 and 2007" (25 October 2011). Online: http://www.cbo.gov/doc.cfm?index=12485 (accessed 16 October 2013).

83   **Figure: Personal pre-tax income, 2010–11**: "Personal Income by Tax Year," HMRC. Online: http://www.hmrc.gov.uk/statistics/income-by-year.htm (accessed 16 October 2013).

82   **more small businesses disappeared than started**: See Brian Head, "Declining Bankruptcies among Promising Indicators," *Small Business Quarterly Bulletin*, fourth quarter 2012. Online: http://www.sba.gov/sites/default/files/files/SBQB_2012q4pdf.pdf (accessed 14 November 2013).

83   **"9% chance of surviving 10 years"**: Moya K. Mason, "Research on Small Businesses" (2013). Online: http://www.moyak.com/papers/small-business-statistics.html (accessed 16 October 2013).

84   **Figure: Impact of parental income on secondary school achievement**: OECD, "Economic Policy Reforms: Going for Growth 2012." Online: http://www.oecd.org/economy/monetary/economicpolicyreformsgoingforgrowth2012.htm (accessed 14 November 2013).

85   **"maintain their advantage in society"**: The Sutton Trust, "What Prospects for Mobility in the UK?" (November 2011). Online: http://www.suttontrust.com/public/documents/1sutton-trust-crita-summary-23-11-11.pdf (accessed 16 October 2013).

86   **"lower social mobility"**: BIS, "Social Mobility: A Literature Review" (March 2011). Online: http://www.bis.gov.uk/assets/biscore/economics-and-statistics/docs/s/11-750-social-mobility-literature-review (accessed 16 October 2013).

86   **Table: Income mobility in the US: 1988–1998**: Katharine Bradbury, "Trends in U.S. Family Income Mobility 1969–2006" (working paper, Federal Reserve Bank of Boston, no. 11-10, 20 October 2011). Online: http://www.bos.frb.org/economic/wp/wp2011/wp1110.pdf (accessed 16 October 2013).

86   **Table: Income mobility in the US: 1996–2005**: Ibid.; US Department of the Treasury, "Income Mobility in the U.S. from 1996 to 2005" (13 November 2011). Online: http://www.treasury.gov/resource-center/tax-policy/Documents/incomemobilitystudy03-08revise.pdf (accessed 16 October 2013).

86   **"Yes, Virginia, there is [an American market dream] Santa Claus"**: Response to letter to the editor, the *Sun* (New York), 21 September 1897. Online: http://www.newseum.org/yesvirginia (accessed 16 October 2013).

87   **"Consumers thus reign over the economy as sovereign rulers"**: "Consumer Sovereignty," AmosWEB. Online: http://www.amosweb.com/cgi-bin/awb_nav.pl?s=wpd&c=dsp&k=consumer%20sovereign (accessed 13 November 2013).

87   **Box: Limited Sovereignty: Advertising in the US**: Matthew J. Slaughter, *How U.S. Multinational Companies Strengthen the U.S. Economy* (Business Roundtable/USCIB, March 2010). Online: http://www.uscib.org/docs/foundation_multinationals_update.pdf (accessed 16 October 2013); Douglas Galbi, "Coen Structured Advertising Expenditure

Dataset," Purple Motes (blog). Online: http://spreadsheets.google.com/pub?key=p9LENaiKJeoyBX4eR1FZEEw (accessed 16 October 2013).

88 **"ensure change is implemented and maintained"**: you:unlimited, "Customer Service in the NHS" (2009). Online: http://www.you-unltd.co.uk/downloads/WhitePaper-CustomerServiceinNHSTrusts-Feb09.pdf (accessed 16 October 2013).

89 **"as Karen Jennings of Unison [the NHS employee union] suggested"**: Ibid.

89 **"embrace this new way of thinking"**: Ibid.

89 **"for-profit universities"**: Randeep Ramesh, "NHS Management Increasing Five Times Faster than Number of Nurses," *Guardian*, 25 March 2010. Online: http://www.guardian.co.uk/society/2010/mar/25/nhs-management-numbers-frontline-staff (accessed 16 October 2013).

90 **"to assess the quality of patient experiences"**: "Medical Mystery Shopping," Baird Group. Online: http://baird-group.com/mystery-shopping (accessed 16 October 2013).

91 **"financial difficulties building up in the system"**: Tom Clark, "Ratings Agencies in the NHS? It's a Blame-Game Wheeze," *Guardian*, 19 January 2012. Online: http://www.theguardian.com/commentisfree/2012/jan/19/ratings-agencies-nhs (accessed 14 November).

91 **"referees of the financial system"**: Tom Clark, "Ratings Agencies in the NHS? It's a Blame-Game Wheeze," *Guardian*, 19 January 2012. Online: http://www.guardian.co.uk/commentisfree/2012/jan/19/ratings-agencies-nhs (accessed 16 October 2013).

91 **"the *laissez faire* solution for medicine is intolerable"**: Kenneth J. Arrow, "Uncertainty and the Welfare Economics of Medical Care," *American Economic Review* 53, no. 5 (December 1963). Online: http://www.who.int/bulletin/volumes/82/2/PHCBP.pdf (accessed 16 October 2013).

94 **"poor, nasty and brutish"**: Read Thomas Hobbs, *Leviathan* (1651) at http://www.gutenberg.org/ebooks/3207 (accessed 16 October 2013).

95 **Figure: US household income and debt, 1960–2010**: Council of Economic Advisers, *Economic Report of the President* (Washington, DC, February 2011). Online: http://www.gpoaccess.gov/eop/tables11.html (accessed 13 October 2013).

96 **"will yield the highest possible utility to global consumers"**: Wikipedia, "Free Trade Debate." Online: http://en.wikipedia.org/wiki/Free_trade_debate (accessed 16 October 2013).

96 **"continually optimise their production processes and develop new products"**: "Opening Economies Succeed," Deutsche Bank Research, 11 November 2005. Online: http://www.dbresearch.com/PROD/DBR_INTERNET_EN-PROD/PROD0000000000189232.PDF (accessed 14 November).

97 **"double-digit increases in trade"**: http://goglobaltowin.com/?p=81 (web page since discontinued).

97 **"it should make the world more green, not less"**: Mark Horowitz, "Jagdish Bhagwati: Keep Free Trade Free," *Wired*, 22 September 2008.

Online: http://www.wired.com/politics/law/magazine/16-10/sl_bhagwati (accessed 16 October 2013).

97 **"*stable* venture-capital model"**: Ibid. (emphasis added).

98 **"gain a foothold in the global marketplace"**: "Encourage Sustainable Trade," Greenpeace. Online: http://www.greenpeace.org/international/en/campaigns/trade-and-the-environment (accessed 16 October 2013).

98 **"join us and demand a [genetically engineered] free world"**: Ibid.

98 **"this is precisely the period that has been most heavily liberalized"**: World Bank, *Global Economic Outlook* (Washington, DC: World Bank, 2000), executive summary.

98 **"the rich get richer and the poor get poorer"**: World Bank, *Inequality and Growth: Lessons for Policy* (Washington, DC: World Bank, 1999), ch. 3. Online: http://siteresources.worldbank.org/INTPOVERTY/Resources/WDR/English-Full-Text-Report/ch3.pdf (accessed 15 January 2013).

99 **"preeminent buff"**: Bhagwati, "The Pure Theory of International Trade," *Economic Journal* 74 (1964): 1–78.

100 **"Oh, the tangled web we weave when first we practice [theory] to deceive"**: Sir Walter Scott, *Marmion* (1808), canto vi. Online: http://www2.hn.psu.edu/faculty/jmanis/w-scott/marmion.pdf (accessed 17 December 2013).

101 **"sectors that intensively use labour as a factor of production"**: Raphael Auer and Andreas Fischer, "The Impact of Low-Income Economies on US Inflation," Vox, 13 June 2008. Online: http://voxeu.org/index.php?q=node/1223 (accessed 16 October 2013).

101 **"vent for surplus"**: Adam Smith, *An Inquiry into the Nature and Causes of the Wealth of Nations*, bk 5, ch. 1. Online: http://www.econlib.org/library/Smith/smWN.html (accessed 12 November 2013).

102 **"search in vain for evidence to support it"**: See Karl Bietel, "US Farm Subsidies and the Farm Economy: Myths, Realities, Alternatives," Food First, 23 August 2005. Online: http://www.foodfirst.org/backgrounders/subsidies (accessed 16 October 2013).

102 **"trade policy to tug at middle-class heart strings"**: See for example the misplaced faith in trade as a poverty reducer in *The Bottom Billion* by Oxford University and ex–World Bank economist Paul Collier.

104 **"farm implements and other heavy equipment"**: Louis Uchitelle, "Factory Jobs Gain, but Wages Retreat," *New York Times*, 29 December 2011. Online: http://www.nytimes.com/2011/12/30/business (accessed 16 October 2013).

104 **"US consumers feasted on cheap imported goods"**: Jon Hilsenrath, Laurie Burkitt and Elizabeth Holmes, "Change in China Hits U.S. Purse," *Wall Street Journal*, 21 June 2011.

103 **Box: Free Trade and Capital Flows Create Employment (But Not in the USA)**: *Economic Report of the President* (2013), annex tables B 18, B 19, B 46, B 105.

Chapter 6

107   **"Governments are notoriously bad at managing the money they collect"**: Ronald Sokol, *International Herald Tribune*, 28 December 2012, 6.

107   **"For a long time the degree of concentration [of income and wealth] fluctuated"**: Samuel Brittan, *Financial Times*, 21 December 2012, 11.

107   **"Road to Serfdom"**: The title of Friedrich Hayek's 1944 polemic against the role of the public sector.

108   **"no sense of responsibility at the other"**: Ronald Reagan, quoted in *New York Times Magazine*, 14 November 1965, 174.

108   **"That is the essence of human freedom"**: Quoted in Sanjeev Sabhlok, "Free Markets and Free Men," India I Dare You to Be Rich! (blog), 16 December 2010. Online: http://sabhlokcity.com/2010/12/free-markets-and-free-men-by-milton-friedman (accessed 16 October 2013).

108   **"burdening taxpayers"**: Joe Murphy, "High Speed Train Tunnel in London," *Evening Standard*, 10 January 2012. Online: http://www.standard.co.uk/news/high-speed-train-tunnel-in-london-7306003.html (accessed 14 November 2013).

110   **"unless we're absolutely sure we know where the money is coming from"**: "Ed Miliband Hits Back at Len McCluskey's Criticism of Labour," *Telegraph*, 17 January 2012. Online: http://www.telegraph.co.uk/news/politics/ed-miliband/9020108/Ed-Miliband-hits-back-at-Len-McCluskeys-criticism-of-Labour.html (accessed 14 November 2013).

110   **"we are totally opposed to them and we are fighting them"**: "Ed Miliband Returns Unite Union Leader's Fire," *Guardian*, 17 January 2012. Online: http://www.theguardian.com/politics/2012/jan/17/labour-spending-cuts-harman (accessed 14 November 2013).

112   **"public schooling in the United States is free enterprise"**: Jacob G. Hornberger, "Letting Go of Socialism," Future of Freedom Foundation, 1 September 1990. Online: http://fff.org/explore-freedom/article/letting-socialism/ (accessed 14 November 2013).

113   **"Texas congressman Ron Paul and Kentucky senator Rand Paul might be exceptions"**: See the video at http://www.esquire.com/blogs/politics/ron-paul-elizabeth-warren-socialist-6552974 (accessed 16 October 2013).

113   **"43,000 college students will lose all or part of their financial aid"**: Tanya Somanader, "Rick Perry's Budget Cuts Will Leave 49,000 Teachers without a Job and 43,000 College Students without Financial Aid," Think Progress, 29 September 2011. Online: http://thinkprogress.org/economy/2011/09/29/332152/perry-budget-cuts-teacher-financial-aid/ (accessed 14 November 2013).

115   **"the opportunity to achieve and enjoy good health"**: Franklin D. Roosevelt, State of the Union address, 11 January 1944.

114   **"put the government's budget and *the American economy* at risk"**: Andrew G. Biggs, "Entitlements: Not Just a Health Care Problem," American Enterprise Institute, 8 August 2008 (emphasis added). Online: http://www.aei.org/outlook/28443 (accessed 16 October 2013).

115 **"Social security is a milk cow with 310 million tits"**: Ezra Ritchin, "An Interview with Sen. Alan Simpson," *The Politic*, 2 January 2013. Online: http://thepolitic.org/take-part-or-get-taken-apart-an-interview-with-sen-alan-simpson (accessed 14 November 2013).

116 **Box: University Reform in the UK: Value for Money**: Leslie J. Calman and Linda Tarr-Whelan, *Early Childhood Education for All: A Wise Investment* (New York: Legal Momentum, 2004). Online: http://web.mit.edu/workplacecenter/docs/Full%20Report.pdf (accessed 16 October 2013).

117 **"For my part I think that capitalism"**: J. M. Keynes, "The End of Laissez-Faire" (Sydney Ball Foundation Lecture, Cambridge, 1926). Online: http://www.maynardkeynes.org/john-maynard-keynes-reparations-probability-gold.html (accessed 14 November 2013).

118 **"most of them are still below the prewar existing levels"**: World Bank, "New World Bank and UNDP Survey on Somalia" (press release, 14 January 2004). Online: http://siteresources.worldbank.org/SOMALIAEXTN/Resources/WBpressreleaserev3.pdf (accessed 16 October 2013).

Chapter 7

122 **"under 3%, in line with European rules"**: "Dutch Socialists Show Major Gains Ahead of Netherlands Elections," *Guardian*, 26 August 2012. Online: http://www.theguardian.com/world/2012/aug/26/dutch-rookie-party-netherlands-elections (accessed 14 November 2013).

123 **"the deadweight of debt that has been built up over time"**: Polly Curtis, "How Nick Clegg Got It Wrong on Debt," *Guardian*, 9 May 2012. Online: http://www.guardian.co.uk/politics/reality-check-with-polly-curtis/2012/may/09/nickclegg-davidcameron (accessed 17 October 2013).

124 **only 19% in favor and a third unsure**: Gallup, "U.S. Economic Confidence Remains Low Post-Fiscal Cliff Deal," 8 January 2013. Online: http://www.gallup.com/poll/159734/economic-confidence-remains-low-post-fiscal-cliff-deal.aspx (accessed 13 November 2013).

124 **"I don't want to leave my successor and my children to pay for France's debt"**: Kim Willsher, "François Hollande Announces 10bn Cut in Public Spending," *Guardian*, 10 September 2012. Online: http://www.theguardian.com/world/2012/sep/10/francois-hollande-cut-public-spending (accessed 14 November 2013).

124 **no sane politician ever complained about their "burden"**: "Take a Closer Look at War Bonds," National World War II Museum. Online: http://www.nationalww2museum.org/learn/education/for-students/ww2-history/take-a-closer-look/war-bonds.html; "British World War II Economics: Financing the War," Historical Boy's Clothing. Online: http://histclo.com/essay/war/ww2/eco/cou/w2ec-brit.html (accessed 17 October 2013).

125 **the shortest maturing to 2.69% for bonds of several years**: Bank of England statistics. Available online: http://www.bankofengland.co.uk/statistics/Pages/default.aspx (accessed 14 November 2013).

127 **following his dubious ascent to the presidency in 2001**: OECD, "Economic Outlook No 93 – June 2013 – OECD Annual Projections." Online: http://stats.oecd.org/Index.aspx?QueryId=48234 (accessed 14 November 2013).

129 **"the shadow of one of the greatest economic catastrophes of modern history"**: J. M. Keynes, "The Great Slump of 1930." Online: http://www.gutenberg.ca/ebooks/keynes-slump/keynes-slump-00-h.html (accessed 14 November 2013).

130 **"more than 10% of GDP, in excess of $1.6 trillion"**: Council of Economic Advisers, *Economic Report of the President* (Washington, DC, February 2013), annex tables B 78, B 79. Online: http://www.gpoaccess.gov/eop/tables11.html (accessed 14 November 2013).

130 **about 40% of the interest to other US government agencies**: US Government Accountability Office, "Federal Debt Basics." Online: http://www.gao.gov/special.pubs/longterm/debt/debtbasics.html (accessed 14 November 2013).

130 **its infamous "stabilization" programs**: See the IMF pamphlet "Guidelines for Fiscal Adjustment." Online: http://www.imf.org/external/pubs/ft/pam/pam49/pam49con.htm (accessed 14 November 2013).

131 **the percentage rose to 20%, and higher still in 2009–2010**: Council of Economic Advisers, *Economic Report of the President* (2013), annex tables B 78, B 79.

131 **the primary deficit never exceeded 4%**: Ibid.

132 **deficit vultures of the political Right**: Ibid.

132 **unemployment fund paid out almost $150 billion in 2010**: Ibid., annex table B 81.

133 **Table: US GDP and Public Finances, 2005–2010**: Office of Management and Budget, "Analytical Perspectives." Online: http://www.whitehouse.gov/omb/budget/Analytical_Perspectives (accessed 14 November 2013).

134 **"A good crisis should not be wasted"**: Scott Rohter, "Government Shutdown, Slim Down, or Show-Down?" Less Gov Is the Best Gov. Online http://lessgovisthebestgov.com/government-shutdown-slim-down-or-show-down.html (accessed 14 November 2013).

134 **Box: US Growth, Recessions and Deficits, 1991–2013**: Council of Economic Advisers, *Economic Report of the President* (2013).

137 **"we hate you guys, but there is nothing much we can do"**: Henny Sender, "China to Stick with US Bonds," *Financial Times*, 11 February 2009. Online: http://www.ft.com/cms/s/0/ba857be6-f88f-11dd-aae8-000077b07658.html (accessed 14 November 2013).

137 **Table: US public debt, end of 2010:** Council of Economic Advisers, *Economic Report of the President* (Washington, DC, February 2011). Online: http://www.gpoaccess.gov/eop/tables11.html (accessed 17 October 2013); OECD, Economic Outlook 89 database. Online: http://stats.oecd.org/Index.aspx?QueryId=48237 (accessed 13 November 2013).

138 **"unless there is some calamity as gigantic as a nuclear war"**: Mark Weisbrot, "Moody's Threat to Downgrade US Debt Is Political, Not

Fiscal," *Guardian*, 13 September 2012. Online: http://www.theguardian.com/commentisfree/2012/sep/13/moodys-threat-downgrade-us-debt-political-fiscal (accessed 14 November 2013).

139   **Table: Interest payments on public debt, percentage of GDP, 2010**: OECD, Economic Outlook 89 database. Online: http://stats.oecd.org/Index.aspx?DataSetCode=SNA_TABLE11 (accessed 14 November 2013).

Chapter 8

141   **"not very or not at all concerned"**: Dennis Jacobe, "Inflation Worries Permeate U.S.," Gallup, 3 May 2010. Online: http://www.gallup.com/poll/127616/Inflation-Worries-Permeate-US.aspx (accessed 17 October 2013).

141   **"despite falls in the headline rate [to less than 3%]"**: Ben Chu, "Dilemma for Bank of England as Public Fears Even Higher Inflation," *Evening Standard*, 8 June 2012. Online: http://www.newsrt.co.uk/news/dilemma-for-bank-of-england-as-public-fears-even-higher-inflation-511864.html (accessed 14 November 2013).

142   **"inflation is always and everywhere a monetary phenomenon"**: Milton Friedman, *Inflation: Causes and Consequences* (New York: Asia Publishing House, 1963).

145   **"itself being regulated by the market process"**: Friedrich Hayek, *Choice in Currency* (London: The Institute of Economic Affairs 1976), 79–80.

145   **"The purpose of a central bank is to deceive and defraud the public"**: Ron Paul, quoted in "The Purpose of a Central Bank Is to Deceive and Defraud the People," RonPaul.com, 11 July 2011. Online: http://www.ronpaul.com/2011-07-11/ron-paul-the-purpose-of-a-central-bank-is-to-deceive-and-defraud-the-people/ (accessed 14 November 2013).

146   **Box: The US "Money Supply," 2000–2011**: Council of Economic Advisers, *Economic Report of the President* (Washington, DC, February 2013). Online: http://www.gpoaccess.gov/eop/tables11.html (accessed 17 October 2013).

147   **rose by about 1% a year, 11% for the decade**: Council of Economic Advisers, *Economic Report of the President* (Washington, DC, February 2010), annex table B 3. Online: http://www.gpoaccess.gov/eop/tables11.html (accessed 14 November 2013).

147   **rising by 115% in the US**: Council of Economic Advisers, *Economic Report of the President* (2013), annex tables B 3, B 60.

148   **Figure: US Inflation, 1992–2010: Too Much Money Chasing?**: Ibid.

148   **Figure: Actual Inflation and Fuel-Only Effect, 1993–2010**: Ibid.

151   **(imports about double production)**: US Energy Information Administration, "Countries." Online: http://www.eia.gov/countries/index.cfm?topL=exp (accessed 14 November 2013).

152   **"Have you seen the inflation monster?"**: "What Is Inflation?" European Central Bank. Online: http://www.ecb.int/ecb/educational/hicp/html/index.en.html (accessed 17 October 2013).

154 **"the civilization and the progress of our generation"**: J. M. Keynes, *The Economic Consequences of the Peace* (1919). Online: http://www.gutenberg. org/files/15776/15776-h/15776-h.htm (accessed 14 November 2013).

154 **these countries rarely experienced annual rates above 10%**: World Bank, "World DataBank: World Development Indicators." Online: http://databank.worldbank.org/data/views/variableSelection/ selectvariables.aspx?source=world-development-indicators (accessed 14 November 2013).

155 **average debt service across Latin America declined below 4%, falling further in the 2000s**: For Germany: Scott Minerd, "Market Perspectives," Guggenheim Partners article, March 2013. Online: http:// guggenheimpartners.com/getattachment/21f2508d-d87e-4c22-8a07- 33f235926af0/Winning-The-War-In-Europe;;.aspx (accessed 14 November 2013). For Latin America: World Bank, "World DataBank: World Development Indicators."

156 **exchange rate depreciation relative to the dollar**: Council of Economic Advisers, *Economic Report of the President* (2010), annex table B 3.

156 **barely 2% in the 2000s**: Ibid.

157 **Figure: Inflation across 18 high-income countries, 1972–2012**: J. M. Keynes, *The General Theory of Employment, Interest and Money* (London: Macmillan, 1936), 300.

158 **(to paraphrase John Kenneth Galbraith)**: *Guardian*, 20 November 1991.

159 **"they are curses to the country"**: *Forum*, February 1895.

Chapter 9

163 **"The best government is that which governs least"**: John Louis O'Sullivan, in the *United States Magazine and Democratic Review* (1837), and certainly not Thomas Jefferson, to whom it is frequently attributed.

164 **"My aim is not to pass laws, but to repeal them"**: Barry Goldwater, *Conscience of a Conservative* (Shepardsville: Publishers Printing Company, 1960), 15.

164 **Richard Nixon would win 60.7% in 1972**: "United States Presidential Election Results," Dave Leip's Atlas of US Presidential Elections. Online: http://uselectionatlas.org/RESULTS/ (accessed 14 November 2013).

165 **"intellectual corruption in the economics profession from the get-go"**: Paul Krugman, "Is Our Economists Learning?" *New York Times*, 14 July 2012. Online: http://krugman.blogs.nytimes.com/2012/07/14/is-our- economists-learning (accessed 18 October 2013).

165 **"remove regulatory impediments to energy production and innovation"**: R. Glenn Hubbard, N. Gregory Mankiw, John B. Taylor and Kevin A. Hassett, "The Romney Program for Economic Recovery, Growth, and Jobs." Online: http://bloximages.newyork1.vip.townnews.com/ theshorthorn.com/content/tncms/assets/v3/editorial/1/e7/1e7c3e70- 0d20-11e2-b8ef-001a4bcf6878/506bd5693d551.pdf.pdf (accessed 14 November 2013).

165   **"a concerned effort by three economists [...] to destroy their own reputations"**: Paul Krugman, "Unconventional," *New York Times*, 29 August 2012. Online: http://krugman.blogs.nytimes.com/2012/08/29/unconventional/ (accessed 14 November 2013).

165   **"even if the taking is sanctioned by a majority of the citizenry"**: N. Gregory Mankiw, "Defending the One Percent," *Journal of Economic Perspectives* 27, no.3 (2013). Online: http://scholar.harvard.edu/files/mankiw/files/defending_the_one_percent.pdf (accessed 14 November 2013).

168   **Figure: Fiscal balance (% of GDP) and the unemployment rate, 1955–2011:** Council of Economic Advisers, *Economic Report of the President* (Washington, DC, February 2012). Online: http://www.gpoaccess.gov/eop/tables11.html (accessed 18 October 2013).

168   **Figure: Inflation rate and the public sector balance, 1960– 2012**: Council of Economic Advisers, Economic Report of the President (Washington, DC, February 2013). Online: http://www.gpoaccess.gov/eop/tables11.html (accessed 17 October 2013).

169   **Figure: Federal bonds interest rate and public sector balance (% GDP), 1980–2012**: Ibid.

170   **"confidence fairy"**: Paul Krugman, "The Confidence Fairy, The Expectations Imp, and the Rate-Hike Obsession," *New York Times*, 9 June 2013. Online: http://krugman.blogs.nytimes.com/2013/06/09/the-confidence-fairy-the-expectations-imp-and-the-rate-hike-obsession/ (accessed 14 November 2013).

173   **weighed in at only £121 billion**: OECD, "General Government Gross Financial Liabilities, % of Nominal GDP" and "General Government Net Financial Liabilities, % of Nominal GDP." Online: http://www.oecd.org/statistics/ (accessed 14 November 2013).

172   **Figure: GDP growth and changes in the UK deficit, 1992–2010**: Office for National Statistics, "Public Sector Finance." Online: http://www.statistics.gov.uk/hub/economy/government-receipts-and-expenditure/public-sector-finance (accessed 14 November 2013).

172   **Figure: UK government borrowing, interest rate on borrowing and the $/£ exchange rate**: Ibid.

175   **central bank of Germany, Deutsche Bundesbank**: See *Europe's Unfinished Currency* (London: Anthem Press, 2012) by Thomas Mayer (ex-IMF and ex–Goldman Sachs).

176   **barely 40%, better than Germany could claim**: OECD, "General Government Gross Financial Liabilities."

178   **Figure: Annual working hours in six EU countries, 2007 (private sector)**: OECD, "Average Annual Working Time." Online: http://www.oecd.org/statistics (accessed 14 November 2013).

178   **Figure: Public sector social spending in six EU countries, 2007**: OECD, "Government Social Spending, % of GDP." http://www.oecd.org/statistics (accessed 14 November 2013).

179   **Figure: Gross public debt of the PIIGS minus that of Germany, 1998–2011**: OECD, "General Government Gross Financial Liabilities,

% of Nominal GDP." Online: http://www.oecd.org/statistics (accessed 14 November 2013).

179   **Figure: Overall fiscal balances of the PIIGS minus the German balance, 1994–2011**: Ibid.

182   **Figure: Trade balances of Germany and PIIGS, US$ bns, 2000–2011**: OECD, "Trade Balances for Goods and Services, US $ Billions." Online: http://www.oecd.org/statistics (accessed 14 November 2013).

184   **"change the world market situation in their favour"**: K. W. Rothschild, "Price Theory and Oligopoly," *Economic Journal* 57, no. 227 (September 1947): 299–320.

Chapter 10

186   **"they who rule industrially will rule politically"**: Quoted in Michael Foot, *Aneurin Bevan: A Biography*, vol. 1, *1897–1945* (London: Faber & Faber, 1962), ch. 2.

186   **"the explosion in unfair pay that followed their abrupt decline"**: Polly Toynbee, "London 2012: Danny Boyle's Opening Ceremony History Is Only a Partial Truth," *Guardian*, 30 July 2012. Online: http://www.theguardian.com/commentisfree/2012/jul/30/danny-boyle-olympics-ceremony-partial-history (accessed 14 November 2013).

186   **"The distinction between service and servitude will blur"**: Jeff Faux, "The Hunger Games Economy," *American Prospect*, June 2012. Online: http://jefffaux.com/?p=254 (accessed 18 October 2013).

186   **"do a disservice to the cause of democracy"**: John F. Kennedy, "Special Labor Day Message from Democratic Presidential Candidate John F. Kennedy," 5 September 1960. Online: http://www.presidency.ucsb.edu/ws/?pid=60413 (accessed 14 November 2013).

187   **"to bring financial decision making under public authority"**: Carter Dougherty, "Stopping a Financial Crisis, the Swedish Way," *New York Times*, 22 September 2008. Online: http://www.nytimes.com/2008/09/23/business/worldbusiness/23krona.html (accessed 14 November 2013).

188   **"no good deed goes unpunished"**: The putative source is Clare Booth Luce, US playwright, congresswoman and ambassador.

188   **"A fool and his money are soon elected"**: A live recording of Rogers saying this can be found here: http://www.mainquotes.com/quote/32913.html (accessed 14 November 2013).

189   **Box: Strikes, Unions and Earnings, USA 1964–2010**: Council of Economic Advisers, *Economic Report of the President* (Washington, DC, February 2012). Online: http://www.gpoaccess.gov/eop/tables11.html (accessed 18 October 2013); Bureau of Labor Statistics, "Work Stoppages." Online: http://www.bls.gov/wsp/ (accessed 14 November 2013).

189   **"The institution of a leisure class has emerged gradually"**: Thorstein Veblen, *Theory of the Leisure Class* (New York: Macmillan, 1899), 7.

191   **"Or a thug for J. H. Blair"**: Florence Reece, 1931, Harlan County, Kentucky, miners' strike. "J. H. Blair" refers to one of the mine owners.

195   **rate three times greater than that of males:** All numbers from the *Economic Report of the President* (2013).

197   **"products such as cars, refrigerators, radios and cookers":** "Boom and Bust," BBC Bitesize. Online: http://www.bbc.co.uk/bitesize/higher/history/usa/boombust/revision/1/ (accessed 18 October 2013).

199   **"that government is best which is most indifferent":** Franklin D. Roosevelt, speech at Madison Square Garden, New York City, 31 October 1936.   Online: http://millercenter.org/president/speeches/detail/3307 (accessed 14 November 2013).

203   **"that would be splendid":** J. M. Keynes, "The Future," in *Essays in Persuasion* (London: Macmillan, 1931) Online: http://gutenberg.ca/ebooks/keynes-essaysinpersuasion/keynes-essaysinpersuasion-00-h.html (accessed 15 December 2013).

203   **"Let us never forget that government is ourselves":** Franklin D. Roosevelt, address at Marietta, Ohio, 8 July 1938. Online: http://www.presidency.ucsb.edu/ws/?pid=15672 (accessed 14 November 2013).

204   **"specialists in mental disease":** J. M. Keynes, "The Future."

INDEX

CPSIA information can be obtained at www.ICGtesting.com
Printed in the USA
LVOW12s1514130414

381507LV00001B/271/P

9 780857 281081